AF539443

BASIC EDUCATION

By

D. Vijaya Lakshmi

M.A., M.Ed.

M.P.E. School

Nunna

Krishna Distt.,

Andhra Pradesh

General Editor

Dr. Digumarti Bhaskara Rao

M.Sc., M.A., M.A., M.Ed., Ph.D.

Reader

R.V.R. College of Education

Srinivasa Nagar Colony

Guntur–522 006

Andhra Pradesh

India

DISCOVERY PUBLISHING HOUSE

NEW DELHI-110002

First Published – 2004
Reprinted – 2017

ISBN: 978-81-7141-881-7

Basic Education

Published by:
DISCOVERY PUBLISHING HOUSE PVT. LTD.
4383/4B, Ansari Road Darya Ganj
New Delhi - 110 002 (India)
Phone: +91-11-23279245, 43596064-65
Fax: +91-11-23253475
E-mail: discoverypublishinghouse@gmail.com
sales@discoverypublishinggroup.com
web: www.discoverypublishinggroup.com

Printed at:
Infinity Imaging Systems
Delhi

PREFACE

Education is a huge structure and Basic Education is its foundation. As per logic and scientific attitude, Basic Education is the basis of the system of education. Unfortunately, in our country, Basic Education is treated as the poorest member of the family. The primary teachers are least paid and are treated in the worst manner. But, in fact, Basic Education is the first ladder, which is most important in its own right. So, our planners and policy makers should lay all stress on Basic Education. The thrust of Education System should be on the first stage alone.

Basic Education has its peculiar problems and a particular attitude is demanded for dealing with them. And for that, are required exclusive books on the subject for making educationists and teachers aware of the real issues and all the related aspects. This work is meant for filling this vacuum only.

The undersigned feels pride in accomplishing a challenging task, which in turn should benefit students and as well as teachers, engaged in various schools.

—Author

Contents

1

INTRODUCTION

Education may be called the 'mother' which has given birth to concepts like teaching etc. Education is like an ocean and as broad in its dimensions that all other concepts may be considered as rivers and streams of this vast ocean. Education and the status of its components may be explained in the following form:

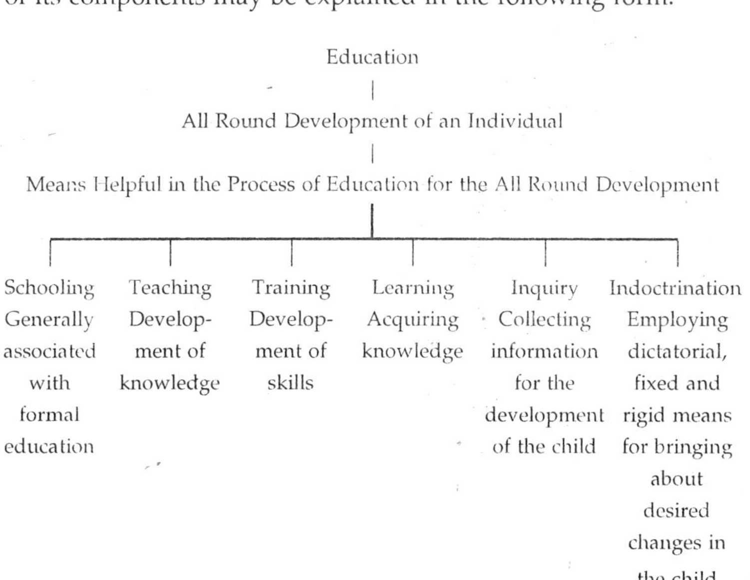

Training is only a part of education. It is concerned with attaining skill and proficiency in a field; for example training to become a teacher, an engineer and a doctor.

S. No.	Education	Training
1.	Scope of education is very wide.	1. Training is limited in scope.
2.	Education has three aspects formal, informal and non-formal.	2. Training is, by and large, formal.
3.	Education is imparted at home, in educational institutions, cultural institutions etc.	3. Training is mainly imparted only in a training institution i.e. training school or college.
4.	Education is a life long process.	4. The period of training is fixed.
5.	Education aims at the all round development of an individual.	5. The aim of training is to develop proficiency in a particular skill or some skills in an individual.
6.	Theoretical and practical aspects are stressed.	6. More stress is laid on practical aspect.
7.	Curriculum is broad and flexible.	7. Curriculum is usually fixed.
8.	The range of methods used is very wide.	8. In training, range of methods is not so wide as in education.
9.	Social discipline is prominent.	9. Discipline is usually strict and authoritarian.
10	Objectives and means of evaluation are very wide.	10. Proficiency in the skill of the profession is tested.
11.	There are many sources of inspiration in education.	11. Economic aspect is the primary source of inspiration.
12.	There is flexibility in the provision of teachers.	12. There are fixed teachers.
13.	Certificate or degree is usually awarded after the successful completion of a course.	13. Certificate or degree is usually awarded after the completion of a course.

Instruction is a part of education. It helps in the attainment of aims of education.

S. No.	Education	Instruction
1.	The scope of education is broad.	1. The scope of instruction is narrow.
2.	Education has three aspects: formal, informal and non-formal.	2. Instruction is basically formal.
3.	Education is imparted by the home, educational institutions and cultural groups etc.	3. Instruction is imparted in educational institutions.

Contd.

S. No.	*Education*	*Instruction*
4.	Education goes on from birth to death.	4. The period of instruction is limited.
5.	Education aims at the many sided development of the individual.	5. Instruction primarily aims at intellectual development.
6.	Theoretical and practical aspects are taken into consideration.	6. Instruction is more or less theoretical.
7.	The entire environment is the curriculum.	7. Curriculum in instruction is usually in terms of certain disciplines or subjects.
8.	A variety of methods are employed in education.	8. Lecture method is the most prominent method according to traditional mode.
9.	Stress is laid on self-discipline and social discipline.	9. Command is usually the basis of discipline.
10.	Several categories of people engaged in the educational enterprise take part.	10. Teachers dominate the scene.
11.	Development of proper behaviour and conduct is more important.	11. Scoring good marks by the students is the key factor.
12.	Child is given more importance.	12. Teacher assumes more importance.

Difference between Education and Schooling

S. No.	*Education*	*Schooling*
1.	Very broad.	Part of the broader field of education.
2.	Natural process.	Artificial process.
3.	It has three aspects: formal, informal and non-formal.	Formal aspect alone is visible.
4.	Continuous and life long process.	Starts from child's entry or admission to school and ends with his withdrawal or leaving the school or college.
5.	It is imparted at a variety of institutions-home, educational institutions, cultural, social, religious and commercial institutions.	The place of schooling is limited to an educational institution i.e. school or college.
6.	It aims at the all round development of an individual-his cultural, ethical, emotional, mental, physical, spiritual, social and professional.	Though schooling also aims at all round development but more attention is paid to mental development.
7.	Formal education has a fixed curriculum but non-formal has a flexible and sometimes an open curriculum.	Curriculum is fixed and usually in term of various subjects.

Contd.

S. No.	Education	Schooling
8.	The range of methods of education is very wide.	It is usually confined to lecture, discussion, experiment and question-answer methods.
9.	There is social discipline and social control.	It is associated with strictness.
10.	Formality and informality between the teacher-pupil go side by side.	Formality is observed between the teacher-pupil relations.
11.	Practical aspect is more important.	Theoretical aspect is predominant.
12.	Techniques of evaluation are very comprehensive. Various aspects are evaluated.	Evaluation of a student is done to test his theoretical and practical knowledge of subject and activities.

Definition and Meaning of Technology: Teaching has been defined in various ways. Here, a few important definitions are given to throw light on the meaning and various dimensions of teaching.

B.C. Smith defines "Teaching as a system of action which intends to introduce learning through interpersonal relations."

In the words of H. C. Morrison "Teaching is an intimate contact between a more mature and a less mature personality which is designed to further the education of the latter.

John Brubacher writes, "Teaching is an arrangement and manipulation of a situation in which there are gaps and obstructions which an individual will seek to overcome and from which he will learn in the course of doing so."

Ned. A Flanders observes, "Teaching is an interaction process. Interaction means participation of both teacher and students and both are benefited by this. The interaction takes place for achieving desired objectives."

N. L. Gage (1962) has defined, "Teaching is a form of interpersonal influence aimed at changing the behaviour potential of another."

According to Burton, "Teaching is stimulation, guidance, direction and encouragement of learning".

Yoakman and Simpson write, "Teaching is a means whereby society trains the young in a selected environment as quickly as possible to adjust themselves to the world in which they live."

Teaching as a Relationship. Teaching is a relationship which is established between three focal points in education; the teacher, the child and the subject. Teaching is the process by which the teacher brings the child and the subject together. The teacher and the taught are active, the former in teaching and the latter in learning.

Important Characteristics of Teaching

1. Teaching is causing to learn.
2. Teaching is helping the child to respond to his environment in an effective manner.
3. Teaching is helping the child to adjust himself to his environment.
4. Teaching is encouragement and stimulation to the child.
5. Teaching is imparting information.
6. Teaching is training the emotions of the child.
7. Teaching is both a conscious and unconscious process.
8. Teaching is formal as well as informal.
9. Teaching is a linguistic process i.e. communication by the use of language.
10. Teaching is an interactive process or face to face encounter between the teacher and the taught.
11. Teaching is an art as well as a science.
12. Teaching is modifiable by the mechanism of feed back devices.

The Factors

1. Effective teaching depends on the skills of the teacher, his personality and behaviour.
2. Effective teaching depends on careful planning by the teacher.
3. Effective teaching depends on healthy interactive relations between the teacher and the taught.

4. Effective teaching depends upon proper classroom environment intellectual as weli as physical.
5. Effective teaching depends upon the active involvement of the learners.
6. Effective teaching depends upon the use of appropriate strategies, methods, techniques and teaching aids.

Education and Teaching. Teaching is one of the instruments of education and its special function is to impart understanding and skill. We limit our outlook to the work of teaching, omitting those more important means of education which are involved in the school as a systematically organized social community, including its tone or general moral atmosphere, its government and discipline, and that potent influence-the personality of the teacher. James Welton thinks, "We talk of teaching by itself, because it is an aspect of school life which can be singled out in thought, though it cannot be separated, in reality, from the whole of which it forms a part and because, it covers a fairly consistent body of doctrine. It is true that the value and success of all school teaching depends on those wider and deeper elements of school life-tone, discipline, etc. which are omitting. But it is also true that whilst the latter may be excellent the former may be of poor quality."

EFFECTIVE LEARNING

Definition and Meaning: Several attempts have been made by thinkers to define learning but so far no one has been successful in giving an accepted definition. Nevertheless following definitions provide a comprehensive view of learning.

According to Freeman, "It (learning) is the process of developing the ability to respond adequately to a situation which may or may not have been previously encountered."

Harriman views learning as, "It is the improvement in efficiency of adjustment as a result of practice, insight, observation, imitation and conditioning."

Gates and others remark, "Learning may be thought of as the progressive change in behaviour which is associated, on the one hand with successive presentations of a situation, and on the other, with repeated efforts of the individual to react to it effectively."

In the words of Heidgerken, "Learning is not an addition of new experiences, 'per se', nor is it old experience summed up, rather it is synthesis of old and the new experiences which result in completely new organisation or pattern of experience."

J.F. Travers defines learning as "a process that results in the modification of behaviour".

According to M.L. Bigge, "Learning may be considered as a change in insights, behaviour, perception, motivation or a combination of these."

Munn defines learning as "the process of being modified, more or less permanently, by what happens in the world around us, by what we do, or by what we observe."

Hunter and Hilgard, observe, "Learning is the process by which behaviour (in the broader sense) is originated or changed through practice or training."

Kingsley and Gary define it as follows: "Learning is the process by which an organism in satisfying its motivations adopts and adjusts its behaviour in order to overcome obstacles or barriers."

As a sequences of events, the learning process is as follows:

1. The individual has needs and therefore, he is in a state of readiness to respond. These are antecedent conditions within the learner.
2. He meets a learning situation or problem. A new interpretation is required because previously learned responses are not adequate for reaching the goal and satisfying his need. He encounters something new or unexpected, and must search for a different response.
3. He interprets the situation with reference to his goals, and tries a response or responses which seem to satisfy his need. The way he perceives the situation and the

response he makes depends both on his 'readiness,' and on external conditions of the situation.

4. If his response leads to devised goals or satisfaction, he will tend to interpret and respond to similar future situations in the same way. If not, he keeps on trying and reinterpreting until consequences are attained. The learning process is the whole sequence.

The Characteristics

1. Learning is growth of the learner.
2. Learning is adjustment by the learner.
3. Learning is an addition of new experience.
4. Learning is a synthesis and integration of the old and new experience.
5. Learning is purposeful.
6. Learning is intelligent comprehension.
7. Learning is insight.
8. Learning is both individual as well as social.
9. Learning is a product of heredity and environment.
10. Learning is change in behaviour.

Learning is influenced by various conditions of life and school. Our attempts should be to create such conditions as are conducive to effective learning and which help students to make the most satisfactory adjustment to life. The following factors influence learning:-

1. Hereditary factors.
2. Physical conditions of the learners.
3. Goals set before the learners.
4. Stimulation of the learners.
5. Effective association of things, ideas and experiences.
6. Suitable teaching or instruction by the teacher.
7. Purposeful guidance and counselling to the learners.

8. Physical conditions of the classroom.
9. Intellectual environment in the class.
10. Use of appropriate teaching aids.
11. Sympathetic but firm attitude of the teacher.
12. Sense of security to the students.
13. Proper involvement of the students in the teaching-learning process.

Meaning and Significance : Undoubtedly, the teaching-learning process is the heart of education. on it depends the fulfilment of the aims and objectives of education. It is the most powerful instrument of the educator to bring about desired changes in the students.

Teaching and learning are related terms. When we talk of teaching, we have in mind the teacher, the students and the subject matter. Likewise when we talk of learning, we have in mind the students, the teachers and the subject-matter. The needs and interests of the students are the guiding factors in the teaching-learning process. It is a process in which the teacher, the learner, the curriculum and other variables are organised in a systematic way to attain some pre-determined goal. It implies that all the various elements of the teaching-learning situation have to be brought into relationship and built into an intelligible whole. The teacher learner activities which are varied and complex have to be harmonised. These elements and activities include learners and their individual differences, the methods of teaching, the material to be taught, class-room conditions, teaching devices and aids, questioning and answering, assignments, thinking, enjoying, creating, practical skills, discussions and many others.

Relationship between Teaching and Learning. Burton has stated the relationship as under:

(a) Teaching can become effective only by relating it to the process of learning.

(b) Teaching objectives cannot be realised without being related to learning situations.

(c) We may create and use teaching aids to create some appropriate learning situations.

(d) The strategies and devices of teaching may be selected in such a manner that the optimal objectives of learning are achieved.

(e) The knowledge of relationship will be helpful for teacher education to produce and train desired type of teachers.

(f) The concept of relationship of the two will be an aid to understand the principles, goals and objectives of education in the right perspective.

(g) The appropriate learning situation condition may be created for congenial and effective teaching.

Teaching-learning process is affected by the totality of the situation. Teaching learning is fruitful and permanent if the total situation is related to life situations. Teachers can play an important role in facilitating learning.

If teaching-learning process is effective then the child is able to make the best use of the things in the world around him. If an individual has not learnt the art of living harmoniously with others, he will find himself beset with more difficulties than the person who has learnt how to establish social relations with his fellows. So the acquisition of knowledge, skills and attitudes which enable the students to adjust themselves in an effective manner to the environment may be said to be the aim of teaching-learning.

Following are the important factors which affect the teaching-learning process.

Organisation and Planning of the Subject-matter. First of all the success of the teaching-learning process depends upon the thoroughness of knowledge of the subject-matter to be taught. There are no two opinions about this important aspect. The soul of effective teaching-learning is good command of the subject-matter on the part of the teacher.

Once it is taken for granted that the subject matter is thoroughly mastered, the next question is how to present that effectively. Here we enter into the field of planning and methods of teaching. The teacher must use dynamic and progressive methods of teaching. The students should be guided how to learn through his own efforts.

Psychology of Learners. A teacher must realize the fact that with all his knowledge of the subject-matter, his ability to present it methodically and effectively and his ability to control the class situation ably, teaching-learning will never be effective if he does not try to take into consideration the interests, abilities, aptitudes and limitations of the learners. A teacher must learn to understand his learners and encourage them. He has to be sincere and honest towards his learners. An ideal teacher is always humble. He has to practise tolerance and patience in dealing with the learners. The participation of the learners is very important and necessary if the teaching-learner has to have a brcader and meaningful process. The teaching- learner has to have a broader and meaningful process. The teacher has to be an 'inductor of change' and unifying force of knowledge.

Class Control. A good teacher is one who can control his class not through fear or high handedness but by virtue of his interest in the learner, good command of the subject-matter and the ability to present it interestingly and effectively. The learners also appreciate good teaching and cooperate with the teacher in the teaching-learning process.

Self-evaluation on the Part of the Teacher. The teacher must evaluate himself through the evaluation of what he has thought. Self-introspection and self-evaluation by both the teacher and the learner are very important.

Meaning of Inquiry. The dictionary meanings of inquiry are:

(i) A systematic investigation often of a matter of public interest.

(ii) A request for information.

(iii) Research often on a matter of public interest.

Inquiry in Relation to Child. This involves inquiry into:

(i) Characteristics of a child at different ages and stages.

(ii) How children are brought up.

(iii) What children inherit.

(iv) How children learn.

(v) What children need at different stages.

(vi) What should be done to make the best of child's innate powers.

(vii) What should be taught.

(viii) How the child should be taught.

Methods of Inquiry. These are :

(i) Observations.

(ii) Experimentation.

(iii) Interviews.

(iv) Tests.

Summary. Inquiry in education relates to philosophical and psychological aspects of child's nature and growth i.e. what type of knowledge and wisdom is needed and how the same could be imparted.

On the basis of inquiry, education should be imparted to the child in terms of 3 A's.

(i) Age of the child.

(ii) Ability of the child.

(iii) Aptitude of the child.

Individual Differences of Children. The most important factor which should be kept in view in the education of children is the aspect of individual differences. No two children are exactly alike. Pupils always differ in their level of intelligence, aptitudes, likes and dislikes and in other propensities and potentialities. Different minds are to be trained by the teacher. There are gifted, backward, retarded, talented and handicapped children. All of them should not be treated in the same manner. Knowledge of Educational Psychology helps the teacher to cater to individual differences of children.

The curriculum, the experiences, the methods of teaching-learning and modes of disciplines etc., will have to be different suiting the age, ability and aptitude of the children. Thus, flexibility would be the key-note in our educational programme. At the same time it has to be ensured that proper balance is maintained between the individual needs and group or social needs. The fact that an individual is a member of the society, cannot be ignored in the educative process.

Following chart explains the difference between old and new learnings:

Paradigm Shift Table

S. No.	***From (Old)***	***Towards (New Learning)***
1.	Teacher centred	Learner centred
2.	Rote learning	Knowledge acquisition
3.	Restricted face to face interaction with hesitation	Unlimited interaction without hesitation
4.	Chalk-talk	Learning resources and/or in combination with chalk-talk.
5.	Passive learning	Active learning
6.	Emphasis on completion of courses	Emphasis on learning outcome
7.	Use of print medium	Use of hypermedia
8.	Class tutorials	Electronic tutorials
9.	Physical lab	Electronic lab as a percursor to physical lab
10.	Evaluation by teacher	Evaluation by teacher plus computer
11.	Linear learning	Linear plus Non-linear learning
12.	Rigid	Flexible systems
13.	Cement and mortar infrastructure for building institutions	Computer and networking infrastructure
14.	Real classroom	Virtual classroom

The process of education revolves round the following:

(a) The learner-his nature, interests, needs etc.

(b) The learning material.

(c) The learning process.

(d) The teacher.

(e) The teaching process.

(f) The teaching-learning situation.

(g) The teaching-learning process.

(h) Evaluation of the learner.

Exercise

1. What is Education in broad terms ?
2. What are basic concepts of education ?

2

Historical Background

(1) Indigenous System of Elementary Education in India in the Beginning of the 19th Century

(2) Gokhale's Resolution on Primary Education (1913-14)

(3) Hartog Committee Report (1929)

(4) Abbot and Wood Report (1936-37)

(5) Zakir Husain Report on Basic Education (1937) and Kothari Commission 1964-66 on Basic Education

(6) Sargent Report (1944)

(7) State of Elementary Education at the time of independence

INDIGENOUS SYSTEM

Characteristics of Indigenous Education. Prof. A.N. Basu in his book 'Education in Modern India' has observed, "The elementary system was intended for the masses. It was widespread system consisting of numerous primary schools scattered all over the country-side. Practically every village had its primary school." In Bengal alone, it is said, there were about the year 1835 a hundred thousand such schools. Similarly MR. Paranjape has stated, "At the beginning of the nineteenth century, there existed a fairly wide spread organisation for primary education in most parts of India."

The second remarkable feature of indigenous education in India was that the schools were not meant for a particular caste class of society. They were open to everyone who wanted to study.

Thirdly attempts were also made to acquire higher education also.

Sir Thomas Monro, the Governor of Madras has said that the state of education exhibited here was low as compared with England but was higher than it was in most European countries.

Reports of Sir Monro and Adams throw a flood of light on the indigenous system of education in India.

Education in Madras

Extent. Each village of Madras had a Primary School.

Number of students per school was very small. In some of the districts, the average number of students per school was about 12. Some people used to educate their children at home. Most of the students were Hindus. Very few of the girls entered the schools.

Courses. Most of the schools provided education in provincial languages. There was no uniformity in courses of study. Primary schools in general taught Arithmetic, reading of manuscripts, beautiful poems and fine stories.

Duration. Generally boys of well-to-do families started going to school at the age of five and continued their studies upto the age of 14 or 15 years.

Ceremony While Starting Studies. 'Havan' and 'Ganesh Pujan' were performed to which the kith and kin of the boy were invited. Afterwards the 'Guru' caused the boy recite the prayer of 'Ganeshji'. The parents of the boy gave 'Dakshina' (gift) to 'Guru'.

Daily Routine. Routine was same for the students. The school used to start at about 6 with 'Saraswati Vandana' i.e. prayer of goddess of learning.

School Discipline. Discipline was very hard. Guilty students were severely caned.

Methods of Teaching. Students started writing the alphabets on sand or ground with their fingers. Afterwards they started writing on small wooden planks, i.e., patti and chalk and pen of wood (Kalam).

Monitorial System. The teachers used monitorial system. Good students of higher classes were given chance to teach the students of lower classes.

Salary of Teachers. Teachers were mostly ill paid. Their pay could hardly feed them.

Education in Bombay

School Buildings. There were no separate school buildings. Education was carried on in temples, houses of teachers and residence of respectable persons.

Number of Schools. There was at least one school in every village. The average number of students per school was fifteen. The highest number in a school was 150.

Fees. Teachers were paid 'Sidha' one rupee per month by the guardians of a student.

Courses of Study. Students were taught to read, write and do ordinary and practical arithmetic. They were made to learn, by heart the 'Pahara' and 'Ginti' (counting of numbers etc.).

Duration. Students started schooling at the age of 6 and continued upto the age of 14 years.

Discipline. Hard punishments were generally given to the students for not maintaining discipline and learning lessons.

Status and Conditions of Teachers. They did not teach from economic point of view. Generally they were Brahmans but sometimes Marathas, Bhandaries and Vaishyas were also working as teachers. They were generally invited at festivals and received some gifts and presents on particular occasions. As a tradition, they got 3 to 5 rupees per month.

Education in Bengal

William Adam was appointed in 1835 by Lord Bentick to make a survey of indigenous education of some districts of Bengal and Bihar. Adam worked on his enquiry for three years (1835-38) and submitted three valuable reports at different times.

Adam classified different educational agencies into seven categories :

1. Indigenous elementary schools.
2. Elementary schools not indigenous, i.e., new types of elementary schools run by missionaries and others.
3. Domestic education.
4. English schools and colleges.
5. Native female schools.
6. Indigenous schools for advanced learning.
7. Adult instruction.

Extent of Education. Adam says that no village in Bengal was without a primary school. There were about one lakh of schools scattered in all the villages. Adam called the places and homes where education was given as 'schools'.

Teacher's Salary. Teachers were paid Rs. 5 per month.

Duration of Schooling. The students started education at the age of 8 and read upto the age of 14 years.

Course of Studies. The Hindus were generally reading Bengali and Sanskrit and Muslims were reading Arabic and Persian.

Education of Women. Adam states that the very name of women education made people afraid of.

Schools Open for All. Schools were not meant for a particular caste or class of society. They were open to every one who wanted to study. Adam suggested the following measures for reforming the system.

1. Publication of a graded series of new textbooks (I-IV) in Bengali, Hindi and Urdu, to be prepared by Indians and Europeans in collaboration.

2. Appointment of an examiner for each district. It was suggested that the examiner should survey his area, supply and explain textbooks to teachers, examine teachers on the context of textbooks already provided after a period of six months, distribute grants and records to teachers according to the percentage or passes in school examinations, and supervise the work of teachers.
3. Appointment of inspectors for supervising the work of examiners.
4. Training of teachers. Adam proposed to convert Vernacular Departments of English schools into normal schools for training teachers of indigenous schools. He suggested that these teachers should be required to study in these schools for three months in a year for four successive years.
5. Award of small grants of land to village schools for their maintenance.
6. Organisation of experimental farms for agricultural education.

Adam's recommendations were not accepted by the Government. Before he submitted his third Report. Macaulay as the Chairman of the Committee had pronounced his verdict. Macaulay was wedded to the Filtration Theory and believed firmly in the superiority of western civilisation. According to Macaulay, indigenous schools were useless. He observed, "I am little inclined to doubt, however, whether we are at present ripe for any extensive practical measure, which he (Adam) recommends. Our work is to educate the school masters for the next generation." The Committee regarded Adam's plan as impartial and accepted the views of Macaulay. Adam submitted his resignation.

F. W. Thomas thinks, "From the accuracy of its information, the candour, sense and statesmanship of its author (Adam) it is among the most valuable and interesting publication on education in India." S.N. Mukherji regards Adam's Reports "as one of the ablest reports ever written on Indian education" and he laments on the fate of this report. "A golden opportunity for building up a national system of education, based on culture and language of the people, was thus lost."

Early Missionary Schools

Important Contribution. There is no doubt that the early missionaries played an important role in the spread of education in the 19th century of India. It is sometimes stated that modern system of education was started in India by the schools established by the missionaries. Missionaries made a good deal of attempt for the spread of education in India with the primary objective of spreading Christianity.

Portuguese Missionaries. Portuguese missionaries were the first among Europeans to start educational institutions in India, The main centres of activities were Bombay, Goa, Daman, Diu, Ceylon Chittagong and Hugli. Those who followed Christians were given free education. The children of the poor Christians were also given free food, books, etc. The name of St. Francis Xavier who came to India in 1542 is associated with many institutions even today.

Dutch Missionaries. Dutch Missionaries did not make their educational institutions as centres of religious propaganda. Their educational institutions did not survive for long as they could not compete with the Britishers in supremacy over India.

French Missionaries. The missionaries started their schools at Pondicherry, Mahi, Yaman and Karikal but in due course these schools were taken over by the English when they took possession of these territories.

Danes. Danish religious preachers started schools for boys who became Christians and they were taught Tamil. They also started a training college for teachers in Travancore. Schools were also started in Madras Fort William, St. David, Trichnapalli and Tanjore where English was also taught, besides other subjects.

Early Mission Schools. Following were the striking features of early mission schools.

1. Religious instruction according to the tenets of Christianity was compulsory and the Bible was used as a class-book.
2. The curriculum was wide and included subjects like grammar, history and geography.
3. Printed textbooks were also introduced.
4. Classes were held regularly at fixed hours. Sunday was a holiday.
5. A regular, clear-cut class-system was introduced, since most of the schools had more than one teacher.
6. Instruction was imparted through the languages of the people.

GOKHALE'S RESOLUTION (1913-14)

Gopal Krishna Gokhale (1866-1915). A champion in the field of compulsory primary education in India: Professor and Principal of Poona Fergusson College for a number of years; President of Indian National Congress (1905); founder of the Servants of Indian Society; Member of Imperial Council.

Gokhale's Efforts. Gokhale contacted the Maharaja Sayaji Rao Gaikwad of Baroda who had in 1906 made primary education free and compulsory within the territory of his state and got great inspiration from his efforts.

In 1910, Gokhale, as a Member of the Imperial Council moved the following Resolution:

"That this Council recommends that a beginning should be made in the direction to make elementary education free and compulsory throughout the country, and that a mixed commission of officials and non-officials be appointed at an early date to frame definite proposals."

Important suggestions contained in his resolution, moved in the Legislative Council, were as follows:

(a) That in the area where 35% boys were receiving education, elementary education should be made free and compulsory. This provision should apply to the age group of 6 to 10 years.

(b) The cost of primary education should be shared by the Provincial Government and Local Bodies. The Local Bodies and the Government Bodies should bear the expenditure in the ratio of 1:2.

(c) A secretary should be appointed to organise, supervise and look after the primary education.

(d) There should be a separate Department in the Central Government to draw up scheme for the expansion of primary education; and in the budget statement there should be a portion describing the progress of primary education.

On the assurances of the government, Gokhale withdrew the Bill.

Gokhale's Second Attempt to Introduce the Bill. Gokhale was not discouraged. He made further attempts to draw the attention of the Government of India and that of the Government of England towards the conditions of education. He grided up his loins to wage a fierce struggle against the Government. He moved the Bill in 1912 but the Bill was rejected. on this occasion his memorable words were: "My Lord, I know that any Bill will be thrown out before the day closes. I make no complaint. Moreover, I have always felt and have often said that we of the present generation in India can only hope to serve our country by our failures. The men and women who will be privileged to serve her by their successes will come later...... The Bill, thrown out today, will come back again and again, till on the stepping stones, of its dead-shelves, a measure ultimately rises which will spread the light of knowledge throughout the land."

Main suggestions contained in the Bill are given below:

(a) Local Bodies were to have the right to introduce compulsion in the whole or part of the area under their jurisdiction.

(b) Local bodies to be given the right to levy cess to meet the cost of free and compulsory primary education.

(c) Expenditure on education be shared by the Local Bodies and the Provincial Government in the ratio of 1: 2.

(d) Primary Education should be made compulsory for the boys of the age-group of 6 to 10, and the defaulting should be penalised for non-compliance of the provisions of sending their wards to recognised schools.

(e) The primary education to be made compulsory for girls.

(f) Guardians whose monthly income is less than Rs. 10/- should not be asked to pay any fee.

Although Gokhale's Bill was rejected, yet it served a great purpose. It focused the attention of entire country on education. The work of Gokhale was taken up by Shri Vithalbhai J. Patel at Provincial level. His bill for compulsory primary education was accepted by the Bombay Legislative Council and became the Bombay Primary Education Act of 1918, popularly known as Patel Act.

Hartog Committee Report (1929)

The Committee was appointed in 1929 to review the position of education in the country. The Committee covered the position of education at the school level and made valuable observations regarding equality and status of teachers. Sir Phillip Hartog was the Chairman of the Committee. He had been a Vice-Chancellor of the Dacca University. The Committee's observations on primary education still find an important place in the educational literature.

Committee on Primary Education

Throughout the whole educational system there is waste and ineffectiveness. In the primary system, which from our point of view should be designed to produce literacy and the capacity to exercise an intelligent vote, the waste is appalling. So far as we can judge, the vast increase in number in the primary schools produces no commensurate increase in literacy, for only a small proportion of those who are at the primary stage reach Class IV, in which the attainment of literacy may be expected. The wastage in the case of girls is more serious than in the case of boys......"

Wastage and Stagnation of Primary Education. According to the Committee, "Wastage meant the pre-mature withdrawals of children from schools at any stage before the completion of the primary course."

Stagnation means detention in lower classes of a child for a period more than what was needed for that class. The Committee made the following recommendations;

1. Primary education should be made compulsory but there should be no hurry about it.
2. Instead of increasing the number of primary schools qualitative development should be made.
3. At least four years should be devoted to primary education.
4. Curriculum of primary schools should be made more liberal and scientific.
5. Due attention should be paid to include subjects of practical utility to the students in life.
6. Primary schools should serve as centres for rural uplift, medical relief, adult education, mass literacy, sanitation, recreation etc.
7. Standard of teachers of primary schools should be improved.
8. Salary and conditions of service of teachers of primary schools should be improved.
9. Inspecting staff should be increased so as to exercise adequate control of these schools.

ABBOT AND WOOD REPORT (1936-37)

Appointment of Two Experts. on its revival in 1935, the Central Advisory Board of Education (C.A.B.E.) recommended the appointment of a Committee to make recommendations for the reorganization of education in view of the fact that a large number of graduates going out of the universities were unable to secure employment of the kind for which the education qualified them. Two experts, Messrs Abbot and Wood were accordingly invited to advise the Government "on certain problems of educational reorganization and particularly on problems of vocational education." The report had two parts, Technical and General. Abbot was the author of the report on technical education and Wood on general education.

Abbot, formerly Chief Inspector of Technical Schools, Board of Education, England, and S.H. Wood, Director of Instruction, Board of Education, England visited the country for making necessary suggestions during the winter of 1936-37 and submitted their report in June 1937.

Observations on Education

1. Infant classes should as far as possible, be entrusted to trained teachers and for this and other reasons the development of educational provision of girls and women is of paramount importance.
2. The education of children in the primary schools should be based more upon the national interests and activities of young children and less upon book-learning. Concentration on narrow learning is unsound.
3. The curriculum of the rural middle school should be closely related to children's environment; and if English is taught to any children of middle school age it should not be allowed to result in an excessive amount of linguistic load.
4. The mother-tongue should, as far as possible, be the medium of instruction throughout the high school stage, but English should be a compulsory language for all pupils at this stage. The teaching of English should be made more realistic.

5. More systematic attention should be paid to the teaching of Fine Arts, and steps should be taken to secure for high schools a supply of qualified teachers of Fine Arts.
6. The pre-service education course of teachers of primary and middle schools should be a three-year course following without any gap in the completion of middle school course.

Observations. The recommendations made were workable and well thought out. Unfortunately due to the outbreak of the Second World War within a year and a half of the submission of the report, no action could be taken on these recommendations.

ZAKIR HUSAIN REPORT

The Zakir Husain Report is a fundamental document on Basic Education/Nai Talim, or Wardha Scheme of Basic Education. It is based on the ideas of Gandhiji on education. Gandhiji placed his views on education before the public in a series of articles written in the Harijan in early 1937. He described this new "educational process in the following words":

1. The course of primary education should be extended at least to seven years and should include the general knowledge gained up to the matriculation standard less English and plus a substantial vocation.
2. For the all-round development of boys and girls all training should, so far as possible, be given through a project-yielding vocation.
3. This primary education should equip boys and girls to earn their bread by the State guaranting employment in the vocations learnt or by buying their manufactured articles at prices fixed by the state.

CONFERENCE OF NATIONAL WORKERS

In October 1937, at a Conference of National Workers at Wardha under the Chairmanship of Gandhiji, his ideas were considered and the following resolutions passed which became the fundamental features of the scheme:

(a) That in the opinion of the conference, free and compulsory education be provided for seven years on a nation-wide scale.

(b) That the medium of instruction be the mother-tongue.

(c) That the Conference endorses the proposal made by Mahatma Gandhi that the process of education throughout this period should centre round some form of manual productive work, and that all the other abilities to be developed or training to be given should, as far as possible, be integrally related to the central handicraft chosen with due regard to the child.

(d) That the conference expects that this system of education will be gradually able to cover the remuneration of the teachers.

A Committee was appointed under the Chairmanship of Dr. Zakir Husain to prepare a detailed syllabus on the lines of the above resolutions. The Committee submitted its report on 2nd December, 1937.

Fundamental Features

The fundamental features of the scheme having undergone some changes are as follows:

1. A school of say 5½ hours could roughly be divided on the following basis:

Physical activities	20 minutes
Mother Tongue	40 minutes
Social Studies and General Science	60 minutes
Art	40 minutes
Arithmetic	40 minutes
Craft work including study of correlated subjects	2½ hours

Thus the craft work to have 2½ hours instead of 3 hours

and 20 minutes as originally proposed.

2. Free and compulsory education to be given in 8 years (from 6 to 14 years) in two stages, instead of 7 to 14. The junior stage will cover five years and the senior 3 years.
3. The medium of instruction is to be the mother-tongue.
4. Education is to centre round some form of productive work. The social and physical environment should be used for correlation in addition to craft.
5. The self-supporting aspect is not to be over-emphasised. The sale-proceeds of the finished goods should be able to help the school to cover some part of its expenditure.
6. External examinations are to be abolished. The day-today work of the students is to be the determining factor.
7. Text-books to be avoided as far as possible.
8. Cleanliness and health, citizenship, play and recreation are to be given sufficient importance.

Zakir Husain Report

Craft Work in Schools

Modern educational thought is practically unanimous in commending the idea of educating children through some suitable form of productive work. This method is considered to be the most effective approach to the problem of providing an integral all-sided education.

Psychologically, it is desirable, because it relieves the child from the tyranny of a purely academic and theoretical instruction against which its active nature is always making a healthy protest. It balances the intellectual and practical elements of experience, and may be made an instrument of educating the body and the mind in co-ordination. The child acquires not the superficial literacy which implies, often without warrant, a capacity to read the printed page but the far more important capacity of using hand and intelligence for some constructive purpose. Thus, if we may be permitted to use the expression, is the literacy of the "whole personality".

Socially considered, the introduction of such practical productive work in education, to be participated in by all the children of the nation, will tend to break down the existing barriers of prejudice between manual and intellectual workers, harmful alike for both. It will also cultivate in the only possible way a true sense of the dignity of labour and of human solidarity—an ethical and moral gain of incalculable significance.

Economically considered, carried out intelligently and efficiently, the scheme will increase the productive capacity of our workers and will also enable them to utilize their leisure advantageously.

From the strictly educational point of view greater concreteness and reality can be given to the knowledge acquired by children by making some significant craft the basis of education. Knowledge will thus become related to life, and its various aspects will be correlated with one another.

Distinctive Merits

"This basic education," according to a pamphlet published by the Ministry of Education, "is not only a valuable and integral part of the priceless legacy that Mahatma Gandhi left to the nation but embodies certain educational ideas and principles of great significance that have been welcomed and endorsed by distinguished and discerning educationists in India and abroad." "Economically considered, carried out intelligently and efficiently, the scheme will increase the productive capacity of our workers, and will enable them to leisure advantageously", reported the Zakir Husain Committee.

The Basic Education has the following distinctive merits.

Craft Centred Education. Gandhiji remarked, "By education, I mean an all-round drawing out of the best in child and man —

body, mind and spirit. Literacy is not the end of education nor even the beginning. It is only one of the means whereby men and women can be educated. Literacy in itself is no education. I would therefore begin the child's education by teaching it a useful handicraft and enabling it to produce from the moment it begins its training".

The craft is the centre of all education in the Basic System. Gandhiji was of the opinion that the method of training the mind through village handicrafts from the very beginning as the central focus would promote the real, disciplined development of the mind resulting in conservation of the intellectual energy and indirectly also the spiritual. According to him, the highest development of the mind and the soul was possible only through handicrafts. This could be done very easily if handicraft was taught scientifically, i.e., the child should know the why and wherefore of every process.

Craft work done under proper conditions not only makes the acquisition of much related knowledge more concrete and realistic but also adds a powerful contribution to the development of personality and character and instils respect and love for all socially useful work.

Craft work helps the child to acquire sensory and motor-co-ordination and to appreciate the value of honest labour.

Craft work gives the child practical sense and skills and prepares him to earn a living.

Craft work is the meeting point of all subjects. The correlated teaching arouses greater interest and enthusiasm because it gives teaching and learning a relevance born of practical and living purpose and need.

Social Activities and Community Life. The corner-stone of Basic education lies in the activities and' the community life of the school. Apart from craft, productive activities and occupations find an important place in the curriculum of a basic school. Living together and doing together is the soul of any progressive system of education and Basic system fully incorporates this in its curriculum and methods of teaching.

Self-sufficiency. Gandhiji felt that the New Education must not only be work-centred but must also be self-supporting.

"......You have to start with the conviction that looking to the need of the villages of India our rural education ought to be made self-supporting if it is to be compulsory. This education ought to be for them a kind of insurance against unemployment.

Not only from economic point of view, this education must be self-sufficient, but also from social and moral points of view. This means that at the end of the period of basic education the individual should become self-reliant and self-supporting."

Views of Mahatma Gandhi. Dr. Zakir Husain Committee pointed out the danger of overdoing of craft work and warned that oral work, drawing and expression work should not be lost sight of. The educative aspect is more important than the economic aspect. It thus shifted the emphasis from complete support to partial self-support. Now it is felt that with the earnings through sale of craft products, uniform for the students or mid-day meal or purchase of some necessary equipment may be made.

Emphasis from Economic to Philosophical Self-sufficiency. Today the emphasis is on philosophical self-sufficiency that Basic education should inculcate in the students ability to pull their weight in the society afterwards and be able to live as efficient workers and self-supporting citizens.

Free and Compulsory Education. Seven year's free and compulsory education is one of the fundamentals of this scheme and this cardinal principle has been emphasised due to two reasons:

(1) India is a democratic country and success of democracy depends upon the enlightened citizens. Our great leaders like Gokhale worked for the introduction of compulsory education for a long time In his historic speech, Gokhale said that if elementary education was to spread in India, it must be made compulsory and if it was to be compulsory it must be free.

(2) Gandhiji's dream of a classless society, free of exploita-

tion, economic and social can be realised only if everyone is educated.

Mother Tongue as Medium of Instruction. It is now universally recognised that the young child can learn with great facility if the medium of instruction is its mother tongue, Gandhiji asserted that no education is possible through foreign medium and all elementary education must be imparted through the medium of the mother tongue.

Education Through Correlation. Correlation is one of the important features and crux of Basic education. The Basic education is, therefore, an effort to correlate the life of the child with his immediate, physical and social environments. It is an effort to make knowledge easier and at the same time more meaningful.

Learning by Doing. Learning by doing sums up the educational methods of Basic education. It is absolutely wrong to think that true knowledge is acquired from books alone. There are other methods and sources which are more helpful in acquiring true knowledge. 'Chalk' and 'Talk' lessons are also not very useful. All educationists have condemned bookish knowledge. Gandhiji believed that school must be a doing thing and therefore a thinking thing in the real sense of the word rather than a talking thing.

Significance of the Word

The word 'Basic' is derived from the word 'Base' which means the bottom or the foundation of a thing upon which the whole thing rests or is made.

1. It is considered basic because it is based on ancient Indian culture.
2. It is basic because it lays down the minimum educational standards which every Indian child is entitled to receive without any distinction of caste or creed.
3. It is basic because it is closely related to the basic needs and interests of the child.
4. It is basic because it makes use of the native potentialities of the child.

5. It is basic because it is intimately related to the basic occupations of the community.
6. It is basic because it is for the common man of the country who is the foundation and backbone of our nation's life.
7. It is basic because it comes first in the primary period of our education.

Limitations and Causes

There is no denying the fact that Basic Education has not been a success. Even Dr. Zakir Husain was constrained to remark "Basic Education as practised is a fraud." Some of the causes for the failure of Basic Education are discussed here.

Misunderstanding about Concept. There had always been confusion about understanding the concept of Basic Education. In the words of Professor Saiyidain, "The Basic Education Movement is in some ways, a radical departure both in theory and practice and it requires a careful reorientation of ideas, attitudes and techniques. It is therefore, a matter of no great surprise—though it is certainly one of disappointment—that the full implication of basic approach has not yet been realized by many teachers and educational administrators".

Economic Aspect Over-emphasised. Too much emphasis was laid on economic aspect or the productivity aspect and this fact was responsible for the unpopularity of Basic Education. Teachers remained busy either in the garden or in the workshop and they lost sight of educational objectives of the craft.

Lack of Competent Teachers. Most of the teachers who taught in basic schools were not trained for this type of education.

Dearth of Textbooks. Suitable books to teach in accordance with the requirements of Basic Education were not made available.

High Cost of Basic Education. A good Basic school can only be established with a good deal of initial cost on the purchase of equipment for different crafts. In addition to this cost, there is always a recurring expenditure on the successful running of a good craft. The income from the products is not commensurate with the financial outlay.

Lack of Provision for Individual Differences. It failed to provide for the individual differences of the pupils and, therefore, the drawbacks of traditional system of education continued to harm the individuality of the child.

Artistic and Aesthetic Aspects Neglected. In some of the Basic schools, these aspects were not attended to. Children did very little art work which was generally confined to the drawing of charts depicting the techniques of correlation. The appreciation of art or beauty was altogether neglected.

Rigidity. The scheme was rigid in several aspects and did not accept even sound and practical suggestions. Any such technique for primary school children must be flexible and must accept suggestions with the change of time and objectives of education.

Apathy of Administration. In the words of Assessment Committee on Basic Education (1956), "It is at the administrative level today, more than any other that serious difficulties arise in the development of Basic Education. Departments are concerned with innumerable problems. Basic Education is a small and side item in their programmes of work. In none of the States did we find a Director of Public Instruction, to whom Basic Education was an issue of utmost importance nor did we find any of them fully conversant with the problems of Basic Education in their respective States."

Sargent Report (1944)

The report derives its name from the name of its author, Sir John Sargent, the Education Adviser to the Government of India who was asked to draw up a memorandum for the development of Indian Education in the Post-war Reconstruction Period. He submitted his report to the Central Advisory Board of Education and the Board accepted it in 'toto' and recommended its enforcement. It is also known as: 1. Sargent Report. 2. Post-war

Educational Development Scheme. 3. Report by Central Advisory Board of Education.

Important Recommendations

Basic Education

(a) A system of universal, compulsory and free education for all boys and girls between the ages of six and fourteen should be introduced as speedily as possible though in view of the practical difficulty of recruiting the requisite supply of trained teacher it may not be possible to complete it in less than forty years.

(b) The Senior Basic (Middle) School, being the finishing school for the great majority of future citizens, is of fundamental importance and should be generously staffed and equipped.

Nursery Education

(a) An adequate provision of pre-primary instruction in the form of Nursery Schools or classes is an essential adjunct to any national system of education.

(b) In urban areas, where sufficient children are available within a reasonable radius, separate Nursery Schools or departments may be provided; elsewhere Nursery classes should be attached to Junior Basic (Primary) Schools.

(c) Nursery Schools and classes should, invariably be staffed with women teachers who have received special training for this work.

(d) Pre-primary education should in all cases be free.

(e) The main object of education at this stage is to give young children social experience rather than formal instruction.

Important Features of the Plan

1. It was spread over a period of 40 years (1945-84).

2. An annual expenditure of Rs. 3,126 million to be incurred on the then estimated population of 290 million; i.e., Rs. 11/- per head of population at the 1939 prices.
3. Provision of facilities for one child in every 21 at the pre-primary stage.
4. Free and compulsory education on basic lines for all children in the age-group 6-11.
5. Compulsory senior basic education for three years for four-fifths of children in the age group 11-14.
6. Secondary education for selected and gifted children (for one child out of every five who completed the primary course).
7. University education for one out of every fifteen students who completed the secondary school.
8. A fair sized programme of technical education and the provision of other ancillary services.
9. Liquidation of adult illiteracy.

The Report thus estimated that the total annual expenditure on the educational system proposed by it would come to as 3,126 million out of which a sum of about Rs. 356 million (or about 13%) would come from fees and other sources and the balance of Rs. 2,770 million (or about 89%) would have to be provided from public taxation.

Critical Analysis

1. The estimates were based on Pre-second world war level of prices and should have been adjusted for any subsequent rise in them.
2. The estimates were based on an estimated population of 290 million and no allowance was made for any increase in population, although the period to be covered by the plan was deemed to extend over 40 years.
3. The plan gave estimates for the recurring expenditure only.

4. The plan provided for the intensive development of certain areas and such an approach is hardly suitable for a democratic country like ours.
5. The plan did not give concrete suggestions to find out the resources for the financing of the plan.
6. The plan was spread over too long a period. It was deemed to extend over 40 years. The Kher Committee appointed by the Central Advisory Board of Education examined the matter and recommended that the plan should be implemented in a period of 16 years instead of 40.

Financial Estimates

(Rs. in million)

	Estimated gross annual expenditure	*Estimated income from sources other than public funds*	*Estimated net expenditure to be met from public funds*
1. Basic (Primary and Middle) Education	2,000	—	2,000
2. Pre-primary Education	32	—	32
3. High School Education	790	290	500
4. University Education	96	29	67
5. Technical, Commercial and Art Education	100	20	80
6. Adult Education	30	—	30
7. Training of Teachers	62	17	45
8. School Medical Service	—	—	—
9. Education of the Handicapped	—	—	—
10. Recreative and Social Activities	10	—	10
11. Employment Bureau	6	—	6
12. Administration	—	—	—
Total	3,126	356	2,770

Merits of the Report

Valuable Contribution

Shri K.G. Saiyidian stated as: "What is the wider significance of this scheme?" It is the first comprehensive scheme of national education.

"Secondly, it is inspired by the desire to provide equality of opportunity at different stages of education. At the primary stage it envisages not merely the provision of free schooling but also of other facilities without which the poorer children cannot fully avail themselves of the educational opportunities—mid-day meal, books, scholarships, medical inspection and treatment."

"Thirdly, it stresses in clear terms the importance of the teaching profession and makes proposals for increasing its miserable standard of salaries and poor conditions of service. It lays down a minimum national scale of salaries, and provides for its adjustment in accordance with the rise in the cost of living."

Criticism of the Report

Sayed Nurullah and J.P. Naik observed: "It placed a very tame ideal before the country. As the report itself admitted, India would reach the educational standard of the England of 1939 in a period of not less than 40 years. In other words, even assuming that the plan fully implemented, the India of 1984 would still be nearly 50 years behind England. This idea did not naturally satisfy any ardent educationist."

"The financial implications of the Report also came in for a good deal of comment. It was, therefore, opined that, on financial grounds, the scheme is too utopian to be practicable."

"It has been pointed out that the only ideal held up by the Report is that of the educational system of England."

It is difficult to compare the statistics of 1946-47 with those of 1936-37 on account of the establishment of Pakistan. But the figures for 1945-46 which are for undivided India, show that there was an actual fall in the number of schools (owing to the stress of war conditions and only a relatively small rise in the number of pupils).

State of Elementary Education At The Time of Independence Expansion of Basic Education 1881-82 to 1946-47

Year	No. of Primary Schools	No. of Pupils
1881-82	82,916	2,061,541
1901-02	93,604	3,076,671
1921-22	155,017	6,109,752
1936-37	192,244	10,224,288
1945-46	167,700	13,027,313
1946-47	134,866	10,525,943

Compulsory Basic Education 1947-48

Province	Age-Group under Compulsion	Area with Boys only under Compulsion		Area with Boys and Girls under Compulsion	
		No. of Towns and Cities	No. of Villages	No. of Towns and Cities	No. of Villages
Bihar	6-10	17	—	—	—
Bombay	7-8,6-11	9	134	110	5,100
C.P. and Berar	6-11,7-12	34	1,031	—	—
East Punjab	6-11	37	1,420	—	—
Madras	6-14, 6-12	16	31	12	1,607
Orissa	6-12, 6-13	1	1	—	—
U.P.*	6—11	36	1,371	3	3
West Bengal	6—10	1	—	—	—
Delhi	6—12	1	7	—	—

*Figures relate to 1946-47.

TEACHER TRAINING

In 1716, a Danish missionary Ziegenbalq established an institution for training of teachers to be employed in the Charity Schools.

In 1802, another missionary, William Gary established a Normal School for the training of teachers.

In 1819, the Calcutta School Society started the training of teachers for indigenous schools.

Position of elementary teacher training was as under during the period of British Rule in India

Year	*Institutions (Normal Training Schools)*			*Students*		
	Boys	*Girls*	*Total*	*Boys*	*Girls*	*Total*
1881-82	93	15	108	3,458	515	3,973
1901-02	133	46	179	4,410	1,292	5,702
1921-22	926	146	1,072	22,774	4,157	26,931
1941-42	476	239	615	22,435	9,265	31,700
1946-47	443	206	649	28,038	10,835	38,873

Salary of Teachers

According to Adam, a primary teacher in Bengal got about Rs. 3 to 5 per month in 1835. By 1921, this had increased to Rs. 8 or so per month. But in the meanwhile the cost of living had increased so many times that it would be perfectly correct to say that the teacher of an indigenous school of 1835 was really better off than a teacher in the aided school of 1921. When salaries at two different periods are compared in terms of money, due allowance has to be made for the rise or fall in the purchasing power of the rupees.

The position of the emoluments of the primary teachers in 1936-37 was not materially different from that given above on account of the 1929 depression and its aftermath effects.

The problem of low emoluments became very acute during the Second World War period (1939-45). In due course trade union methods began to be adopted by the teachers. The first great strike took place in 1946 in the Province of Bombay. About 45000 primary teachers struck for 54 days. Consequently, the public conscience was aroused and in every Province, the scale of teachers were revised. They were given more liberal dearness allowances. The remunerations therefore, were far better than that in 1936-37 but the rise in the cost of living was so high during this interval that the lot of the primary teachers was far from happy even in 1946-47.

In 1946-47 the average salary of a primary teacher in the country was about Rs. 32 per month.

The Hartog Committee 1927 gave the following comparative figures regarding the salary of primary teachers in different provinces:

Provinces	*Rs.*	*Annas*
Bombay	47*	0
Punjab	25	8
Central Provinces	24	8
United Provinces	18	8
Madras	15	4
Assam	14	4
Bihar and Orissa	11	5
Bengal	8	6

*Probably the salary relates to Bombay city. Average salary of a primary teacher in Bombay was Rs. 33.

KOTHARI COMMISSION

The Kothari Education Commission made the following observations regarding Basic Education: "The movement of basic education launched by Mahatma Gandhi more than 25 years ago, proposing a new type of elementary education for the nation which would centre round some form of manual and productive work and have intimate links with the life of the community, was a landmark in the history of education in India. It was a revolt against the sterile book-centred, examination-oriented system of education that had developed along traditional lines during several decades of British rule. It created a national ferment, which may not have transformed the quality of education at the primary stage, but which has certainly left its impact on educational thought and practice on a much wider sphere. We believe that the essential elements of the system are fundamentally sound and that with necessary modifications these can form a part of education, not only at the primary stage but at all stages in our national system. These elements are (1) productive activity in education; (2) correlation of the curriculum with the productive activity and the physical and social environment; and (3) intimate contact between the school and the local community."

The Commission popularised the concept of 'work experience' and saw that the two ideas work experience and basic education—were essentially similar:

"In the curricula of most contemporary school systems, particularly in the socialist countries of Europe, a place is found for what is variously called 'manual work' or 'work-experience'. In our country, a revolutionary experiment was launched by Mahatma Gandhi in the form of basic education. The concept of work experience is essentially similar. It may be described as a redefinition of his educational thinking in terms of a society launched on the road to industrialisation."

The Commission gave a call for the reorientation of the basic education programme in view of the changed character and need of the new society. It is not difficult to miss the clear shift of emphasis in terms of a new science-oriented social order in the following words:

"The programme of basic education did involve work-experience for all children in the primary schools, though the activities proposed were concerned with the indigenous crafts and the village employment patterns. If in practice basic education has become largely frozen around certain crafts, there is no denying the fact that it always stressed the vital principle of relating educa-tion to productivity. What is now needed is a reorientation of the basic education programme to the needs of a society that has to be transformed with the help of science and technology. In other words, work-experience must be forward looking in keeping with the character of the new social order."

NATIONAL EDUCATION SYSTEM

Five-Year Plans

Since the Government of India had earlier accepted basic education as the national system of education, sincere efforts were made in all directions to popularise it. A systematic effort to encourage basic education was made in the First Plan and a number of schemes on all-India basis were launched. The pace of progress increased in the Second Plan. The progress was maintained in the Third Plan, but a lukewarm attitude was creeping in as a result of some opposition from public quarters. The progress of basic education in the four plans is set out below:

Schools	*1st Plan*	*2nd Plan*	*3rd Plan*	*4th Plan*
Junior basic schools	33,379	42,971	1,00,000	1,53,000
As percentage of total primary schools	15.9	15.4	9.2	30.9
Senior basic schools	318	4842	11940	16700
As percentage of total middle schools	1.9	22.3	30.2	28.9
Basic training schools	114	520	715	1424
As percentage of total number of training schools	15	56	70	100

After the Report of the Education Commission (1964-66) the phrase 'work-experience' came in more frequent use than that of 'basic education'. The Government of India's Resolution of National Policy of Education (1968) has not made any mention of 'basic education'. It, however, declares that work-experience should become an integral part of education.

The National Institute of Basic Education set up by the Government of India which functioned as an important department of NCERT for the purpose of research, extension and training in basic education, has been wound-up.

Some educators consider that recommendations of the Kothari Commission came as 'Death Certificate' of Basic Education.

If the recommendations of the Kothari Commission are any indication, Basic education will remain 'a matter of history of education'.

Again in the National Policy on Education, 1986, there is no mention of Basic system of education at the school stage.

Exercise

1. Give a brief account of the indigenous system of elementary education in India in the beginning of the nineteenth century.
2. Write short notes on:
   (i) Gokhale's effort regarding primary education,
   (ii) Hartog Committee Report,
   (iii) Wood-Abbot Report.
3. Why was the Basic System of education in India introduced?
4. Explain the significance of the Zakir Husain Committee Report. What were the chief features of the report?
5. Discuss the merits and demerits of the Basic System of Education. State the reasons for its failure in India.
6. Write briefly on:
   (i) Expansion of elementary teacher training institutions in India before independence.
   (ii) Salaries of primary teachers.
7. What were the salient features of Sargent Report? Why was it not acceptable to the people of India?

3

The Development

The Meaning

The term 'education' has a very wide connotation. Philosophers and thinkers from Yajnavalkya (Around 1000 B.C.) to Gandhiji (1869-1948 A.D.) in the East and from Socrates (469-399 BC) to Dewey (1859 to 1952 A.D.) have given the meaning of education in accordance with their philosophy of life with the result there have emerged divergent concepts of education and different definitions. The concept of education is like a diamond which appears to be of a different colour when seen from a different angle. Like the proverbial elephant and the blind men, everybody i.e. an artist, a biologist, an educator, a farmer, a merchant, a moralist, a philosopher, a psychologist, a religious preacher, a sociologist and a statesman, a student and a teacher seems to have his version of education, which is influenced by his own outlook on life and his experiences in a limited field.

In brief, concept of education has different meanings on account of the following factors:

1. Cultural setting.
2. Economic set-up.

3. Geographical considerations.
4. Political philosophy and system.
5. Philosophical thought.
6. Religious moorings.
7. Sociological thinking.

All these singly or in combination of one or more factors exercise their influences on the aims, contents, organisation, discipline and methods etc. of education.

The Derivations

Different educational theorists have given different derivations of the term education. Among the important ones are:

(a) According to some, the word 'education' is derived from the Latin word 'educare' which means 'to rear' 'to nourish' and 'to bring up'.

(b) Some are of the view that 'education' means to 'draw out' 'to bring up', 'to foster'.

(c) Some trace the derivation of education to another Latin word 'educo'-'e' meaning 'out of and 'deco' meaning 'to lead'. Thus education implies 'to draw out' something and 'to lead' or simply 'leading out' something from 'within'.

(d) One school of thought believes that 'education' is derived from the Latin word 'educaturn' which means the 'act of training'. Hence education is 'training of the child'.

From a close study of the above meaning of education, it is revealed that each derivation is concerned with one or two aspects of education. However key words are:

(i) To bring up.
(ii) To draw out.
(iii) To lead out.
(iv) To nourish.

(v) To rear.

(vi) To teach.

(vii) To train.

A synthesis of these words would give us the clear meaning of the word 'education'. So when we synthesise these words we find that education is to draw out and to lead out by bringing up, by rearing, by nourishing up, by teaching and training.

Thus, the parents as well as the teachers educate the children. In this context we may quote Gandhiji: "By education I mean all round drawing out of the best in child and man-body, mind and spirit".

What is to be drawn out? Here we may refer to the definition of Pestalozzi. "Education is the natural, harmonious development and progressive development of man's innate powers".

Now the key question arises as to how the innate powers are to be brought out, developed, nourished and trained. Here comes the environmental factor which includes the family, the neighbourhood, the school, the community and the society at large. Thus, education is a means to provide the proper environment for the all round development of the individual. The development of the individual has to be a balanced one and not lopsided. An individual is one whole. Since the needs of the various communities, societies and countries differ, emphasis on methods of rearing and education differs. Naturally, the concept of education differs. It is related to time and space and also situation.

Education and Values of Universal Nature. However, there are some values which all societies and countries cherish. Accordingly from a larger view, by education we mean the bringing up and training an individual who is aesthetically refined, culturally rich, emotionally stable, mentally alert, morally upright, physically strong, spiritually sound and socially efficient.

Wider Meaning of Education. William H. Kilpatrick views education as "From the broad point of view, all life thoughtfully lived is education". Education is thus life and life is education. It includes all influences, social, cultural, political, domestic, geographical etc. Even the soil, climate and surroundings educate us. From broader sense "Whatever broadens our horizons, deepens our insight, refines our reactions, stimulates thought and feeling, educates us."

In the words of John Stuart Mill, "Not only does education include whatever we do for ourselves and whatever is done for us by others for the express purpose, of bringing us somewhat nearer to the perfection of our nature, it does, more, in its largest acceptance, it comprehends even the indirect effects produced on character, and on human faculties, by things which the direct purposes are quite different, by laws, by forms of government, by the industrial arts, by the modes of social life, nay even by physical facts not dependent on human will, by climate, soil and local position. Every environment, every surrounding, every activity helps to shape the human being. A human soil is in constant interaction with his environment. The interaction results in the modification of human behaviour and education."

It is observed by Lodge, "In the wider sense, all experience is said to be educative. The bite of a mosquito, the taste of water melon, the experience of falling in love, or flying in an aeroplane, of being in storm in a small boat-all such experiences have direct educative effect on us. The child educates the parents, the pupil educates his teachers ....Everything we say, think or do educates us no less than what is said or done to us by other beings, animate or inanimate. In the wider sense, life is education and education is life."

Salient Characteristics of Education. These are as under:

1. Education is a process of drawing out the best in child and man-body, and spirit.
2. Education is a process of modification of natural tendencies of an individual.
3. It is a process of self-realisation.

4. It is a deliberate process.
5. It is a tri-polar process involving the interaction of the educator and that of the child in social setting.
6. It is a psychological and sociological process.
7. It is a life-long process.

Chief Elements of the Educative Process

(1)	(2)	(3)	(4)	(5)	(6)	(7)
Why to Educate (Aims and Objectives of Education)	Whom to Educate (Child)	Who is to Educate (Teacher, Formal and Non-formal Agencies of Education)	Where to Educate (Educational Institution, Distance and Open System)	What to Educate (Subjects, Experiences, Skills, Values)	How to Educate (Methods and Techniques of Teaching-Learning)	When to Educate (Developing Interest and Motivation Stages and Levels.

Why to Educate. This includes aims of education. The educator and the educand must be clear about the aims of education so that efforts are made in the right direction. Aims of education depend upon a host of factors: political, economic, social, geographical, religious etc. In a nutshell, education must produce socially efficient individuals.

Whom to Educate. The educator must understand the educand thoroughly-his aptitudes, interests, temperaments etc., so that the 'best of him' is 'drawn out'.

Who is to Educate. The teacher is to educate and he must thoroughly understand himself also. He must get rid himself of all the blemishes and remember 'Woe to the teacher who teaches one thing with the lips and carries another in the heart.'

Where to Educate. The child is to be educated in a school which must 'simplify' `purify' and 'idealise' the environment. Likewise there are several other agencies that supplement school's work.

What to Educate. This leads to the contents of the curriculum which has been described as 'the environment in motion'. In a broader sense it includes all the courses, readings, associations and activities that go in the school, in the classroom, library, laboratory, workshop, playgrounds and in the numerous informal contacts between teachers and pupils.

How to Educate. This involves the knowledge and technique of various methods of teaching for making the teaching-learning process dynamic, effective and inspirational.

When to Educate. This is concerned with the different stages of the child so that 'motivational' aspects may be handled and attended to psychologically.

Education has been defined differently in the light of the needs of the times in different countries. In this regard Clark has very highly observed, "No writer on education, however, much he may strive after universality of thought, can wholly shape himself free from the influence of time and place". Likewise Kandel has observed, "In order to understand, appreciate and evaluate the real meaning of the educational system of a nation, it is essential to know something of its history and tradition, of the forces and attitudes governing its social organization and the political and economic conditions that determine its development." Thus, education has been developed, shaped and defined in the light of various factors, like culture, economy, geography, philosophy, polity and religion. In recent years, scientific and technological developments have played a significant role in the conceptual development of education.

Definition by Indian Thinkers

- Building of the powers of the human mind and spirit.

  Aurbindo

- Leading from the unreal to the real, from darkness to light, from death to immortality.

  Brihadaranyaka 'Upanishad'

- Formation of character.

  (Swami) Dayanand

- All-round drawing out of the best in child and man.

  (Mahatma) Gandhi

- Helping the individual to grow greatly in love and goodness.

  J. Krishnamurthi

- Making youngman as embodiment of the finest in his culture.

  K. M. Munshi

- Enabling the individual to be a producer as well as a good citizen.

  Nehru

- Training the intellect, refinement of heart and discipline of the heart.

  Radhakrishnan

- Purification of the mind and heart.

  Ramakrishna

- Noble thoughts coming from everyside.

  'Rigveda'

- Making life harmonious with existence.

  Tagore

- Manifestation of perfection already in man.

  (Swami) Vivekananda

- Helping the mind of the educand to realize the absolute moral and intellectual values.

  Zakir Hussain

Main Thrust

- Creation of a sound mind in a sound body.

  Aristotle

- Development of the whole man.

  Comenius

- Increasing social efficiency.

  Dewetry

- Controlling the mind.

  Emerson

- Developing real wisdom.

  Erasmus

- Leading and guiding for peace and unity with God.

  Froebel

- Developing morality.

  Herbart

- Adjusting with the ultimate nature of cosmos.

  Horne

- Fashioning the will of the individual to enable him to move in harmony with nature.

  Huxley

- Attainment of a sound mind in a sound body.

  Locke

- Complete development of individuality.

  Nunn, P.C.

- Development from within.

  Rousseau

- Leading the human souls to what is best and making what is best out of them.

  Ruskin

- Dispelling error and discovery truth.

  Socrates

- Preparing for complete living.

  Spencer

- Disciplining the feelings, restraining the passions, inspiring worthy motives and inculcating pure morality.

  Webster Daniel

Evaluation of Definitions

The definition given by Redden seems to be one of the most acceptable definitions of education. According to Redden, "Education is the deliberate and systematic influence extended by the mature person upon the immature through instruction and discipline for the harmonious development of physical, intellectual, aesthetic, social and spiritual powers of the human-being according to their essential hierarchy by and for the individual and social uses and directed towards the union of the educand with the creator as the final end."

Reddens' definition touches almost all aspects-hereditary and environmental and all phases of the development of the individual and society. It also takes into consideration the ultimate unity. The only limitation of this definition is that it ignores informal form of education.

The definition given by Gandhiji also deserves careful attention. Gandhiji had a spiritual as well as scientific attitude to issues. He observed facts, sorted them before accepting them and after weighing them well, he drew his conclusions. Gandhiji felt that while physical and intellectual development was necessary, the training of a child's heart and spirit was more important. He remarked, "By education I mean all-round drawing out of the best in child and man-body, mind and spirit. Literacy is not the end of education nor even the beginning. It is one of the means whereby man and woman can be educated. Literacy in itself is no education." This aim is in conformity with the one accepted by the Board of Education in England, viz. "The aim of education should be to the full potentialities of every child at school, in accord always with the general goods of the community of which he is a member."

'Drawing out' and not 'pouring in'-`Drawing out' and not pouring in' has been stressed by Gandhiji. He wrote, "We have upto now concentrated on stuffing child's mind with all kinds of information without even stimulating or developing them."

Gandhiji fully realized that nature has endowed children and youth with tremendous vitality. They have within them the springs of youth, joy and vigour. They have the God-given curiosity of wishing to know things for themselves. The task of education is to use these powers. It would be wrong to suppress them. This energy should be utilised and harnessed properly.

Conceptual Development of Education

Following table illustrates the conceptual development of education in historical perspective.

Stages of Development	*Aims*	*Curriculum*	*Classroom Authority*	*Process*	*Concern*	*Context*
First Stage	Mortification of soul	Ethics, Religion and allied subjects.	Religious institutions, churches, etc.	Discourses, Memorisation of spoken/ written word	Moral	Dominance
Second Stage	Enquiry into the nature of things and universe	Logic, ethics, Science of universe	Reformers, Thinkers and their disciples	Discourses Experiences Memorisation	Social and Educational	Renaissance (Reaction to Church dominance)
Third Stage	Productive	Scholastic, Professional, Vocational	Teacher	Controlled and conditioned learning	Political Dominance	Industrialised Society, Vocational
Fourth Stage	Learning and Earning	Integrated but more biased towards professional courses	Partnership of teacher-taught	Self-learning Programmed learning Group interaction	Socialization of Individual	Equalization of Opportunities

What do we understand by "All-round?"—Man is neither mere intellectual nor the gross animal body, nor the heart or soul alone. A proper and harmonious combination of all these three is required for the making of the whole man and constitutes the true essence of education. Any programme of education that puts exclusive emphasis on one of these aspects of the human personality is against the basic concept of education.

Meaning of the term 'best in man'. The best man has three fields i.e., body, mind and spirit. Education, therefore, must cater to the physical, mental and spiritual needs. No field should remain neglected. The best in man will include the harmonious development of the various faculties of man and child.

How can we draw out the Best?—The best can be drawn out by touching the hearts of the students. Gandhiji wrote, "If I were to be their real teacher and guardian I must touch their hearts. I must share their joys and sorrows, I must help them to solve the problems that face them, and I must take along the right channel the surging aspirations of their youth."

TRADITIONAL CONCEPT

The most distinctive feature of modern society is its science-based technology which has been making a profound impact not only on the economic and political life of a country but also on its educational system. The changes that occur as a result of the impact are broadly described as 'Modernisation'. This modernisation has affected the teaching-learning process in many ways. The recent changes in the concept of educative process (teaching-learning process) have led to the development of newer areas of educational endeavour. In a traditional society the aim of teaching-learning was the preservation of the accumulated stock of knowledge. But in the modern society, the main aim of teaching-learning is not acquision of knowledge alone. It is the awakening of curiosity, the stimulation of creativity, the development of proper interests, attitudes and values and the building of essential skills such as independent study. Teaching-learning process has to serve as a powerful instrument of social, economic and cultural transformation of the society. Teaching-learning process is conditioned by the nature and demands of society to which the learner should get adapted and attuned. One of the main aims of teaching-learning in the modern society is to keep pace with the advancement of knowledge and skills. In the modern society educative process cannot be undertaken passively.

Emerging Concerns

The world has never changed so rapidly as in recent years. Eminent thinkers in the world began to contemplate in the 1990s on the emerging modern society and its impact on the modern education. UNESCO took the lead and in 1993 appointed an International Commission on Education for the 21st Century to consider the various dimensions of modern education. The Commission gave its report in 1996.

Major Issues Confronting the Society

According to the Commission, modern education must take note of the following:

1. Tension between the global and local situations.
2. Tension between the universal and the individual.
3. Tension between tradition and modernity.
4. Tension between long term and short term considerations.
5. Tension, on the one hand the need for competition and on the other, concern for equality of opportunity.
6. Tension between the extraordinary expansion of knowledge and human beings capacity to assimilate it.
7. Tension between the spiritual and the material.

Important Elements

The Commission suggested the following:

1. Four Pillars of Education. These are: (i) Learning to know. (ii) Learning to Do. (iii) Learning to Live Together (iv) Learning to Be.

Traditional Education and Modern Education at a Glance

S. No.	*Aspect*	*Traditional Education*	*Modern Education*
1.	Aim	Knowledge of 3 R's- Reading, Writing and Arithmetic i.e. knowledge of subjects.	1. Training in 7 R's i.e. Reading, Writing and Arithmetic i.e. Teaching of subjects, Rights, Responsibilities and relationship. 2. Development of total personality. 3. Social Efficiency.
2.	Function	Broadly Religious	Broadly Social
3.	Contents/ Curriculum	Subjects-centred	Subjects and experiences
4.	Agencies	Family, School and Church	School, Several Agencies, Mass Media.
5.	Teacher	Autocrat, Policeman	Democrate, Humanist.
6.	School	A place for the pouring in of knowledge	1. Place for training in citizenship and democracy. Art of living together. 2. Idealised miniature society.
7.	Child	Like Dumb-driven cattle, Passive.	Human being. Active
8.	Individual Differences	Not recognised	Utmost consideration to individual differences
9.	Methods of Teaching	Bookish, Memorisation, Mechanical	Dynamic and Challenging, Question answer. Project Method. Discovery method etc.
10.	Courses	Usually single track	Diversified
11.	Life Experiences	Very few	Related to life.
12.	Media	Mainly Chalk and Board	New Electric Media
13.	Discipline	Rule of the 'rod'	Self and social discipline
14.	Examination	Rigid. Essay Type	Comprehensive and Continuous, Objective Tests etc.
15.	Chief Concern	Religious and spiritual	1. Sociological. 2. Several new concerns like environmental education and population education etc. 3. New Technologies.

2. Life long education.
3. Teachers as partners in education.
4. Collaboration of education with industry etc.
5. Incorporation of information technology in education.

Formal and Non-formal Education

Formal Education. Formal education implies:

1. Planned education keeping in view some definite aim.
2. Education imparted through well planned means or formal lessons.
3. Education having a definite course to be covered during a definite period.
4. A teaching-learning process with which the teacher and the learner are acquainted.
5. Education organised by some agency, say the Government or the private agency.
6. Education imparted through institution having building/premises.
7. Education starting and ending at a particular age.
8. Education associated with a degree or certificate.
9. Education usually associated with some sort of mental strain on the teacher and the taught.

Non-formal Education. It means:

1. Flexibility in various aspects of education, i.e. admissions, place of education, curriculum, age, co-curricular activities, modes of teaching, evaluation etc.
2. Covering life span of an individual.
3. Guided by motivation of the individual for self-growth, self- renewal.
4. Diversified curriculum responsive to learner and environmental needs.

5. Process of sharing, exploring, analysing and judging with maximum participation of the learner.
6. Preparation for future needs.
7. Part-time education.

Informal Education. Following are its main characteristics:

1. Unconscious learning.
2. No fixed aim.
3. No fixed curriculum, methods of teaching etc.
4. No organised body or institution behind this process.
5. Life-long learning.
6. Natural outcome.

Life Long Education

Origin. The concept of life-long education is said to have originated in the 1970s with publication of a UNESCO report entitled "Learning to Be-The World of Education, Today and Tomorrow" in 1972. Thereafter several international conferences were held to work out the details of this concept. The International Commission on Education for the Twenty-first Century (1993-96), popularly known as Delors Commission laid great emphasis on life-long education in the context of technological advancements. It observed, "Learning throughout life must take advantage of all the opportunities offered by society."

Meaning of Lifelong Education. An individual learns step by step every moment, every day, every month and every year if given an opportunity. According to UNESCO, "Lifelong education embraces all forms of education and especially out-of-school education." Main Features of Life-long Education are :

1. It is a "cradle-to-the- grave" educational process.
2. It is self-education.
3. It has no terminal stage.
4. Television and other mass media become important allies in the educational enterprise.

5. Computer and internet etc. are expected to play a significant role in lifelong education.
6. Life-long education is for all.
7. Lifelong education is a cooperative affair.

A Balanced View. The use of new information technology in education has narrowed down the difference between different concepts of education. T.V. is increasingly being used in normal classrooms teaching. Distance and open education systems have brought about great flexibility in all the components of the traditional system. Non-formal education has accepted several characteristics of formal education and vice versa. Homes are becoming educational institutions with the use of computers and internet as modes of learning.

Education in Ancient India. Education in India was considered as a liberating force as the aim of life was 'Moksha' (Liberation or salvation from the cycles of births and deaths). Therefore, emphasis in education was laid on those elements that assisted an individual in the fulfilment of this objective. Philosophy to our ancestors was a practical aid that showed the right way of living. This task was performed through education.

With a view to understand the central teaching of Indian philosophy and accordingly to understanding the chief features of the educational system it would be very relevant to explain in brief a few concepts like 'Purushartha' (Action or value), `Artha' (Wealth or material prosperity), 'Kama' (Pleasure or enjoyment), `Dharma' (Righteousness) and 'Moksha' (Liberation or salvation).

'Purushartha'. Each individual has several desires-desire for children, desire for wealth, desire for power, desire for prestige, desire for common good, desire for communion with the God or unseen.

Thus, it follows from above that 'Moksha' or salvation can be attained only by earning wealth through 'Dharma' i.e. in a righteous way and enjoying the fruit of wealth in the proper manner. It is clear from this that Indian philosophy does not aim at producing 'sanyasis' or ascetics. Here chief emphasis is on

'Dharma' i.e. righteousness. Indian philosophy does not decry possession of wealth and its enjoyment. The idealist in India, while talking of the infinite good does not neglect the immediate objectives of life. Self-realization is to be realised in the society. The Indian seers very clearly prescribed four stages of life, each involving certain duties. Education aimed at preparing the individual for meeting effectively the challenges of each stage. It may be stressed that knowledge and wisdom were meant for making a man moral and thereby assisting him in self-realization. A great seer Swami Vivekananda, who is considered as an embodiment of Indian culture has observed, "So long as the millions live in hunger and ignorance, I hold every man a traitor who, having been educated at their expense, pays not the least head to them...... I call him a 'mahatma' who feels for the poor. Let these people be your God—think of them, work for them".

'Selflessness' is the essence of Indian philosophy and its main concern is 'sarvajana Sukhino Bhavantu' (happiness for all) and education's function is to serve this end.

Exercise

1. What does Education mean ?
2. What are different definition ?
3. What does the term, 'best in man' mean ?
4. What is meant by Life Long Education ?

4

The Expansion

Number of Educational Institutions (since 1950-51)

During the period 1950-51 to 1999-2000, the number of primary schools increased three fold, from 210,000 in 1950-51 to 6,42,000 in 1999-2000. The number of upper primary schools increased by about 13 times, from 13,596 in 1950-51 to 198,000 in 1999-2000. The ratio of upper primary schools to primary schools also came down from 1:15 in 1950-51 to 1:3.2 in 1999-2000. There are now 245 universities, 52 deemed universities, five institutions established through State and Central legislations, nearly 11,831 colleges including 1,520 women's colleges in the country, in addition to the unrecognised institutions in the higher education sector.

Enrolment at the Elementary Stage (since 1950-51)

The total enrolment at the primary and upper primary school levels in India witnessed a steady increase. Total enrolment at the primary stage (grades I-V) increased by 5.91 times, from 19.2 million in 1950-51 to about 113.61 million in 1999-2000. Out of this, the relative share of girls' enrolment increased from 28.1 per cent in 1950-51 to 43.6 per cent in 1999-2000. Total enrolment at the Upper Primary levels (grades VI-VIII) increased by 14 times from 3.1 million in 1950-51 to 42.06 million in 1999-2000. The relative share of girls' enrolment which was only 16.1 per cent in 1950-51 rose to about 40.4 per cent in 1999-2000. During 1950-51 to 1999-2000, the growth rate of girls' enrolment at the elementary levels was higher as compared to that of the boys. Participation of girls at all levels of school education has improved appreciably over the years.

Sex-Wise Enrolment by Stages/Classes Since 1951— Second Level (In Million)

Year	*Primary*			*Middle/Upper Primary*			*High/Hr.Sec./Inter/ Pre-degree*		
	Boys	*Girls*	*Total*	*Boys*	*Girls*	*Total*	*Boys*	*Girls*	*Total*
1950-51	13.8	5.4	19.2	2.6	0.5	3.1	1.3	0.2	1.5
1955-56	17.1	7.5	24.6	3.8	1.0	4.8	2.2	0.4	2.6
1960-61	23.6	11.4	35.0	5.1	1.6	6.7	2.7	0.7	3.4
1965-66	32.2	18.3	50.5	7.7	2.8	10.5	4.4	1.3	5.7
1970-71	35.7	21.3	57.0	9.4	3.9	13.3	5.7	1.9	7.6
1975-76	40.6	25.0	65.6	11.0	5.0	16.0	6.5	2.4	8.9
1980-81	45.3	28.5	73.8	13.9	6.8	20.7	7.6	3.4	11.0
1985-86	52.2	35.2	87.4	17.7	9.6	27.1	11.5	5.0	16.5
1990-91	57.0	40.4	97.4	21.5	12.5	34.0	12.8	6.3	19.1
1991-92	58.6	42.3	100.9	22.0	13.6	35.6	13.5	6.9	20.4
1992-93	57.9	41.7	99.6	21.2	12.9	34.1	13.6	6.9	20.5
1993-94	55.1	41.9	97.0	20.6	13.5	34.1	13.2	7.5	20.7
1994-95*	62.3	46.8	109.1	24.5	15.8	40.3	16.0	8.4	24.4
1995-96*	62.4	47.4	109.8	25.0	16.0	41.0	16.1	8.8	24.9
1996-97*	62.5	47.9	110.4	24.7	16.3	41.0	17.2	9.8	27.0
1997-98*	61.2	47.5	108.7	23.7	15.8	39.5	17.1	10.2	27.2
1998-99*	62.7	48.2	110.9	24.0	16.3	40.3	17.3	10.5	27.8
1999-2000*	64.1	49.5	113.6	25.1	16.9	42.0	17.2	10.9	28.1

* Provisional

Source:- Selected Educational Statistics 1999-2000, Ministry of Human Resource Development, Government of India

Enrolment during 1950-51 and 1999-2000

	1950-51	*1999-2000*	*Increase (Approximate)*
1.	Primary Stage (Class I to V) 19.2 Million	13.61 Million	5.91 Times
2.	Upper Primary Stage (Classes VI to VIII) 3.1 Million	42.06 Million	14 Times

Gross Enrolment Ratios (GER) since 1950-51

	1950-51	*1999-2000*
1.	Primary Stage (Class 1 to V)42.6%	94.90%
2.	Upper Primary Stage (Class VI to VIII) 12.7%	58.79%

Gross Enrolment Ratios

The Gross Enrolment Ratio (GER) at Primary and Upper Primary levels improved perceptibly from 1950-51 to 1999-2000 (see Tables). The GER rose at the primary level from 42.6 per cent in 1950-51 to 94.90 per cent in 1999-2000. Enrolment for girls rose from 24.8 per cent to 85.18 per cent during this period. The boys/girls differential also declined substantially, from 35.8 percentage points in 1950-51 to 18.90 percentage points in 1999-2000. The GER at the Upper Primary level improved from 12.7 per cent in 1950-51 to 58.79 per cent in 1999-2000 with that for girls increasing from 4.6 per cent to 49.66 per cent for this period. The boys/girls differential at the Upper Primary level which had increased to 29.6 percentage points in 1990-91 had been in the range of 16-18 percentage points in 1996-97 to 1999-2000. Though the participation of girls at all levels of school education has increased substantially, the proportion of girls enrolled both at the Primary and Upper Primary levels continues to be lower than the gross enrolment of boys. Vast disparities exist among the States/UTs in terms of enrolment.

Trends in Gross Enrolment Ratios in India

(in percent)

Year	*Primary (I-V)*		*Upper Primary (VI-VIII)*		*Elementary (I-VIII)*	
	Boys	*Girls*	*Boys*	*Girls*	*Boys*	*Girls*
1950-51	60.6	24.8	20.6	4.6	46.4	17.7
1960-61	82.6	41.4	33.2	11.3	65.2	30.9
1970-71	95.5	60.5	46.5	20.8	75.5	44.4
1980-81	95.8	64.1	54.3	28.6	82.2	52.1
1990-91	114.0	85.5	76.6	47.0	100.0	70.8
1991-92	112.8	86.9	75.1	49.6	101.2	73.2
1992-93	95.0	73.5	72.5	48.9	87.7	65.7
1993-94	90.0	73.1	62.1	45.4	80.2	63.7
1994-95	114.8	92.6	79.0	55.0	101.8	78.8
1995-96	114.5	93.3	79.5	55.0	101.8	79.3
1996-97	98.7	81.9	70.9	52.8	88.9	71.8
1997-98	97.7	81.2	66.5	49.5	86.4	70.0
1998-99	100.9	82.9	65.3	49.1	87.6	70.6
1999-2000	104.1	85.2	67.2	49.7	90.1	72.0

Source: Selected Educational Statistics, 1999-2000 (D/o. Education, M/O. Human Resource Development, GOI.

Drop-Out Rates

Whereas the rising enrolment in elementary schools is a source of satisfaction, there is concern about the percentage of students actually attending school and those dropping out of the education system altogether. Nearly 79 per cent of the 6-14 age group are attending school that is of the population of 200 million in this age group in the year 2000, the number of children attending school was about 158 million. The student retention rate at the primary school stage was about 58 per cent (1990-95). Dropout rates at the primary and upper primary level have decreased over the years. From 64.9 per cent at the primary level in 1960-61 the dropout rate decreased to 40.25 per cent 1999-2000 and from 78.3 in upper primary level in 1960-61 it decreased to 54.53 per cent in

1999-2000. Though dropout rates at the elementary education stage have declined over the years, they are still relatively high especially in the case of girl students for whom the rates are 42 per cent and 58 per cent at the Primary and Upper Primary stages respectively.

Teachers and Pupil-teacher Ratio

In absolute terms, the number of teachers registered at the elementary level increased five fold from 6,24,000 in 1950-51 to 3.2 million in 1999-2000. The percentage share of female teachers to total teachers during this period increased from 15.2 per cent in 1950-51 to 35.81 per cent in 1999-2000. Despite the fact that the number of teachers has increased, this increase has not kept pace with the growth of enrolment. From 1:24 in 1950-51, the Pupil-teacher Ratio (PTR) at the Primary Education level worsened to about 1:43 in 1999-2000. Similarly from 1:20 at the Upper Primary level, the PTR increased to 1:38 in 1999-2000. Apart from the worsening Teacher-pupil Ratio, problem areas to be addressed are the distribution of teachers among the schools in various states/regions, non-attendance of teachers on a regular basis, presence of single-teacher schools, inefficient teaching methods and the general quality of education.

New Schemes at the Elementary Stage

Within the education sector, elementary education has been given the highest priority in terms of sub-sectoral allocations. Several schemes have been launched by the Central Government to meet the needs of the educationally disadvantaged and for strengthening the social infrastructure for education viz. Operation Blackboard (OB), District Primary Education Programme (DPEP), Education Guarantee Scheme and Alternative and Innovative Education (EGS&AIE), Manila Samakhya, Teacher Education (TE), Mid-day Meals Scheme, Lok Jumbish, Shiksha Karmi Project (SKP), Janashala etc. The details of these schemes are given separately. In 2001-02 significant steps were taken towards achievement of the goals of UEE through a time bound integrated approach in partnership with the States through launching of the "Sarva Shiksha

Abhiyan" (SSA). The planning in SSA will be decentralised and highest priority accorded to community ownership and monitoring. This programme will subsume all existing programmes including externally aided programmes in due course within its overall framework with district as the unit of programme implementation.

Goals of "Sarva Shiksha Abhiyan"

- All children of age 6-14 to be in schools/Education Guarantee Centres/bridge course by 2003
- All children of age 6-14 to complete five year primary education by 2007
- All children of age 6-14 to complete eight years of schooling by 2010
- Focus on elementary education of satisfactory quality with emphasis on education for life
- Bridging all gender and social category gaps at primary stage by 2007 and at elementary education level by 2010 and
- Universal retention by 2010.

Primary Education : A Fundamental Right

One of the measures for achieving the goal of Education For All (EFA) was the Ninety Third Amendment of the Constitution passed in the Lok Sabha on November 28, 2001 to make the right to free and compulsory education for children for 6-14 years of age a Fundamental Right and also to make it a Fundamental Duty of the parents/guardian to provide opportunities for education to children in the age group of 6-14 years.

Literacy as Seen in the 2001 Census

The progress of literacy rates in India since 1951 is listed in Table. While the rates for the years 1951, 1961 and 1971 Censuses relate to the population in the five years plus category, those for 1981, 1991 and 2001 relate to the population which is seven years and above. The literacy rates for the country as a whole increased from 18.33 per cent in 1951 to 65.38 per cent in 2001 (Table), with literacy rate for males at 75.85 per cent and that for females at 54.16 per cent. The literacy rate recorded an increase of 13.17 percentage points to from 1991 to 2001, the highest increase in any one decade. An encouraging feature is that the growth rate of literacy has been higher in case of females at 14.87 per cent than for males at 11.72 per cent during this decade. The gap in male-female literacy rates decreased from 24.84 percentage points in 1991 to 21.70 percentage points in 2001. The rate of growth of literacy in the decade ending 2001 has been higher in the rural areas, at 14.75 per cent as compared to the 7.2 per cent increase in urban areas. Despite these improvements literacy in urban areas was 80.3 per cent and that in rural areas 59.4 per cent.

Kerala which has the highest literacy rate of 90.92 per cent, occupies the top slot in both male and female literacy, at 94.20 and 87.86 per cent respectively. Bihar has the lowest literacy rate of 47.53 per cent, along with the lowest literacy rate for males at 60.32 per cent and for females, at 33.57 per cent.

Rural-Urban Literacy Rates 1951-2001

Year	*Male*	*Female*	*Persons*
1951			
Rural	19.02*	4.87*	12.10*
Urban	45.60*	22.33*	34.59*
Total	**27.16**	**8.86**	**18.33**
1961			
Rural	34.30	10.10	22.50
Urban	66.00	40.50	54.40
Total	**40.40**	**15.35**	**28.30**
1971			
Rural	48.60	15.50	27.90
Urban	69.80	48.80	60.20
Total	**45.96**	**21.97**	**34.45**

Contd.

Year	*Male*	*Female*	*Persons*
1981			
Rural	49.60	21.70	36.00
Urban	76.70	56.30	67.20
Total	**56.38**	**29.76**	**43.57**
1991			
Rural	57.90	30.60	44.70
Urban	81.10	64.00	73.10
Total	**64.13**	**39.29**	**52.21**
2001			
Rural	71.40	46.70	59.40
Urban	86.70	73.20	80.30
Total	**75.85**	**54.16**	**65.38**

Note:

(*) For 1951, the population male, female and persons refers to effective literacy rates and the break up of Rural, Urban and male-female components and crude literacy rates.

(1) Literacy rates for 1951, 1961 and 1971 Censuses relates to population aged live years and above. The rates for the 1981, 1991 and 2001 Census relate to population aged seven years and above.

(2) The 1981 Literacy rates exclude Assam where census could not be conducted and the 1991 literacy rates exclude Jammu & Kashmir where Census could not be conducted due to disturbed conditions.

(3) The 2001 Census, literacy rates exclude entire Kachchh district, Morvi, Maliya-Miyana and Wankaner talukas of Rajkot district, Jodiya taluka of Jamnagar district of Gujarat State and entire Kinnaur district of Himachal Pradesh where population enumeration of Census of India, 2001, could not be conducted due to natural calamities.

Source: Census of India 2001

Comparative Data on Primary Education and Other Indicators of Development (Around 2000)

S. No.	Country	Total Population In thousand	GNP Per Capita (US$)	Life Expectancy	Adult Literacy Rate	Primary School Enrolment Rate (Gross)	% of Primary School Students Reaching Grade V
1.	Afghanistan	21900	250	46	32	29	49
2.	Bangladesh	126900	370	59	56	97	75
3.	Bhutan	2061	510	62	42	72	86
4.	Brazil	167900	4420	67	85	128	71
5.	Canada	30901	19320	79	97	102	99
6.	China	1266840	780	70	84	104	91
7.	Ethiopia	61000	100	44	33	42	51
8.	Germany	82201	25350	77	99	104	100
9.	India	998000	450	63	58	91	52
10.	Indonesia	20900	580	66	86	114	85
11.	Japan	126500	32000	80	99	102	100
12.	Myanmar	45000	220	61	83	101	45
13.	Nepal	15800	220	58	45	122	44
14.	Pakistan	152300	470	65	45	84	50
15.	Russian Federation	147196	2270	67	99	107	NA
16.	Sri Lanka	18601	820	74	90	107	NA
17.	Switzerland	7344	38351	79	99	107	101
18.	U.K.	58700	22640	78	99	104	99
19	U.S.A.	276218	30600	77	99	102	99

Development in other Countries

The table includes comparative data on the following aspects:

1. Total Population, 2. GNP Per Capita (US$), 3. Life Expectancy, 4. Adult Literacy Rate, 5. Primary School Enrolment Ratios (Gross)

Exercise

1. Write a brief note on the expansion of education in India ?
2. Is primary education a fundamental right ?

5

Scope and Sphere

Objectives of education including primary education are determined by the objectives of a nation as contained in its Constitution. Accordingly objectives of education in India derive their origin from our Constitution. Broadly speaking objectives of education in India are to prepare individuals for a democratic, secular and socialist state. Within the framework of the national objectives of education, educational objectives for different levels of education are worked out. Regarding formation of objectives at the primary stage, it must be pointed out that for a large number of children, primary stage is terminal. It should, therefore, be necessary to provide an education to them which prepares them for life and for self-learning.

The Objectives

Junior Primary Classes I-IV

1. To acquire a rudimentary knowledge of Reading, Writing and Number and the appropriate skills.
2. To learn and practise the basic principles of healthful living.

3. To gain an elementary knowledge and appreciation of his environment—social, physical and cultural.
4. To appreciate in a rudimentary way of the gifts of science in our every day life.
5. To express himself freely and creatively through both verbal and non-verbal media.
6. To lay in himself proper foundations of an intelligent patriotism through an appreciation of national symbols and national festivals.
7. To learn to use his hands and also to develop a respect for dignity of labour.
8. To grow socially by acquiring habits of courtesy; cooperation and adjustment and of working with others for a common purpose.
9. To have respect for all places of worship, irrespective of the religion he follows.
10. To learn in an elementary way important skills like listening attentively, observing carefully and thinking logically.
11. To acquire a spirit of inquiry in respect of the immediate environment.
12. To gain some idea of the values to be cherished and also of the culture of the country.
13. To appreciate the inter-dependence of people in all spheres of life inside the country and outside.

For Senior Primary Classes V to VII

14. To acquire knowledge of basic facts and principles in different subjects, skills and competence to apply them in appropriate situations.
15. To express himself adequately through oral and written language to meet his every day needs.
16. To appreciate and use number and the symbolic language of mathematics and to understand spatial relationships.

17. To learn the basic principles of personal and social health and to act upon them.
18. To develop an appreciation of the unity that runs through our diverse cultural practices.
19. To develop a sense of healthy patriotism and legitimate pride in the nation—its past, present and future.
20. To comprehend the ways in which science helps in our lives and to start using the scientific method in whatever he does.
21. To acquire work-experience through the pursuit of crafts.
22. To develop respect for religion other than his own and to live and work co-operatively with others, regardless of all considerations of language, caste or religion.
23. To include such personal qualities of character as well enrich his social living, e.g., cooperation, respect of other's views, tolerance, sincerity, patience and leadership.
24. To become aware of his responsibility as a member of his family, community and nation and to discharge them as best as his age and capacity permit.
25. To take an active part in programmes for the betterment of the community.
26. To develop the capacity for, and the habit of thinking critically on all kinds of problems.
27. To ensure proper habits of study.
28. To appreciate how the different nations of the world are coming closer every day and are more dependent on one another.

The Curriculum for the Ten-Year School : A Framework (1975), NCERT, mentions the following objectives of education.

Primary Stage. (Age 6+ to 11+ studying in classes I to V or 5+ to 10+ or 5+ or 5 to 9 or 6 to 10 classes I to IV).

1. The first objective is 'literacy'. The child should learn the first language, which would generally be his mother-tongue to a level where he can communicate easily with others through articulated speech and in writing.
2. The second objective is attainment of 'numeracy'. The child should develop facility in the four fundamental numerical operations and be able to apply these in the life of the community to solve practical problems.
3. The third objective is 'technicracy'. The child should learn the method of enquiry in science and should begin to appreciate science and technology in the life and world around it.
4. The child should develop a respect for national symbols, like the flag and the anthem, and for the democratic processes and institutions of the country. He should know about the composite and plural culture of India and learn to denigrate untouchability, casteism and communalism.
5. The child should acquire healthy attitudes towards human labour and its dignity.
6. The child should develop habits of cleanliness and healthful living and an understanding of the proper sanitation and hygiene of its neighbourhood.
7. The child should acquire a taste for the good and the beautiful and should take care of its surroundings.
8. The child should learn to cooperate with others and appreciate the usefulness of working together for the common good. Other desirable qualities of charity and personality such as initiative leadership, kindness, honesty should also be developed as well as understanding of its role as an individual in the home, the school and the neighbourhood.
9. The child should be able to express itself freely in creative activity and should acquire habits of self-learning.

Middle Stage

The classes VI to VIII cover the middle stage when the normal age group should be from 11+ to 14+. This period can become a very difficult period for some children on account of the adolescence period. However children become more mature in emotional, intellectual, physical and social development. This stage is also terminal for a large number of children who enter life after this. Following are, therefore, the main objectives of education at this stage:

1. Developing capacities and attitudes for productive work.
2. Developing an understanding, of the matter of national integration through the knowledge of history, geography and other subjects.
3. Inculcating a sound knowledge of the democratic processes, structures and institutions in our country.
4. Acquainting the students with the salient features of the Constitution.
5. Deepening and widening the knowledge of the students of world culture and civilisation.
6. Developing language competencies.
7. Developing competencies in science so as to relate it meaningfully to life.

Ishwarbhai Patel Committee

The Committee was appointed primarily to review the stage-wise and subjectwise objectives of education and to scrutinise the NCERT syllabi and curriculum. While listing the objectives of primary education the Committee observed, "It should be remembered that the objectives of primary education have to be distinct from those of the other stages of education in view of the Constitutional obligations to make it universal." The Committee laid down the following objectives:

(1) Acquisition of tools of formal learning, namely literacy, numeracy and manual skills;

(2) Acquisition of knowledge through observation, study and experimentation in the areas of social and natural sciences;

(3) Development of physical strength and team spirit through sports and games;

(4) Acquisition of skills for planning and executing socially useful productive work with a view to making education work based;

(5) Acquisition of habits of cooperative behaviour within the family, school and community;

(6) Development of aesthetic perception and creativity through participation in artistic activities and observation of nature.

(7) Development of social responsibility by inculcating habits (individually as well as collectively) of appreciation of the culture and life styles of persons of other religions, regions and countries; and readiness to serve the weaker and the deprived;

(8) Development of the desire to participate in productive and other processes of community life and to serve the community.

Developmental Objectives

An NCERT publication entitled Psychology of the Child and the Curriculum (1983) has described the developmental objectives of education at the primary stage in terms of competencies—knowledge, understanding and skills. These have been listed under the following heads:

I. Development of the child as a Learner (26 Objectives)

II. Development of the child as a Person (22 Objectives)

III. Development of the child as a Citizen (26 Objectives)

IV. Development of the child as a Worker (19 Objectives)

Child as a Learner

Competencies—Knowledge, Understanding and Skills

1. Knows that the school can give him much by way of useful knowledge.
2. Understands the importance of learning in school.
3. Possesses reading, writing and computational skills.
4. Is able to acquire information.
5. Is able to listen carefully and with understanding.
6. Is able to read with comprehension.
7. Is able to memorise and retain facts.
8. Is able to express himself in speech and in writing.
9. Is able to express himself in art forms (drawing, painting, music, dance and drama)
10. Is able to observe accurately.
11. Is able to classify information.
12. Is able to analyse, relate and organize facts.
13. Is able to interpret and draw conclusions.
14. Is able to experiment with things and situations to find out solutions.
15. Is able to use imagination.
16. Is able to think independently and come out with ideas of his own.

Attitudes and Appreciations

1. Is eager to understand the physical and social phenomena and events in his environment.
2. Is eager to ask questions.
3. Is not deterred by initial difficulties in learning.
4. Welcomes new ideas and enjoys discussing them with others.

5. Likes originality and novelty in ideas and methods.
6. Welcomes healthy and constructive criticism of his views by others.
7. Uses constructive criticism of others for self-improvement.

Behaviours and Habits

1. Uses acquired knowledge, skills and understanding in different situations of life.
2. Engages himself in extra books, newspapers and magazines.
3. Shares his knowledge with others.

Child as a Person

Competencies—Knowledge, Understanding and Skills

1. Knows the rules of personal health and hygiene.
2. Knows how to behave with others in various relationships.
3. Understands the importance of discipline in day today living.
4. Understands his own strengths and weaknesses.
5. Possesses self-confidence and courage.
6. Is able to formulate his goals and is motivated to achieve them.

Attitudes and Appreciations

1. Has respect for life in its various forms.
2. Is eager to help the weak and the needy.
3. Appreciates what is beautiful.
4. Appreciates what is true.
5. Does not dislike people only because they are different from him.

6. Likes to be rational.
7. Appreciates the value of self-help and self-reliance.

Behaviours and Habits

1. Behaves courteously.
2. Tries for continuous self-improvement.
3. Uses his abilities in socially useful ways.
4. Controls the unhealthy and destructive impulses which he may sometimes experience.
5. Copes with his sorrows, disappointments and anxieties in his day today life.
6. Expresses his emotions and feelings in a socially acceptable manner.
7. Acts courageously for a good cause.
8. Makes worthy use of leisure.

Child as a Citizen

Competencies —Knowledge, Understanding and Skills

1. Knows the national flag of his country.
2. Knows what a national flag stands for.
3. Knows the significance of national emblem.
4. Knows that people belonging to different castes, religions and socio-economic strata are equal in the eyes of law.
5. Knows that we live in a country which believes in secularism, democracy and socialism.
6. Knows the names of different religions.
7. Knows the main teachings of different religions.
8. Knows about the important religious festivals.
9. Knows about basic freedoms of a citizen such as freedom of speech, freedom of worship, etc.
10. Possesses civic sense.
11. Understands the importance of small family.

Attitudes and Appreciations

1. Appreciates the importance of good social relationships.
2. Appreciates the value of country's freedom.
3. Appreciates the cultural heritage of his country.
4. Has respect for all religions and languages.
5. Dislikes injustice in any form.
6. Is sensitive to the sufferings of the weaker sections of the society.

Behaviours and Habits

1. Sings the national anthem.
2. Does not discriminate between people because of differences in caste, creed, religion, sex and nationality.
3. Performs his duties with responsibility.
4. Extends his help and cooperation to others.
5. Avoids causing inconveniencies to others.
6. Participates in activities related to community development.
7. Tries to settle the differences amicably.
8. Participates enthusiastically in group activities as a leader and as a follower.
9. Takes adequate care of public property.

Child as a Worker

Competencies—Knowledge, Understanding and Skills

1. Knows the types of work people do in his environment.
2. Knows the basic tools and materials used in different types of work.
3. Knows broadly the processes involved in various types of work.
4. Understands that all types of work lead to production of goods and services.

5. Understands that planned and organised work saves time, money and materials.
6. Possesses basic skills necessary for doing any work successfully.
7. Possesses skills to express himself creatively in work.
8. Possesses skills of critically appraising his own work.

Attitudes and Appreciations

1. Respects manual work.
2. Appreciates work well done.
3. Likes to cooperate with others in work.
4. Enjoys doing work with one's own hands.
5. Appreciates the value of creative expression in work.

Behaviours and Habits

1. Works with perseverance.
2. Maintains neatness and cleanliness in work.
3. Expresses himself artistically.
4. Avoids wastage of time and materials.
5. Adopts safety measures in the use of tools and materials.

Teacher Education and the Emerging Indian Society (1988) has listed the following essential aims of elementary education:

1. Developing an inquiring or an investigating mind.
2. Developing human qualities in the child, i.e., to develop a positive image of self. This aim is known as the development of self-concept in the child.
3. Developing right concept of work.

Processes and Structures

Elementary education refers to all processes and structures which cover education upto 14 years of age starting from 5 or 6.

Gandhiji used the term primary education. According to him, "The course of primary education should be extended at least to seven years and should include the general knowledge gained up to the matriculation standard less English and plus a substantial vocation." (Harijan 1937)

First Conference of National Education

The First Conference of National Education, held at Wardha on 22nd and 23rd October, 1937, considered the new system of education proposed by Gandhiji. Among others, it passed the following two resolutions:

1. That in the opinion of this conference free and compulsory education be provided for seven years on a nation-wide scale.
2. That the conference endorses the proposal made by Mahatma Gandhi that the process of education throughout this period should centre some form of manual productive work, and that all the other abilities to be developed or training to be given should as far as possible, be integrally related to the central handicraft chosen with due regard to the environment of the child."

Sargent Report (1944)

The Sargent Report (1944) mentions as "Universal compulsory, and free Primary or Basic education for all children between the ages 6 and 14, divided into the Junior Basic (6 to 11) and Senior Basic (11 to 14) stages.

Article 45 of the Constitution neither uses the term elementary education nor primary education. It mentions "Compulsory education for all children until they complete the age of fourteen years."

The Secondary Education Commission 1952-53 has recommended "four or five years of Primary or Junior Basic Education...middle or Junior Secondary or Senior Basic School Stage which should cover a period of 3 years."

The Education Commission 1964-66 used the terms Primary (classes I to VII or I to VIII) as detailed below:

(a) Lower Primary : Classes I to IV or I to V.

(b) Higher Primary : Classes V to VII or VI to VIII.

(c) Lower Secondary Classes : Classes VIII to X or IX to X.

The National Policy on Education 1968 referred to the Directive Principle under 45 of the Constitution seeking to provide free and compulsory education for all children up to the age of 14.

An NCERT publication 'The Curriculum for the Ten-year School: A Framework' (1975) used Primary stage and Middle stage. Primary stage of education "covers roughly, the children of age 6+ to 11+ studying in classes I to V. In some parts the age may be 5+ to 10+. In some cases the classes may be I to IV and age in years may be 5 to 9 or 6 to 10." The same publication further said, "The classes VI to VIII cover the middle stage when the normal age groups should be from 11+ to 14+."

According to the Ishwarbhai Patel Review Committee, Primary Education included classes I to VII/VIII divided into two parts: classes I to IV/V and classes V/VI to VII/VIII. It also used the terms lower primary stage and upper primary stage.

National Curriculum for Primary and Secondary Education: A Framework (1985) has used the term "Primary as referred to here is a substitute for 'Elementary', a terminology used in earlier documents."

The National Policy on Education 1986 has used the term elementary education. In part V it states, "The new thrust in elementary education will emphasise two aspects: (i) Universal enrolment and universal retention of children up to 14 years of age, and (ii) a substantial improvement in the quality of education."

According to, 'National Curriculum for Elementary and Secondary Education: A Framework' (1988) prepared by NCERT, Elementary Education is of 8 years. It includes: Primary Stage (5 years) and Upper Primary Stage (3 years).

Changing Scope

With the attainment of independence new goals, demands and responsibilities necessitated far-reaching changes in the system of education. There was 'Explosion of Expectations' in every walk of life, including education. Education for universal education found its expression in the Article 45 of the Constitution. It was recognised that elementary education was of an immense importance for building up a responsible citizen try for a democratic, secular and socialist society.

Now the trend is to use Elementary Education comprising 8 years of education for the age group 6 to 14 and classes I to VIII. It combines two stages of education earlier known as the primary school stage and the middle school stage.

The three main areas of the elementary education are:

(i) Provision of educational facilities everywhere free of cost;

(ii) Retention of all children in schools; and

(iii) Retention of all the children in schools till they complete the elementary stage of education or the age of 14 years.

Exercise

1. "Elementary stage of education is the terminal stage for a large number of children." Elucidate this statement and point out the objectives of education at this stage.
2. What are the determinants of the objectives of education? In this context describe the objectives of elementary education.
3. Point out the scope of primary/elementary education in India. Do you think that there should be a uniformity in the duration of this stage? Give arguments in support of your answer.

6

The Objectives

A.K.C. Ottaway has rightly stated, "Education is an activity which goes on in a society and its aims and methods depend on the nature of the society in which it takes place". Likewise Clark has observed, "No writer on education, however, much he may strive after universality of thought can wholly shake himself free from the influence of time and space".

Social Aims

Aims are related to real situations in life. Education to be effective must meet the many-sided needs of the society. A child is not to be educated in a vacuum. He is a member of the society in which he lives and education must enable him to become a useful member of the society.

Since, economic, physical, political, religious and social needs differ from place to place, from time to time and from country to country, educational aims also differ.

Economic Factors. Formal education is possible where production exceeds consumption. This may be the result of tremendous industrial development or favourable natural circumstances. This will depend upon fertility of soil, abundant mineral deposits and proper climatic conditions for work. Such conditions provide men with leisure to pursue education. Where there is a subsistence economy, it is a far cry to afford time for formal schooling. This is the reason why poorer and undeveloped countries have a minimum education for their children while industrially advanced countries afford to keep nearly all their children at school and for a longer time.

Geographical Factors. Educational system in ancient Greek States presents an interesting study. Education in Sparta aimed at developing physical strength, courage and endurance and obedience because the immediate aim was to train the Spartan youth as soldiers who could protect the state from foreign aggression. Athian education on the other hand was finer.

Political Factors. Political ideologies go a long way in determining the aims and the system of education. Different political ideologies like totalitarian or fascist, communist or socialist and democratic will call for different systems of education.

The ruled nations had a different educational system than their rulers as they were being exploited by their rulers. The system of British education was implanted in this country from purely political motives.

Religious Factors. The influence of religion is very powerful as it penetrates the emotional depth of human nature. The Brahmanic system of education, the Buddhist education and the early Mohammedan education were dominated by religion. Similarly in Europe the Protestant countries were wedded to the education of the masses and the Catholic countries to the education of the classes.

Social Factors. Education reflects the social pattern of society. The tremendous explosion of science and technology has shaken the old leisurely outlook on life and has created intricate problems of social adjustment. A new emphasis has been placed on literacy. A growing interest is shown in reorganising the curricula at all stages. The new forces in the social structure of the Indian society have provided a fresh incentive for educationists to pattern the educational system.

Education in Primitive Societies. In ancient times men needed training in the use of bows and arrows for their safety. Their needs were simple and a few. The process of production, consumption, distribution and exchange was quite simple. Thus, the educative needs were also simple and these could be met by a process of education which was also very simple.

Aim of Education in a Totalitarian State. The aims of education are determined by the political ideologies. J. F. Brown says "Education in any country and at all periods reflects ideologies of the ruling class". There are many instances in the history of the world when persons with different ideologies from their rulers were threatened, sacked, and even assassinated. In Russia, the individual was to be trained in a way so as to become a Communist, in Germany a Nationalist Socialist and in Italy a Fascist. The aim of education is to force upon every individual an ideology which he must not question. The creed will be reflected in the curriculum, syllabi, methods, and techniques of education.

Aim of Education in Ancient India. Education in ancient India was in the hands of the Brahmans, and religion played an important role in the life of an individual. Indian education aimed at inculcating a spirit of piety and righteousness. Education constituted a real training for living life according to spiritual and moral values.

Aim of Education in Medieval India. The aim was religious and the educator was required to produce pious and religious minded people. Maktabs and Madarsas were the places where education was imparted. These institutions were generally run in mosques.

Aims of Education in British India. There was a radical change in the aims of education with the advent of British rule in India. Lord Macaulay laid down the aims of education in the famous Minutes of 1835. The aim of the educational system was to train an army of individuals who could assist the Britishers in the administration of this country. Macaulay wanted an educational system which might bring about the cultural conquest of the people of India by the British.

Aims of Education in Free India. The ideals and values embodied in the Preamble to the Constitution of India are the guiding sources of educational aims in India. These may be expressed as under:

1. Development of democratic values.
2. Development of egalitarian values.
3. Development of secular values.
4. Development of values related to dignity of individual.
5. Development of values conducive to the unity of the country.

General Aims

1. Aesthetic aim.
2. Complete living aim.
3. Cultural aim.
4. Harmonious and all-round development aim.
5. Happiness aim.
6. Individual aim.
7. International understanding aim.
8. Knowledge aim.
9. Leisure aim.
10. Moral aim.
11. Physical health and well being aim.
12. Political aim.
13. Religious aim.
14. Self-realization aim.
15. Social aim.
16. Spiritual aim.
17. Vocational aim.

Summary. Education to be effective cannot have a single aim. An ideal balance among various aims has to be struck.

Individual Aims

Individual Aim in Education

Individual aim in education has found support from the following:

Individual Aim and the Biologists. Prof. G. Thompson has observed, "Education is for the individual: its function being to enable the individual to survive and live out his complete life."

Individual Aim and the Naturalists. In the words of Rousseau, the most ardent supporter of the individual aim in education, "Everything is good as it comes from the hands of the Author of Nature". Accordingly he and others who also think likewise advocate that education should be in accordance with the nature of the individual.

Individual Aim and the Psychologists. According to psychologists, each individual is a unique one and accordingly education should develop the innate powers of the individual.

Individual Aim and the Spiritualists. The spiritualists are of the view that every individual is a separate identity and responsible for his own actions. Therefore, the main aim of education is to lead the individual to self-realisation.

The Criticism

1. The critics of individual aim believe that the individual left to himself is an animal, selfish and indisciplined. The animal instinct of man, if given, a loose reign is sure to lead him to the state of primitive barbarism where the law of jungle prevailed.
2. The exaggerated claim of the individual may have an adverse effect in the politics and economy of a country. The policy of 'Laissezfaire' is not conducive to national interests in the modern times.
3. Absolute freedom to the individual should not be given. The individual may begin to assert that I must have what I want.

4. According to Raymont, an individual is only a figment of imagination. An individual cannot be conceived in isolation from society.

Supporters of Social Aim

1. Gandhiji formulated the basic scheme with the objective of making people realize that education was not merely for the benefit of the individual but for the needs of a predominantly rural and agrarian population.
2. According to John Dewey, social aim in education is stressed as education should make each individual socially efficient, and this social efficiency must be achieved by the positive use of individual powers and capacities in social occupations. A socially efficient individual is not a drag or parasite on society or any individual. A socially efficient individual is able to earn his livelihood. He also conforms to moral and social standards of conduct.
3. Raymont says that the isolated individual is "a figment of the imagination." The individual being a social animal, will be moulded to the needs of the society. The individual will develop through social contacts.
4. According to the Education Commission 1964-66, "Education cannot be considered in isolation or planned in a vacuum. It has to be used as a powerful instrument of a social, economic and political change and will, therefore, have to be related to the long-term national aspirations, the programmes of National Development in which the country is engaged and the difficult short-term problem it is called upon to face."

Limitations of Social Aim

1. Social aim of education envisages the individual as a non-entity and leaves little scope for his personality development.

2. Extreme form of social aim has led to the concept. "My country! Wrong or right". This emphasis became responsible for the rise of Nazism in Germany and Fascism in Italy. As a result of this, Second World War took place.
3. Undue stress on social aim of education is against the concept of universal brotherhood.

Synthesis between Individual and Social Aim

The individual and the society, both be regarded as realities, neither of the two being absolutely independent of the other. Instead of being regarded as isolated entities, the individual and the society should be considered as functionally related to each other—the individual acting on the society, and the society reacting on the individual. The individual is the product of society which the society in its own turn finds its advancement in the development of its individual members. In the words of John Adam, "Individuality requires a social medium to grow. Without social contacts we are not human."

According to Ross, "Individuality is of no value and personality is a meaningless term apart from the social environment in which they are developed and made manifest. Self-realization can be achieved only through social service, and social ideas of real value can come into being only through free individuals who have developed valuable individuality. The circle cannot be broken."

PRIORITIES OF AIMS

Aims of Education in Accordance with the Nature of Indian Society. The Indian Constitution with its statements contained in the Preamble, Fundamental Rights and Directive Principles forms the chief sources of aim of education in India.

The goals placed before the people by the Constitution are those of a democratic society which recognizes the dignity and the basic rights of the individual and holds the promise of an order in which social, political and economic justice and equality will prevail.

The salient features of the Indian society as envisaged in the Constitution are:

1. Indian society must be based on the principles of secularism, socialism and democracy.
2. Indian society must be based on justice, social, economic and social.
3. Indian society must provide for liberty of thought, expression, belief, faith and worship.
4. Indian society must be based on equality of status and opportunity.
5. Indian society must be based on fraternity, assuring the dignity of the individual and the unity of the nation.
6. Indian society must provide a reasonable standard of living to its members.

Brief History of Aims of Education in India. As stated from time to time the first attempt to list aims of education in India was made by the University Education Commission (1948-49). The aims were confined to higher education only. Besides, these were formulated before the commencement of Indian Constitution. The second attempt was made by the Secondary Education Commission (1952-53). These related to secondary education only.

The Education Commission (1964-66), popularly known as the Kothari Commission went into reforms of all aspects of education including aims of education.

The Education Commission suggested the following aims of education:

1. Vocational aim for increasing productivity.
2. Character development i.e. development of moral, social and spiritual values.
3. National and emotional integration aim.
4. Democratic aim.
5. Modernisation of Indian society through awakening of curiosity.

Two Most Important Aims of Education Relevant to Indian Society: Character Formation and Vocational Efficiency.

Character Development Aim

A man of character is bound to be liberal, appreciative of his duties and responsibilities, above from sectarian, regional and religious considerations. He follows the values of secularism, socialism and democracy. Therefore, character formation is the first aim of education in India.

Character has Two Facets: the one which is personal, and the other which manifests itself in our relationship with society. Both these aspects should be pure and unsullied.

Gandhiji has observed, "All our learning or recitation of the Vedas, correct knowledge of Sanskrit, Latin, Greek and what not will avail us nothing if they do not enable us to cultivate absolute purity of heart. The end of all knowledge must be building up of character." Raymount states, "The teacher's ultimate concern is to cultivate, not wealth of muscle, nor fullness of knowledge, nor refinement of feeling, but strength and purity of character." According to Vivekananda, "The end of all education, all training, should be man making." John Dewey has said, "All education forms character—mental and moral". The Secondary Education Commission has observed, "Education is the training of character to fit the students to participate creatively as citizens."

Character is the product of daily, hourly actions and words and thoughts; daily forgiveness, unselfishness, kindness, sympathies, charities; sacrifices for the good of others, struggles against temptations. What is character without elementary personal purity?

In India today we find a lack of character at various levels so much so that the actions of the V.I.P.'s also create doubts in the mind of the common man. State of affairs is very shocking. The present saying is 'As the ruler, so the people'. Perhaps after independence, morality or character has been the greatest casualty. Education, therefore, must be devoted to character building activities.

Vocational Aim

Moral or character formation aim of education is also one-sided. An individual must be prepared to earn his livelihood otherwise he will not be a happy man. of course, values of life must not be sacrificed for "bread and butter".

Gandhiji has also supported the vocational aim. He observed, "True education ought to be for them (boys and girls) a kind of insurance against unemployment." The vocational aim is also called the `bread and butter aim'. It can train individuals to become socially efficient. They will, therefore, neither be drags nor parasites on the society. They will contribute to increase production and national wealth. The advocates of the vocational aim argue that all the knowledge a pupil gains in the school, all the culture the pupil acquires in the school will be of no use, if he cannot make both ends meet when he enters life.

Synthesis of Character Formation and Vocational Aim of Education. Vocational aim in education has its own importance but man does not live by bread alone. Education must take into consideration the entire personality of the pupil and not one segment of it. Man has to develop himself aesthetically, intellectually, morally, physically and socially. The University Education Commission 1948-1949 has very rightly observed, "If we wish to bring about a savage upheaval in our society, a Rakshas Raj, all that we need to do is to give vocational and technical education to starve the spirit. We will have number of scientists without conscience, technicians without taste, who find a void within themselves a moral vacuum and a desperate need to substitute something, anything for their lost endeavour and purpose".

Pt. Nehru has stated, "Education has mainly two aspects, the cultural aspect which makes a person grow, and the productive aspect which makes a person do things. Both are essential. Everybody should be a producer as well as a good citizen and not a sponge on another person even though the other person may be one's own husband or wife." Gandhiji, it is true, stressed the vocational aspect but at the same time he was very emphatic, "By education I mean an all-round drawing out of the best in child and man-body, mind and spirit". He was convinced that without character, vocational efficiency had no meaning.

Functions and Directions

General Functions of Education in Life. Education is expected to perform the following functions:

1. Development of natural abilities of individuals.
2. Development of such capacities in the individuals that help them to harness the natural resources of the country.
3. Development of character.
4. Development of personality.
5. Preparation for living present life.
6. Preparation for adult life and future life.
7. Sublimation of instincts.
8. Creation of socially efficient individuals.
9. Development of community sense.
10. Conservation and promotion of culture and civilization.
11. Involvement in social welfare.
12. National development.
13. Development of suitable leisure time activities.
14. Developing values of emotional integration.
15. Developing universal brotherhood.

Influencing Factors

As already observed, educational systems is to be transformed in such a way as it fully meets the requirements of a society as envisaged in the Constitution of India. Among the important characteristics of the Indian society are to be (i) Democratic (ii) Socialist (iii) Secular (iv) Modern. Inherent in these are the concept of a welfare state i.e. raising the standard of living can be improved only with increased production and equitable distribution of wealth. All this demands, that education in India should be geared to perform the functions as discussed here.

Social Development. An individual is social by nature. He always resides and works in society. He has to live and act in the society as a social being. Education, therefore, must aim at social development. The social development finds expression in such concepts as 'education for social service' and 'education for social efficiency'.

Education for Human Resources Development. The Education Commission 1964-66 has described the situation as "There can be no hope of making the country self-sufficient in food unless the farmer himself is moved out of his age-long conservation through a science-based education, becomes interested in experimentation, and is ready to adopt techniques that increase production. The same is true of industry. The skilled manpower needed for the relevant research and its systematic application to agriculture, industry and other sectors of life can only come from a development of scientific and technological education. Similarly, economic growth is not merely a matter of physical resources or of training skilled workers, it needs the education of the whole population in new ways of life, thought and work."

The Development of Physical Resources of the Country. This can be made possible through the modernization of agriculture and rapid industrialization. This requires the adoption of a science-based technology, heavy capital formation and investment and the provision of the essential infrastructure of transport, credit, marketing and other institutions.

Education for the Development of Skills. Our principal potential asset is our people. Whether using a plough, driving a truck, designing a steel mill or typing business letters, the human factor is common and vital to all branches of economics activity. Education has an essential role to play in the structure and effectiveness of the country's work force. Education is indispensable in all occupations as it develops proper insight. As economic and productive activities expand there is a greater need for educated people to design, plan, supervise, manufacture, sell and administer. Services of all kinds grow in step with industry. All services need educated personnel for operation and administration.

Ensuring Equality of Opportunity. The National Policy on Education, 1986 has observed, "the New Policy will lay special emphasis on the removal of disparities and to equalise educational opportunity, by attending to the specific needs of those who have been denied equality so far".

Democratization of Education and the Involvement of People. Democratizing education does not only mean giving more education to more people, but also involving more people in educational management.

Meeting the Needs of an Egalitarian Society. Education should develop such attitudes and values in the citizens of India so that they contribute to the building of an egalitarian society.

Development of Secular Values. Education must inculcate such values as are helpful in appreciating the diverse religious points of view and harmonising them.

Exercise

1. What are major objectives of education ?
2. What features affect aims of education ?
3. What are functions and directions of education ?

7

Commissions and Policies

Secondary Education Commission (1950-53)

The Government of India, Ministry of Education appointed this commission with Dr. A. Lakshmanaswami Mudaliar, Vice-Chancellor, Madras University, as its Chairman in September 1952. The Commission submitted its report in June 1952. The terms of reference of the Commission were:

(a) to enquire into and report on the present position of Secondary Education in India in all its aspects; and

(b) suggest measures for the reorganisation and improvement.

The Commission gave its recommendations on the various aspects of secondary education. Only a few references were made in respect to elementary education.

The Recommendations

Pattern of Education. The Secondary Education Commission visualised the following structure of school education including the primary stage:

(a) 4 or 5 years of Primary or Junior Basic Education.

(b) A middle or Junior Secondary or Senior Basic Stage covering a period of 3 years.

(c) A Higher Secondary Stage which should cover a period of four years.

The Commission emphasised that in the planning of the curricula at these three successive stages (including the primary) there must be an organic continuity so that each stage leads on to the next stage and there is no abrupt break. Particular care should be taken to ensure that the education imparted during the first 8 years in the Primary (or Junior Basic) and the Middle (or Senior Basic) stage forms an integrated and complete whole, so that when free and compulsory education is extended upto the age of 14, as envisaged in the Constitution, it should constitute a uniform pattern of education.

Co-education. Separate schools for girls should be established where it is possible as they are likely to offer better opportunities than in mixed schools to develop their physical, social and mental aptitudes. It should be open to girls whose parents have no objection in this matter, to avail themselves of co-educational facilities in boys schools.

Study of Languages. During the middle school stage every child should be taught at least two languages. English and Hindi should be introduced at the end of the Junior Basic Stage, subject to the principle that no two languages should be introduced in the same year.

Curriculum at the Middle Stage. The function of the curriculum at this stage is to introduce the pupil in a general way to certain broad fields of human knowledge and interest. By providing a broad-based and general curriculum, we can help the child to discover his own tastes and talents. Keeping in view these considerations the following broad outline of the middle school curriculum is suggested:

(1) Languages, (2) Social Studies, (3) General Science, (4) Mathematics, (5) Art and Music, (6) Craft, and (7) Physical Education.

Education Commission (1964-66)

The Education Commission popularly known as Kothari Commission after its Chairman D.S. Kothari is the first comprehensive document on education in India which surveyed the entire field of education in India and suggested measures for changing the system of education. The opening sentences of the report are, "The destiny of India is now being shaped in her classrooms. This, we believe, is 'no more rhetoric. In a world based on science and technology, it is education that determines the level of prosperity, welfare and security of the people." The Commission considered education as an instrument of change.

It emphasised that education must be related to the life, needs and aspirations of the people of India. It recommended as:

- education should be related to productivity.
- education should strengthen social and national integration.
- education should consolidate democracy as a form of government and help the country to adopt it as a way of life.
- education should hasten the process of modernisation.
- education should strive to build character by cultivating social, moral and spiritual values.

Kothari Commission

1. *Structure of Education.* Primary stage of 7 to 8 years: (a) Lower primary stage of 4 to 5 years, (b) Higher primary stage of 3 or 2 years.
2. *Admission.* The age of admission to class I should ordinarily be not less than +6.
3. *Enrolment.* Five years of effective primary education should be provided to all children by 1975-76 and seven years of such education by 1985-86.
4. *Part-time Education.* Part-time education for one year should be made compulsory for all children in the age

group 11 to 14 who have not completed the lower primary stage and are not attending school.

5. *Tuition Fees.* Tuition fees at the primary stage should be abolished in all government local authority and aided private schools as early as possible and preferably before the end of the Fourth Plan.
6. *Other Facilities.* Free text-books and writing materials should be provided at the primary stage. Children freshly admitted should be welcomed at a school function and presented with a set of books. Other should be presented with complete set of books for the next year as soon as the results of annual examinations are declared and before the long vacation starts so that they can use the vacations for further study.
7. *Scholarships.* An adequate member of scholarships should be provided for talented students at every stage of education.
8. *Education of the Tribal People.* At the primary stage, Ashrams, schools should be established in sparsely populated areas.
9. *Stagnation and Wastage.* The objective should be to ensure that not less than 80 per cent of the children that enter class I reach class VII in a period of seven years.
10. *Perspective Plan for Primary Education.* Each state and district should prepare a perspective plan for the development of primary education.
11. *Universal Provisions of Schools.* A lower primary school should be made available within a distance of about a mile from the home of every child, and a higher primary within one to three miles.
12. *Improvement of Quality.* Expansion facilities at the primary stage should be accompanied by qualitative improvement.

13. *Education of Girls.* Education of girls requires special attention and measures for fulfilling the constitutional directive.
14. *Study of Languages.* At the lower secondary stage, the pupil will ordinarily study only one language—the mother-tongue or the regional language. At the higher primary stage he will study two languages—the mother-tongue (or the regional language) and the official language of the Union (or the associate language). The teaching of English should ordinarily not begin earlier than class V after adequate command has been required over the mother-tongue.

Observations

1. The Education Commission did not clearly specify the duration of the two stages of primary education.
2. It is very unfortunate that we have not been able to make adequate progress in checking stagnation and wastage even after about 3 decades of the report.
3. Targets regarding universalisation of elementary education still remain eluded. Strategies recommended by the Commission were, by and large, ignored.

National Policy (1968)

The Report of the Education Commission 1964-66 was widely discussed. A national consensus on the national policy on education emerged during the course of discussions at various levels. The Government of India was convinced that a radical reconstruction of education on the broad lines recommended by the Education Commission was essential for economic and cultural development of the country. It was also necessary to change the educational system for national integration and for realising the ideals of a socialistic pattern of society. The Government of India accordingly resolved to promote the development of education in the country and laid down the principles in the National Policy.

National Policy on Free and Compulsory Education. This was the first principle and it observed, "Strenuous efforts should be made for the early fulfilment of the Directive Principles under Article 45 of the Constitution seeking to provide free and compulsory education for all children upto the age of 14. Suitable programmes should be developed to reduce the prevailing wastage and stagnation in schools and to ensure that every child who is enrolled in schools successfully completes the prescribed course."

Observations. The Policy did not fix any target date for achieving the objective of free and compulsory elementary education. Subsequent events showed that the problem of stagnation and wastage could not be tackled with any reasonable degree of success.

National Policy on Education (1986)

Since the adoption of the 1968 Policy on Education, there had been considerable expansion in educational facilities all over the country at all levels. It was, however, felt that an effective strategy could not be worked out in carrying out educational reforms in the country. As a result problems of access, quality, quantity, utility and financial outlay had assumed alarming proportions. Besides, the country was faced with new challenges and social needs. It, therefore, became imperative for the Government of India to formulate and implement a new Education Policy for the country.

Elementary Education in Policy

In Part III, para 3, the duration of the elementary stage has been fixed as 8 years, 5 years of primary education and 3 years of upper primary. Part V, paras 5 to 12 deal with elementary education and they are reproduced here.

The new thrust in elementary education will emphasise two aspects: (i) universal enrolment and universal retention of children up to 14 years of age, and (ii) a substantial improvement in the quality of education.

Child-centred Approach

A warm, welcoming and encouraging approach, in which all concerned share a solicitude for the needs of the child, is the best motivation for the child to attend school and learn. A child-centred and activity-based process of learning should be adopted at the primary stage. First generation learners should be allowed to set their own pace and be given supplementary remedial instruction. As the child grows, the component of cognitive learning will be increased and skills organised through practice. The policy of non-detention at the primary stage will be retained, making evaluation as disaggregated as feasible. Corporal punishment will be firmly excluded from the educational system and school timings as well as vacations adjusted to the convenience of children.

Essential Facilities

Provision will be made of essential facilities in primary schools, including at least two reasonably large rooms that are usable in all weathers, and the necessary toys, blackboard, maps, charts, and other learning material. At least two teachers, one of whom a woman, should work in every school, the number increasing as early as possible to one teacher per class. A phased drive, symbolically called OPERATION BLACKBOARD will be undertaken with immediate effect to improve Primary Schools all over the country. Government, local bodies, voluntary agencies and individuals will be fully involved. Construction of school buildings will be the first charge on NREP and RLEGP funds.

Non-formal Education Programme. A large and systematic programme of non-formal education will be launched for school drop-outs, for children from habitations without schools, working children and girls who cannot attend whole day schools.

Modern technological aids will be used to improve the learning environment of NFE centres. Talented and dedicated young men and women from the local community will be chosen to serve as instructors, and particular attention paid to their training. Steps will be taken to facilitate their entry into the formal system in deserving cases. All necessary measures will be taken to ensure that the quality of non-formal education is comparable with formal education.

Effective steps will be taken to provide a framework for the curriculum on lines of the national core curriculum, but based on the needs of the learners and related to the local environment. Learning material of high quality will be developed and provided free of charge to all pupils. NFE programmes will provide participatory learning environment, and activities such as games and sports, cultural programmes, excursions, etc.

Much of the work of running NFE centres will be done through voluntary agencies and panchayati raj institutions. The provision of funds to the agencies will be adequate and timely. The Government will take over-all responsibility for this vital sector.

The Resolve

The New Education Policy will give the highest priority to solving the problem of children dropping out of school and will adopt an array of meticulously formulated strategies based on micro-planning, and applied at the grass-roots level all over the country, to ensure children's retention at school. This effort will be fully coordinated with the network of non-formal education. It shall be ensured that all children who attain the age of about 11 years by 1990 will have had five years of schooling, or its equivalent through the non-formal stream. Likewise, by 1995 all children will be provided free and compulsory education upto 14 years of age.

Implementation of the National Policy. The most important step for the promotion of elementary education has been the launching of the scheme of Operation Blackboard. Under this scheme, 1.13 lakh schools in 1987-88, 1.40 lakhs in 1988-89 and 0.46 lakhs in 1989-90 were covered. The percentage of primary schools covered was 21.00, 26.40 and 9.90 during these years respectively.

Posts of primary teachers sanctioned during the same period were 36891, 36327 and 5212 respectively.

Non-formal Education. The Non-formal Education (NFE) was introduced during the Sixth Five Year Plan as a centrally assisted scheme. Under the revised scheme, assistance is being given to State Governments in the ratio of 50: 50 and 90: 10 for running general NFE centres and girls NFE centres respectively. More than 350 voluntary agencies are also working in the field of NFE.

Mass Orientation of School Teachers (MOST). A Centrally Sponsored Scheme of teacher orientation was implemented for a number of years after the formulation of the NPE. Annually about 5 lakh school teachers (including primary and secondary) were covered under the scheme.

District Institutes of Education and Training (DIET's). About 200 DIET's have been set up either by upgrading suitable Elementary Teacher Education Institutions, or where necessary, by establishing new ones so as to provide academic training support.

PROJECT OF SHIKSHA KARMI

This project is being implemented in Rajasthan since 1987 with the assistance from the Swedish International Development Agency. It aims at universalisation of primary education in remote and backward villages in selected blocks of the state. It is to cover about 2,000 villages in a phased manner. It envisages the substitution of the single teacher by appointing two qualified local residents who have been termed as Shiksha Karmies. The existing primary school when run by Shiksha Karmis is called a 'Day Centre', in addition, each Shiksha Karmi also runs a 'Night Centre' for children who cannot attend the Day Centre.

Exercise

1. Why was the Secondary Education Commission appointed? State its main recommendations on elementary education.

2. Describe the chief recommendations of the Indian Education Commission 1964-66 on elementary education.
3. What were the circumstances leading to the formation of NPE 1986? Elucidate its main recommendations and the action on them?
4. Write brief notes on:

   (a) Child-centred Education.

   (b) Shiksha Karmi.

8

Ethics and Identity

Concept of Ethics and Identity

Commitment to the Teaching Profession. The concept of professional ethics may be described in the words of Laurie as, "If a teacher has not an ideal aim he had better to take to shopkeeping at once, he will there doubtless find an ideal within his capacity." The Secondary Education Commission 1952-53 has stated in this connection as, "They (teachers) will not look upon their work as an unpalatable means of carrying a scanty, living but as an avenue through which they are rendering significant social services as well as finding some measure of self-fulfilment and self-expression."

The teacher should feel the importance of his profession. He would be showing a dishonesty of purpose if once having entered it he is engaged in other pursuits. Without an exclusive attention to his job he would fail in bringing forth a harvest of young men and women who are able to contribute their best for the welfare of mankind. If a teacher takes to his work just to make his living because nothing else is available, he will lack the essential zeal required by the teaching profession. He must be a teacher first and the teacher last.

The professional ethics demands that a teacher does not try to exploit school influence for private gains because he realizes that if he does it, he signs his moral death-warrant. The result is that no amount of pressure can wean him from the path of duty and justice. Authority cannot coerce him, nor can temptation reduce him into any course of conduct, not conducive to the highest interests of the school.

He fights all temptations to pad his purse with money to which he is not entitled.

A teacher is expected:

1. To keep abreast of the developments in the teaching profession.
2. To maintain membership in some professional organizations relevant to his subject or area of speciality.
3. To manifest ethical behaviour in relations with fellow teachers and educational associates.
4. To keep abreast of subject matter through study of books, periodicals, newspapers and other sources concerning development in his field.
5. To utilise films, filmstrips, T.V. and radio as a means of keeping abreast of new and advanced knowledge in his field.
6. To attend conferences, workshops seminars and meetings; to take field trips which tend to broaden knowledge.
7. To excercise professional discretion in his relations with parents and the community.
8. To attend to the all-round development of the learners under his charge.

A Man of Confidence. The teacher must have an unlimited confidence and faith in himself. It is essential that a teacher should be not only a man of high character but also that he be a man of confidence; confidence in his vocation, confidence in his pupils, confidence in human nature and confidence in his colleagues.

Mutual Respect

1. A teacher should be adept in establishing good human relationships with his colleagues.
2. He should give due regard to their personality.
3. He should not indulge in forming cliques or groups.
4. He should never criticise any of his colleagues before the students, their parents and others.
5. He should not backbite his colleagues to the head of the institution or others.

The Administration

1. He should give due regard to the head, the members of the managing committe and the personnel working in the Education Department.
2. He should be loyal to the institution.
3. He should appreciate the difficulties and limitations of the head of the institution.
4. He should not indulge in loose talk.
5. He should submit timely reports and records to the appropriate authority through the head of the institution.

The Community

1. Participating in parent-teacher and similar activities.
2. Participating in community affairs.
3. Making himself available to parents at scheduled times to discuss pupil progress and behaviour.
4. Evincing a helpful, sympathetic and understanding attitude towards parents and their children's schooling problems.
5. Assuring through personal behaviour in the community that the school-staff image in the community is favourable.

6. Showing due courtesy to the members of the community and especially when they visit the school.

The Students

1. Students should have free access to the teacher.
2. The teacher should give due regard to the individuality of the students.
3. The teacher should take interest in the welfare of the students.
4. The teacher should attend to their individual needs.
5. The teacher should share responsibility with the students.
6. The teacher should be fair and just with the students.
7. The teacher should have faith in the students.

State Education Code

An Education Code includes rules and regulations governing various aspects of education. It is divided broadly into five categories:

1. Rules regarding recognition of schools.
2. Rules regarding instructional issues e.g. age of admission to a school, admission procedure, fees and funds, prescription of teaching material, school discipline, examination and evaluation etc.
3. Rules regarding school inspections.
4. Rules regarding service conditions and welfare of the staff.
5. School community relations.

It is very important to remember that the entire teaching-learning process is carried on in accordance with the provisions of the Education Code. Any deviation from it is likely to land the teachers into trouble.

Acceptable Attitude

A teacher is a member of the society. He lives and works in the society. In view of his special responsibilities and role, he is expected to rise above the average member of the society. His general attitude in the society should be enthusiasm and optimism. He should be man of cooperative attitude. He should be sensitive to the needs of the society. He should be guided by the ideals of democracy, secularism and socialism. He should be sufficiently appreciative of the needs and problems of the society.

Work Ethics

Since he ceaselessly strives to be a model to others, he regards no aspect of his work as trivial or insignificant which can conveniently be passed on to others to be done well or ill. He is too well aware of the truth of that wise statement, "Trifles make perfection and perfection is no trifle." Hence every item—be it the folding of a sheet or the writing or a circular—is done with meticulous care as if it were a religious act.

It is righty said, "Dignity consists in being helpful and doing the right thing in the right manner and at the right time." A teacher would do well to prepare his lessons daily. Bagley has rightly said, "However able and experienced the teacher he could do never without his preliminary preparation. Efforts should be made to ensure that all the work done is neat and clean, systematic and in time.

Exercise

1. Explain the concept professional ethics.
2. Why do we emphasise professional ethics?
3. Write short notes on:
   (a) Professional growth.
   (b) Staff relations.
   (c) Unethical practices.

4. Suggest measures for establishing rapport with the parents and the community.
5. Explain the significance of the Education Code. Why should it be followed? What are the consequences if it is not followed?
6. What types of pressures pose a threat to the professional ethics of a teacher? How can such threats be met successfully?

9

Scientific Attitude

The impact of science is visible in every aspect of man's existence—aesthetic, cultural, economic, physical, political, religious, social, spiritual and vocational. Science is closely related to the process of consumption, production and transportation. In such situations, an understanding of basic and general nature and principles of science becomes essential to live efficiently and successfully.

For a clear understanding of scientific thinking and attitudes it is desirable to survey a few definitions of science.

The Science

Science searches for relations.

(Albert Einstein)

Science is first of all a set of attitudes. It is the disposition to deal with facts rather than with what someone has said about them.

(B.F. Skinner).

Science perfects genius and moderates the fury of fancy which cannot contain itself within the bounds of reason.

(John Dryden)

The belief that science proceeds from observation to theory is still so widely held that my denial of it is often with incredualitу.

(*Karl Popper*)

Science is built up with facts as a house is with stones. But a collection of facts is no more a science than a heap of stones in a house.

(*J.H. Poincare*)

Hurd, Paul, D. explains the concept of science in 'Directions in Teaching Secondary School Science' (1969) as under:

1. Science is the discovery of order among the data that makes the science.
2. Science is an intellectual activity which arises from personal experience and takes place in the minds of men.
3. Science is a way of using human intelligence to achieve a better understanding of nature and nature's laws.

Facts in themselves simply do not make a science. Science is not simply an abstraction from empirical data.

Scientific Thinking

Scientific thinking and attitude imply the following characteristics:

- Critical Observation.
- Careful Recording.
- Critical Analysis.
- Enquiring Mind.
- Exactness and Accuracy.
- Exhaustive Treatment.
- Impartiality.
- Objectivity.
- Precision.
- Rationality.
- Verifiability.

A close observation of the characteristics of science, will indicate that these are needed in every subject in varying degrees. The promotion of scientific thinking and attitude is very helpful in understanding our surroundings.

Four areas of attitudes in science are:

1. Information processing.
2. Problem solving.
3. Creativity.
4. Decision making.
   - The system of education may enable young students to develop skills and acquire scientific knowledge which has a higher probability to produce a better understanding of their environment. It will also make possible for the students to have an acquaintance with the process of discovery of knowledge.
   - Such a curriculum in schools would not lay emphasis on theoretical scientific principles. Emphasis will be on applications of scientific knowledge to the improvement of living conditions. Then we may hope to achieve this laudable objective—'Science for All.'

"Thus Science for All" envisages "Science as a Way of Life" and may help pupils in Thinking, Reasoning and Citizenery Process (TRC Process).

The National Policy on Education, 1986 envisages the following:

Science in democratic societies benefits all people and we must ensure that they become aware of the advantages which science can bring to their lives. We must find a way to change our attitude towards science education especially at the school level.

To arouse interest in science and to make it for all at least upto the secondary level as propagated by UNESCO, we have to change our attitude towards science. This poses a challenge for our developers and curriculum transactors, i.e., teachers and teacher educators. Now the question arises how do we accomplish this task.

Environmental Activities

The importance of nature study and science experience through environment during the early stages is well recognized as a part of the school programme. This leads to the development of structures, practices and attitudes suitable for these children. It is observed that a child from infancy begins to discriminate and generalize environmental data. If the children are provided with suitable stimulating science experiences, abstractions are likely to proceed more readily. Concepts seem to arise out of actual experiences with the objects and situations. Most children attending schools recognize the various sensations received by sense organs and organize them into a framework. They think intuitively and focus their attention on specific objects within their environments.

Scientific Attitudes

(a) Activities relating to introducing and enabling the child to understand the 'how' and 'why' of things around him.

(b) Activities relating to encouraging the child to observe and wait for changes and effects.

(c) Activities relating to encouraging the habits of discovery.

Living and Non-living Objects

(a) Activities relating to classify living and non-living objects, viz., plants.

(b) Activities relating to classify living and moving objects, viz., animals, birds, insects, human beings, reptiles.

(c) Activities relating to classify non-living and non-moving objects, viz., materials, rocks, etc.

(d) Activities relating to classify non-living and moving objects, viz., cycles, trucks, aeroplanes, boats, trains, etc.

Organising Activities

1. Nature study is a very good source of arranging activities.
2. The teacher may take the children after rains have stopped to witness phenomena like waterfall, water pool etc.
3. The teacher may explain aspects pertaining to raining, keeping of water level, collection of water in ponds.
4. The teacher may assist the children in the making of paper boats, floating them in water and explaining the direction of flow of water.
5. Field trips may be organised to draw the attention of the children regarding these distinctions.

Teacher's Role

Every effort should be made to encourage children to participate in the joy or observing, experimenting and discovering. School should be an exciting place where children meet, discover and learn in comfortable safe surroundings. The roles of the teacher in primary schools to develop a good science programme are:

1. Acquiring necessary information about simple problems which may arise in science teaching.
2. Acquiring awareness of the breadth of opportunities to utilize new concepts.
3. Acquiring awareness of how to relate scientific concepts through continuous meaningful experiences.
4. Arranging an environment that excites the child's curiosity, promotes systematic observation leading to discovery; and encourages discussion.
5. Giving careful thought to the component parts of the environment.
6. Developing concepts that lead to basic understanding about science.

7. Using well designed instructional materials in providing activities.
8. Understanding the behaviour pattern of children.
9. Channelising the attention of individual who are not following acceptable social patterns of behaviour.
10. Helping children to develop intellectually at their own individual pace through exploration, investigation, assimilation and reflection.
11. Coordinating environmental activities with other school programmes.

An elementary teacher may have to play manifold roles as given below:

An Organizer

- Selection of activities.
- Selection of material.
- Organizing activities.
- Field trips.
- Excursions.
- Science exhibitions.
- Science clubs.
- Lectures.
- Debates.
- Quizs.
- Paper reading contests.

As a Facilitator

- Introducing a topic.
- Questioning technique.
- Teacher-student relations.

As a Moderator

- Leading discussions.
- Moderating discussions.
- Summarising concepts.

As a Guide

- Peer group learning.
- Helping slow learners.
- Helping talented learners.

As a User of Resources

- Primary science kit.
- Educational technology.
- Audio-visual aids.
- Improvising equipment.
- Community resources.

PROBLEM SOLVING METHOD

Life is full of problems and an important purpose of education is to prepare children for solving these problems. Therefore, from the beginning, children should be trained in the art and science of problem-solving.

Children are curious by nature and they want to find out answers of many happenings of everyday life. They take pleasure when they are involved in this process.

What is Problem Solving? Yoakam and Simpson define problem-solving as, "A problem is a difficulty that is clearly present and recognised by the thinker. It may be a purely mental activity or it may be physical and involve the manipulation of data. The distinguishing thing about a problem, however, is that it impresses the individual who meets it as needing a solution. He recognises it as a challenge."

Problem solving is needed in the teaching-learning of every subject. For instance in nature study, students may be interested to find out whether a given plant or a variety of cultivated vegetables will flourish under given conditions of soil, water etc.

'How to organise an exhibition' may be the problem before the students.

Steps in Problem Solving

1. The formation and appreciation of the problem. The nature of the problem should be made very clear to the students. They must also feel the necessity of finding out a solution for the problem.
2. The collection of relevant data and information. The students should be stimulated to collect data in a systematic manner. Full co-operation of the students be secured. The teacher may suggest many points to them. He may ask them to organise a few educational trips to gather the relevant information.
3. *Organisation of data.* The students should be asked to sift the relevant material from the superficial one and put it in a scientific way.
4. *Drawing of Conclusions.* Panton suggests that the teacher's aim "should be to secure that, as far as possible, the essential thinking is done by the pupils themselves, and that their educative process produces the particular solution, formulation or generalisations at stake". Care should be taken that judgment is made only when sufficient data is collected.
5. *Testing Conclusions.* No conclusion should be accepted without being properly verified. The students must be taught to be critical to examine the "truths" which they "discover" and to see "whether they fit all the known data". We should have our minds free from every bias in the process of problem-solving.

Teacher's Role in Problem-solving

Valentine Davis quotes Prof. Pasher who suggests the following points in problem-solving:

1. Get them (the students) to define the problem clearly.
2. Aid them to keep the problem in mind.
3. Get them to make many suggestions by encouraging them:
   (a) to analyse the situation in two parts.
   (b) to recall previously known similar cases the general rules that apply.
   (c) to guess courageously and formulate guesses clearly.
4. Get them to evaluate each suggestion carefully by encouraging them:
   (a) to maintain a state of doubt or suspended conclusion.
   (b) to criticise the suggestion by appeal to know facts, miniature experiments, and scientific treatises.
5. Get them experience to organise the material by proceeding:
   (a) to build an outline on the board.
   (b) to use diagrams and graphs.
   (c) to take stock from time to time.
   (d) to formulate concise statement of the net outcome of the discussion.

It has been stated that for the success of problem-solving teaching technique, we need "a teacher who has the ability to see problems clearly, the power to analyse with a keen discernment and the facility to synthesize and draw conclusion with an uncanny accuracy."

Essential Features

1. The problem should be meaningful, interesting and worthwhile for children.

2. It should have some correlation with life.
3. It should have some correlation with other subjects.
4. It should arise out of the real needs of the students.
5. The children must possess some background of the problem which they are going to discuss.
6. The problem should be clearly defined.
7. The solution of the problem should be found out by the students themselves working under the guidance and supervision of the teacher.
8. The problem must have some educational value.

The Merits

1. It helps to stimulate thinking.
2. It develops reasoning power.
3. It helps to improve knowledge.
4. It helps in developing good study habits.
5. It affords opportunities for participation in social activities. Problems are solved with the joint efforts of many students. The students learn to appreciate the different points of view and thus become tolerant.
6. The students learn to be self-dependent.
7. Discussions help to develop the power of expression of the students.
8. The method provides opportunities to the teachers to know in detail his pupils. They learn which students are shy in nature and which are very active and accordingly they assist them.
9. Students learn facts which are meaningful and which have been discovered by their own efforts.
10. It helps in the maintenance of discipline. The students remain busy in finding out the answer to their own problem.

11. Knowledge is easily assimilated as it is the result of a purposeful activity.
12. Education becomes more interesting in place of a dreadful affair.
13. It develops the power of critical judgment.
14. It helps to verify an opinion.
15. It satisfies curiosity.
16. It helps to learn how to act in a new situation.

The Demerits

1. Generally speaking problem-solving involves mental activity only. There is less of bodily activity.
2. Small children do not possess sufficient background information and therefore they are reluctant to participate in discussions.
3. There is a lack of suitable reference and source books for children.
4. It involves a lot of time and the teachers find it difficult to cover the prescribed syllabus.

Exercise

1. State the various elements of scientific enquiry and attitude.
2. Describe the various measures for promoting scientific enquiry and attitude.
3. Explain the role of the teacher as developing and promoting scientific attitude in daily life.
4. What is problem-solving? How is it helpful in promoting an attitude of enquiry in the students?
5. What is the role of the teacher in problem-solving in and outside the class? How can he obtain the involvement of the students in the teaching learning process? What are the limitations in this approach?

10

Teacher Training

National Council

The National Council for Teacher Education (NCTE) has been established as a national level statutory body by the Government of India vide its notification dated August 17, 1995 with the objects of achieving planned and coordinated development of teacher education, regulation and proper maintenance of norms and standards of teacher education and for matters connected therewith. The mandate of the NCTE is quite wide and includes regulatory as well as developmental functions. Some of the major functions are laying down norms for various teacher education courses, recognition of teacher education institutions, laying down guidelines in respect of minimum qualifications for appointment of teachers, surveys and studies, research and innovations, prevention of commercialisation of teacher education, etc.

During the brief period that the Council has been in existence, the Council has laid down norms and standards for pre-primary, elementary and secondary level teacher education institutions. Norms for B.Ed, through distance education mode and M.Ed, have also been prepared. on the basis of the recommendations of an expert committee, the NCTE has taken a decision that the education for the first degree/diploma should be only through face to face institutional course of teacher education of minimum of one year academic duration. The decision has been communicated to all State Governments, Universities, Boards of Education, etc. However, with a view to providing avenues for professional growth of in-service teachers and to clear the backlog of untrained teachers in some regions of the country, B.Ed, through correspondence/distance education is being continued on a limited sale. For this purpose, NCTE has issued regulations laying down guidelines for the universities/institutions running B.Ed, through correspondence/ distance education mode.

National Curriculum

The NCTE published a discussion paper seeking a country wide debate on the document to develop a national consensus on guidelines for improving teacher education, designing futuristic programmes, developing curriculum and evolving transactional strategies to meet the demands of the 21st country.

Important Considerations

1. Teacher education as an integral part of educational and social system.
2. Teacher education and national and social goals.
3. Plural society and national integration.
4. Homogeneous curriculum in a heterogeneous society.
5. Nature of the State and nature of polity.
6. Human resource and economic development.
7. Migration from rural to urban areas and alienation of educated youth.
8. Unemployment.
9. The philosophy of equality and the ramification of teacher education.
10. The philosophy of social justice.
11. Role of teacher education, values and nation building.

12. The scientific philosophy and nature.
13. Panchayati Raj and traditional power structure.
14. Teacher in the community.
15. Teachers for the 21st century.
16. Education : Theory and practice.
17. Changes in schools demand concomitant changes in teacher education.
18. Competencirs and skills in education of teachers unrelated to work situation.
19. Clarity in curriculum.
20. Universalisation of elementary education.
21. Facing the challenges of science and technology.
22. Manpower planning in teacher education.
23. Mismatch between the training and nature of work in teaching.
24. Teaching as a profession.

Specific Objectives

- To equip teachers with sufficient theoretical and practical knowledge and skills.
- To develop a proper understanding of the psychological and sociological principles implicit in the elementary education.
- To empower teachers for promoting all round development of children.
- To generate the capacities for greater motivation, aspiration and a sense of value commitment.
- To enable teachers to manage learning resources and organise experiences for children at this stage with the focus on the minimum levels of learning.
- To enable teachers to foster problem-solving ability among pupils.

- To acquaint them with methods and techniques of handling children with special needs.
- To develop among them the capacity to solve the social and emotional problems of children.
- To enable pupil-teachers to organise supplementary educational activities for this group of pupils.
- To enable them acquire necessary skills so as to develop curiosity, imagination and self-confidence among children.
- To enable them to perform their varied roles in the educational system as well as in society.
- To develop communication skills.
- To foster the desire for life-long learning.
- To motivate them to undertake action research and employ innovative practices.
- To enable them to use community resources as educational inputs.

PRE-SCHOOL STAGE

- Emerging Indian Society
- Pre-school education in India—Status, problems and issues
- Psychology of the child
- Early childhood care
- Methods and techniques for facilitating the growth and development of the pre-school child through activities for:
    - Physical development
    - Mental development
    - Emotional development
    - Language development
    - Social development

- Neuro-muscular co-ordination
- Self-expression
- Habit formation
- Training observation
- Practical Activities, such as,
- Art and clay work
- Paper and pencil work
- Scissors and paste work
- Music and dance
- Story telling
- Games and sports
- Field trips
- Block making and related games.

State Curriculum

- Emerging Indian Society
- Elementary education in India—status, problems and issues
- Psychology of teaching and learning (with special reference to child)
- Health education and school administration
- Education of children with special needs
- Pedagogical analysis of elementary school subjects with focus on MLLs.
- School experience/internship
- Socially useful productive work with focus on school community relationship.
- Organisation of supplementary educational activities.

- Organisation of activities directed towards physical development, social development, emotional development, personality development and leadership creativity, etc.
- Practical work.

Restructuring and Reorganisation

The Centrally Sponsored Scheme of Restructuring and Reorganisation of Teacher Education which has been functioning from 1987-88 in pursuance of the National Policy on Education 1986 envisages strengthening of the institutional base of teacher training as also taking up special programmes for training of teachers in specified areas and other non-institutional programmes of orientation of teachers. For this purpose, the scheme provides for setting up of District Institutes of Education and Training (DIET) to provide training and resource support to elementary education (both formal and non-formal), and adult education systems at the grass root level; upgradation of selected Secondary Teachers Education Institutions (STEIs) into Colleges of Teacher Education (CTEs)/Institutions of Advanced Study in Education (IASEs) to provide similar training and resource support to secondary education; strengthening of State Councils of Educational Research and Training (SCERTs) and also strengthening and establishment of University Departments of Education (through the UGC). In addition to this Programme of Mass Orientation of School Teachers (PMOST) was also taken up under this scheme during 1986-90 to provide orientation to school teachers in the main thrust area of the NPE and also to improve their general competence. About 17.62 lakh teachers were covered. Another such programme, namely Special Orientation Programme for Primary Teachers (SOPPT) has been taken up since 1993-94 to provide orientation to primary teachers in the use of teaching-learning materials supplied under Operation Blackboard and also to train them in the Minimum Levels of Learning Strategy with focus on teaching of language, mathematics and environmental studies. Under the Special Orientation Programme for Primary Teachers, a total of 45,798 primary teachers have so far been oriented.

The target of establishing 425 District Institutes of Education and Training (DIETs) was met in the year 1996-97. 108 Secondary Teacher Education institutions have so far been upgraded into Colleges of Teacher Education (CTEs) Institutes of Advanced Study in Education (lASEs) against the target of establishing 135 CTEs/ IASEs at the end of 8th Five Year Plan. It is proposed to establish 110 CTEs/IASEs by the end of the plan period.

The progress of Teacher Education Scheme since 1987-88 is as indicated below:

Teacher Education Scheme

Sl. No.	*Nomenclature*	*Cumulative Achievement*
1.	Amount spent (Rs. in crores)	337.225 (as on 31.3.1996)
2.	Number of Teachers oriented under the Special Orientation Programme for Primary Teachers (1986-90)	40 lakh teachers
3.	Number of District Institutes of Education and Training (DIET) sanctioned	425
4.	Number of Secondary Teacher Education Institutes upgraded into CTEs/IASEs.	108
5.	Number of SCERTs Strengthened	18

Exercise

1. What is Elementary Teacher Education ?
2. Discuss NCTE Paper in details.
3. What is Restructuring and Reorganisation Scheme ?

11

TEACHING STRATEGIES

INSTRUCTIONAL STRATEGY

An instructional or teaching strategy refers to a pattern of teaching acts that serves to attain certain outcomes and to guard against others. An instructional strategy is a purposefully conceived and determined plan of action.

According to Broudy (1963), "Method refers to the formal structure of the sequence of acts commonly denoted by instruction. The term method covers both strategy and tactics of teaching and involves the choice of what is to be taught." Method is a wider term. It includes strategies and techniques of teaching. Different strategies may be adopted in following a method. Teaching strategy may include different techniques of teaching. Different techniques may be used within the same strategy and method.

E. Stones and S. Morris, define the term teaching strategy comprehensively. They point out that it is a means to achieve learning objective. According to them, "Teaching strategy is a generalised plan for a lesson which includes structure, desired learner behaviour in terms of goals of instruction and an outline of planned tactics necessary to implement the strategy. The lesson strategy is a part of a larger development scheme of the curriculum."

Main Functions

1. They should aim at inculcating 'love of work'.
2. They should aim at developing the desire to do work with the highest measure of efficiency of which one is capable. The motto of every school and pupils should be "everything that is worth doing at all is worth doing well."—Whether it be making a speech, writing a composition, drawing a map, cleaning the classroom, making a book rack or forming a queue.
3. They should provide numerous opportunities of participation in freely accepted projects and activities in which discipline and co-operation are constantly in demand.
4. They should aim at developing the capacity for 'clear thinking' which distinguishes every truly educated person, "whether a student is asked to make a speech in a debating society or to write an essay or to answer a question in history, geography, or science or to perform an experiment, the accent should always be on clear thinking and on lucid expression which is a mirror of clear thought."
5. They should aim at providing opportunities to pupils to apply practically the knowledge that has been acquired by them. They should aim at transforming present bookish schools into "work schools" or activity schools.
6. They should aim at the quickening of interest and training in efficient techniques of learning and study.

Main Characteristics

1. The term strategy owes its origin to military science.
2. A teaching strategy assumes that teaching is a science.
3. A teaching strategy uses micro-approach to teaching.
4. A teaching strategy makes use of tactics in teaching.

5. The behavioural objectives and learning conditions are the two basic elements of a teaching strategy.
6. A teaching strategy rests on the educational philosophy of the institution and the teacher.
7. A teaching strategy takes into account feedback.
8. A teaching strategy is evaluated in terms of achieving objectives by administering criterion test.

Ten Ways for Strategy

Richard Ober of University of Florida, U.S.A. developed a Reciprocal Category System (RCS) in 1967. This system includes the following functions in classroom strategy building.

Sl. No.	*Teacher Category Talk No.*	*Description of Verbal Behaviour*
1.	*"Warms"* (Informalizes)	the climate, tends to open up, eliminates the tension, praises or encourages the action, accepts and clarifies the feeling tone of the learner in a friendly manner.
2.	*Accepts*	accepts the action, behaviour comments on ideas of learners, positive reinforcement of these.
3.	*Amplifies*	the contribution of the learner, asks for clarification, builds on and develops the action, behaviour, comments, ideas and or contributions of the learner.
4.	*Elicits*	asks a question or requests information about the content, subject or procedure with the intent that the learner should answer.
5.	*Responds*	gives direct answer or response to questions or requests for information that are initiated by the learner; includes answers to one's own question.

Contd.

Sl. No.	Teacher Category Talk No.	Description of Verbal Behaviour
6.	*Initiates*	presents facts, information and/or opinions concerning the content, subject or procedures; expresses one's own ideas.
7.	*Directs*	gives directions, instructions, orders and/or assignments to which the learner is expected to comply.
8.	*Corrects*	tells the learner that his answer or behaviour is inappropriate or incorrect.
9.	*"Cools" (formalizes) the climate:*	makes statements intended to modify the behaviour of the learner from an inappropriate to appropriate pattern, may tend to create a certain amount of tension.
10.	*Silence or Confusion:*	pauses, short period of silence and periods of confusion in which communication cannot be understood.

Teacher-centred and Learner-centred Strategy. In times gone by, teaching was teacher-centred. He did not pay adequate attention to the needs of the young learners. The child was considered very much like clay and it was believed that the teacher could give any shape to him as he liked. The learner was considered as a passive being. The teacher emphasised knowledge and acquisition of facts. The learner was expected to be quiet rather than expressive. Self-activity on the part of the child was not encouraged. The child was kept in the background. The teaching did not socialise the process of learning and on the other hand made the child docile. Individual differences of learners were seldom taken into consideration.

The present century is sometimes called the 'century of the child.' Many educators would like to make him the 'monarch' in the process of education. It is considered that learning by learners is more important than teaching by the teacher. Modern instruction aims at recognising the importance of the individual, at least in theory. In the words of Dr. Stantley Hall, new teaching is to be 'paide-centric'.

"Teach the child rather than the subject" is the important principle of instruction. In the past, stress was on 'Latin' but the progressive educator John stresses also. Education and teaching must fit a learner and be in accordance with his particular needs and reverse process in which learners are made to fit into an educational mould has no place in modern education. The school exists for the learner and not the learner for the school.

Many educators stress that the teacher should make himself somewhat dispensable. The Dalton Plan of curriculum asks the teacher to get aside. Madam Montessori calls herself 'Directoress' and Mckown styles himself as the 'Chief Adviser'.

There is no doubt that more importance should be given to the learner but it is wrong to think that we can dispense with the teacher. His guidance is indispensable although his authority is 'dispensable'. He is a friend who helps his friends to help themselves. He must guide the learners in the right way, at the right time and in the right manner. His function is to promote the growth of the child in self-direction. Instead of facility of speech he has to acquire the power of silence and instead of talking, he has to observe. The modern concept of curriculum thus makes heavy demands on the teacher's ability, skill, time and personality for meeting the individual differences of the learners.

Teaching-learning in Terms of Activities. T.P. Nunn views curriculum "as various forms of activity that are grand expressions of the human spirit and that are of the greatest and most permanent significance to the world wide."

In the words of Norton and Norton, "The curriculum consists of all the experiences which the child has irrespective of their character or when or where they take place."

The adherents of the activity theory are disposed to determine nothing in advance and depend on what may be called as the 'activity curriculum' or the 'activity programme'. According to them pupils should engage in any curriculum activity which is desirable.

Overt Activity Conception—It means that almost any kind of overt or covert or manual activity is a desirable curriculum activity. It may consist of making a dress, constructing a box, building a miniature house, etc., in contrast to such intellectual operations as memorizing, imagination and reasoning. Memorizing, reading, writing, solving mathematical problems, or studying history and geography are not considered activities. Thus in many schools which have this approach the production of articles becomes for a while the dominating factor of the instruction programme.

Centre of Interest Conception Activities—In this conception, activities are related to specific topics called centres of interest. A centre of interest means different things to different people. It is usually conceived in terms of a comprehensive topic that cuts across the ordinary school subjects and includes several other things.

Purpose Conception Activities—The adherents of this view would like to confine the curriculum to purposeful activities. Obviously all desirable curriculum activities cannot be purposeful from beginning to end and some of them that are purposeful may not be desirable.

By living and working in the school community, the young people learn that rights involve responsibilities, freedom implies restraint and that the membership of the school community carries with it a sense of responsibility for the welfare and good reputation of the school as a whole.

An Interactive Process

Teaching-learning necessarily is an interactive process where teacher and learner participate in a reciprocal manner. It is a two-way process. Both teachers and students influence each other.

ACTIVITIES/EXPERIENCE PROGRAMME

The Experience Service. Davis Valentine in 'The Matter and Method of Modern Teaching" has suggested the following programme.

Activities, Experiences and Situations	*Learning Outcomes*
1. Sharing some of the functions of school administration with the students in the form of student council which may be responsible for making rules for discipline and work, organising games and sports, planning co-curricular activities, looking after school property, running a cooperative store and school canteen, preparing school handbook, looking after the school reading room, health and sanitation etc.	1. Students get practical experiences in the working of representative government in choosing their representatives, in making and obeying laws made by them and others in formulating their judgement on matters of conduct and learn the necessity of having rules and regulations for our every day behaviour in various groups and situations.
2. Making surveys of the various needs of the locality.	2. The students develop the sense of belongingness to the community and the part to be played by them.
3. Social service to the school and locality by doing jobs like cleaning the school and surroundings, beautifying school, undertaking social service in community fairs and festivals, rendering first aid to the injured, helping weak children in their studies, making small repairs, digging roads and wells etc.	3. The students develop the sense of responsibility and become acquainted with the social and civic problems and the need to tackle them.
4. Organising excursions to the local surroundings.	4. This helps children to exchange experiences and they learn to appreciate good standards and to decry low standards.
5. Visits to the Legislatures, i.e., Parliament, Assembly, Corporation, Municipality or to Panchayat.	5. This helps children to acquire first hand information of the working of a democratic set-up.
6. Providing Hostel or residential life in the school.	6. The students learn to adjust themselves adequately to the demands of other people and learn how to develop good social relationships. They realise the value and necessity of mutual cooperation and understanding.

Contd.

Activities, Experiences and Situations	*Learning Outcomes*
7. Holding Regular Morning Assembly and congregational prayers.	7. This provides a good start for the daily routine of the school. Students develop qualities like God learning and realise their responsibility to their fellows. They learn audience habits also. They are inspired to do noble deeds.
8. Organising Debates and Discussions.	8. This enables the students to formulate their own judgement and to develop habits of thinking independently, scientifically and creatively. Students learn to become good speakers and debators.
9. Having Clubs for the organisation of musical and dramatic activities.	9. Students develop aesthetic sense.
10. Having common symbols like the school motto and school insignia.	10. This arouses a sense of loyalty and 'esprit de corps'.
11. Organising sports and clubs	11. Students learn to work with a team spirit, forego selfish advantage in view of the greater good of the school as a whole, develop physical well being, build up strong moral qualities, learn the virtues of sustained effort, learn to take success or failure with equal equanimity, learn self-control and self-discipline etc.
12. Having Scouting and Girl Guiding, N.C.C., etc.	12. Such activities develop strong corporate feeling, resourcefulness, initiative, dignity of duty, self-restraint, right attitudes and correct values of life.
13. Organising camps, excursions and educational tours.	13. Students develop a spirit of belongingness to a much large area; their mental horizon is widened. They learn to work together, pool their ideas and to adjust with each other by knowing the qualities or shortcomings of each other.

Contd.

Activities, Experiences and Situations	*Learning Outcomes*
14. Organising Students' Days in schools and assigning them the teaching work along with other school activities; student themselves acting as principals and teachers; the school personnel being busy with the task of guiding them in the staff room.	14. This is a very good method of impressing upon the students to learn virtues of self-discipline. The students working as teachers on that particular day learn how to control classes and develop qualities of leadership.
15. Dispensing with invigilation on certain occasions.	15. Children learn to work honestly and this facilitates the task of removing an atmosphere of suspicion.
16. Celebrating National Days.	16. Children become acquainted with the lives of great men and develop a sense of obligation to the heroes and motherland and a sense of patriotism.

Teaching-learning process implies that all the various elements of the teaching-learning situation have to be brought into relationship and built into an intelligible whole. The teacher-learner activities which are varied and complex have to be harmonised. These elements and activities include learners and their individual differences, the methods of teaching, the material to be taught, class-room conditions, teaching devices and aids, questions and answering, assignments, thinking, enjoying, creating, practical skills, discussions and many others.

Teaching-learning process is affected by the totality of the situation. Teaching-learning is fruitful and permanent if the total situation is related to life situations. Teachers can play an important role in facilitating learning.

Three Variables in the Inter-active Process. Structure of teaching comprises three variables which operate in the process of teaching and creating learning conditions or situations.

1. Teacher as the independent variable.
2. Students as the dependent variable.

3. Content and the strategy of presentation as intervening variables.

Teacher as Independent Variable. The teacher does the planning, organizing, leading and controlling of teaching. He is free to perform various activities for providing learning experiences to the learners.

Student as the Dependent Variable. The student is required to act according to the planning and organization of the teacher. Teaching activities of the teacher influence the learning of the students.

Content and the Strategy of Presentation as Intervening Variables. The intervening variables lead to interaction between the teachers and the students. The content determines the mode of presentation-telling showing, and doing.

Functions of Variables. The variables perform three functions:

1. Diagnostic Function,
2. Prescriptive Function, and
3. Evaluative Function (Achievement).

Diagnostic Function. The teacher as an independent variable is more active and has to diagnose the following:

(a) Entering behaviour of the students,

(b) Teaching problems,

(c) Individual variations, and

(d) Content analysis in view of learning conditions.

The teacher performs two functions in this regard. He administers a diagnostic test for the entering behaviour of the students and analyses the content into elements and arranges from logically in a sequence.

The student as a dependent variable diagnoses on the basis of his perception of his activities and responses. In the process of interaction both the teacher and the student diagnose for initiations and response.

Prescriptive Function. The main objective of this function is to bring desirable changes in the behaviour of the learner. The teacher makes efforts to organize the inventing variables in such a way so as to select teaching techniques and feedbacks that help in the realization of the objectives. The student helps the teacher.

Evaluative Functions. The aims at examining the effectiveness of the prescriptive function. The evaluative function has two main activities:

(i) Construction of criterion test,

(ii) Evaluation of change of behaviour.

Group Discussion

A group discussion is an activity where group members learn through communicating and interacting with each other.

Group discussion is formal when specific rules are followed. It is a systematic approach to a learning situation.

Informal discussion is not a systematic and an organised discussion. It is also useful as it allows more freedom of expression to the learners.

Usually in schools we depend upon group discussion and use the terms group discussion and formal discussion interchangeability.

A group may involve itself into the following types of activities.

1. To discuss a learning issue.
2. To solve a problem.
3. To make a decision.
4. To consider a topic.
5. To view a skill.
6. To carry out role-play.
7. To develop a project.
8. To play a simulation game.

9. To carry out an assignment.
10. To listen and talk to a panel.
11. To hold a tutorial or seminar.
12. To share information.
13. To recommend action.
14. To create new ideas.

The Merits

1. Working in a group produces motivation.
2. All the learners can be involved.
3. Critical thinking can be stimulated.
4. This fits in well with other strategies.
5. The learners can express their difficulties freely.
6. This fosters decision-making skills.
7. It improves independent problem-solving skills.
8. It encourages creative thinking skills.
9. It improves social skills like cooperation and the art of working together.

The Demerits

1. A few talkers may dominate the learning process.
2. The group may side-track the issues.
3. The group learning may become too slow for the ablest and too quick for the slowest.
4. The learners may fail to make necessary preparation for group work.
5. Group cohesion may be poor.
6. Progress may be slow.
7. Shy students may not benefit from this method.

Panel Discussion

A panel is a discussion, held by three to six speakers. It is listened to by an audience who follow the panel discussion wish a general group discussion.

The Seminar

A seminar is a type of group discussion where one learner or several learners prepare a paper on a given topic, issue or problem, which is then presented to the whole group for discussion and analysis.

The Symposium

A symposium consists of several formal speeches, given by experts panels and followed by a general group discussion.

The Workshop

A workshop involves a range of group discussion and practical techniques. While there is basically group activity, learners can work individually for some of the time.

Project Method

Project Method is the practical outcome of the pragmatic education philosophy of Dewey, the well-known American philosopher-cum-educationist. It was developed and perfected by Dr. William Heard Kilpatrick of the University of Columbia. The method is a revolt against the general atmosphere of the school which is marked by one of listlessness and in which there is no keenness, no real life and no desire for good living.

What is a Project Method? Project Method has been defined by various educationists as:

1. *J.A Stevenson.* A project is a problematic act carried to completion in its natural setting.
2. *William Kilpatrick.* A project is a whole hearted purpose-ful activity proceeding in a social environment.

3. *Bollard.* A project is a bit of real life that has been imported into the school.
4. *Burton.* The problem is a project which results in doing. The motor element is not what makes the activity a project but the problem-solving of a practical nature accompanying the activity.
5. *Snedden.* Project is a unit of educative work in which the most prominent feature is some form of positive and concrete achievement.
6. *W. W. Charters.* In the topical organisation principles are learned first while in this projects the problem are proposed which demand in the solution the development of principles by the learner as needed.

The following points have been stressed in the above mentioned definitions of the project:

- Problematic act.
- Purposeful activity.
- Whole-hearted activity.
- Activity in a natural setting.
- Activity in a social environment.
- A bit of real life introduced in school.
- It is problem-solving of a practical nature.
- Positive and concrete achievement is its most prominent feature.
- An activity through which solution of various problems are found out.

Important Principles

The Principle of Purpose. Knowledge of purpose is a great stimulus and motivates the child to realize his goal. The child must have an idea 'why is he doing certain things?' Purpose motivates learning. Interest cannot be aroused by aimless and meaningless activities.

The Principle of Activity. Children are active by nature. They love activity. The instincts of curiosity, construction, pugnacity and herd make them active by nature. Therefore such opportunities should be provided to them that make them active and learn things by doing. Physical as well as mental activities are to be provided to them. They are to be allowed to do and to live through doing.

The Principle of Experience. Experience is the best teacher. What is real must be experienced. The children learn new facts and information through experience.

The Principle of Social Experience. The child is a social being and we have to prepare him for social life. Training for a corporate life must be given to him in his childhood. In the Project Method, the child works in groups.

The Principle of Reality. Life is real and the education to be meaningful must be real. The child who is to live in a life of reality must be trained as such during his education. The project method is a method of educating the child and therefore it must also be real. Real life situations should be presented in the life of the school.

The Principle of Freedom. The desire for an activity must be spontaneous and not forced by the teacher. The child should be free from imposition, restrictions or obstructions so that he may express himself fully and freely. He must be given the freedom to choose an activity, to do an activity according to his interests, needs and capacities.

The Principle of Utility. Knowledge will be worthwhile only when it is useful and practical. The traditional system of instruction simply stressed formal and verbal information for its own sake and was of little utility. The method develops various attitudes and values which are of great significance from the practical point of view.

Various Steps

Providing a Situation. It is not right to force a project on the unwilling students. The students themselves should define, state and choose their problems. of course, the teacher's function would be to provide real and worthwhile situations. He would discover the tastes, temperaments and needs of the students and would provide situations wherein the students feel a spontaneous urge to carry out projects according to their felt needs. Stevenson taught the use of the electric bell to his high school students by the Project Method. The necessity of completely overhauling the bell system in the school building arose and this occasion was utilised in providing a situation.

Choosing and Purposing. It is the centre round which a project moves. The project selected must be such as to satisfy a definite need or purpose. This purpose, as far as possible, must be acceptable to all the students of a class. Dr. Kilpatric remarks, 'The part of the pupil and the part of the teacher in most of the school work depend largely on who does the purposing. It is practically the whole thing." The students themselves should choose the project. Better results and better satisfaction can be had only through self-choice. Many situations should be provided to children. These situations should be discussed and the teacher should give useful suggestions. Decision should always be democratic. The teacher should merely guide and not thrust his opinion. The children must feel that the project is of their own choice.

Planning. When the decision of a project has been arrived at, the next problem is of planning. The teacher should draw the attention of the students to the need of plan before undertaking any activity. Each child should be encouraged to give his suggestions. The teacher should point out to the students to take into consideration their resources. Different proposals should be discussed and alternatives considered.

Executing the Plan. This step is the longest of all and requires a lot of work. The whole project is to be executed through the co-operative efforts of all students. This is the stage at which the students perform many activities and learn various useful experiences. The children keep themselves busy in collecting information, reading and writing in various languages, keeping accounts, calculating prices, looking up maps, collecting specimens of different things, measuring length and area, visiting markets, museums and zoos, visiting fields and crops, seeking help from others and the like.

Judging. The work is to be reviewed when it is completed. Lessons must be learnt from the mistakes that have been made in the various steps of a project. The students must learn to criticise their own work. Self-criticism is a valuable form of training. The students should find out what things they have learnt from the project.

Recording. A complete record of all activities connected with the project must be maintained. The project book should give a comprehensive picture of the project as a whole. It should give the procedure of providing a situation and of choosing the project, duties assigned, difficulties felt and experiences gained, etc.

The Demerits

Neglecting Intellectual Work. There is a wide-spread misconception that the project method glorifies hand work at the cost of intellectual work. The critics argue that the children are kept busy in model-making and the like.

Haphazard and Unconnected Teaching. Projects do not keep the examination factor in view. It is not possible to deal with all the subjects in a single project. There are many topics which cannot be taught through this method.

This difficulty can be met with by setting aside some periods in which the gaps may be covered up.

Upsetting the Time-table. In a project method it is not possible to follow a rigid time-table. It upsets the routine work of the school.

Neglect of Drill Work. This method neglects practice and the development of skill in various subjects. The students do not get adequate drill in arithmetic, reading, spelling, drawing etc.

Difficulty of Suitable Text-books. Preparation of books suitable for the project method is by no means an easy task. Moreover material required for the implementation of a project is very costly. The method is not suitable for ordinary schools.

Artificial Correlation. Sometimes teachers show over-enthusiasm in stretching the projects upon which the class is working beyond it natural limits and try to connect those topics which have remote connections with the projects in hand.

Unsuitable for the Shirkers and Shy. Some students who are not inclined to take responsibility may remain in the background and do very little work.

Too Much Reliance on Young Children. It is not wise to depend too much on the choice of the children.

Lack of Competent Teachers. For the successful working of this method, very learned, efficient and resourceful teachers are needed. The method imposes heavy burden and responsibility upon the teachers.

Unsuitable for Transfers. A child reading in an ordinary school finds it very difficult to adapt himself to a school that follows project method and vice versa.

A review of the above brings us to the conclusion that most of the limitations are unreal and without much significance. Whenever a new method is suggested, criticisms are unnecessarily levelled.

Traditional methods have been tried and found unsuitable to the changing needs of the time. New methods must be tried and if found suitable should be accepted even if they are a bit expensive.

Role of Teacher

The relation of the teacher with his students is very closer in the Project Method than in the ordinary class teaching. The teacher is like a friend, and elder brother who works together with the students and helps them to gain rich experiences. He must stimulate the shy students to put in their best. He must help the students to help themselves. He must see that the project is carried on in a democratic way. He must read intensively as well as extensively.

He should have adequate patience, skill, knowledge, tact and sincerity.

Correlation of Subjects

Name of the Project: Village Survey

History. History of the village, if any, relies and monuments, dwellings of primitive man—caves, huts etc., houses through different ages and at different places.

Geography. Source of water supply, climate, crops, fruits, vegetables and other products.

Economics. Occupation of the people, agricultural yield per acre, village handicrafts, rural indebtedness, co-operative societies.

Civics. Working of the Village Panchayat, co-operative store, educational facilities.

- *General Science.* Health and sanitation of the villlage, water facilities, causes of diseases, village dispensary, ventilation etc.

Arithmetic. Estimate of the cost of the village drainage system, calculation of the per capita income of the village, measurement of land holding, calculation of different items in the family budgets, total area of the village land, area sown and cultivated, calculating agricultural produce per acre.

Language. Description of the various details of the survey.

Art Work. Preparation of charts depicting co[illegible]ions of an ideal village.

Second Project. The pageant on the life of Buddha.

History. The social, religious and political conditions of the Indians at that time, sources of information regarding the life of Buddha.

Geography. Different places connected with the life of Buddha, preparation of maps showing these places.

Language. Study of books which throw light on the life of Buddha, writing of the various details of project.

Religion. Evils of untouchability, love for all, truth and non-violence, teachings of Buddha.

Civics. Co-operative spirit to make the project a success.

Drawing. Preparation of models and charts connected with the events of the life of Buddha.

Craft. Preparation of stage, making lighting arrangement.

Art. Beautification of the various materials used.

Exercise

1. Explain the meaning of instructional strategies. What are the main characteristics of an instructional strategy?
2. "All that is taught is not learnt". Explain this and state the role of a teacher in adopting various classroom strategies.
3. Describe ways and means in building classroom teaching strategies.
4. Compare and contrast teacher-centred and learner-centred teaching-learning process.
5. Suggest a suitable activity-based programme of the school.
6. Explain teaching-learning as an interactive process and bring out the role of the teacher and learner in this strategy.
7. Elucidate the project method of teaching. Suggest a few situations in which this method could be used effectively. To what extent is this method workable in Indian schools.
8. Point out the main merits and limitations of group discussion in teaching-learning.

12

Skills for Teaching

An Interactive Process

Teacher, student, learning process and learning situation. The teacher creates the learning situation. The process is the interaction between student and teacher. Teaching and learning relationship or interaction may be explained with the help of a diagram.

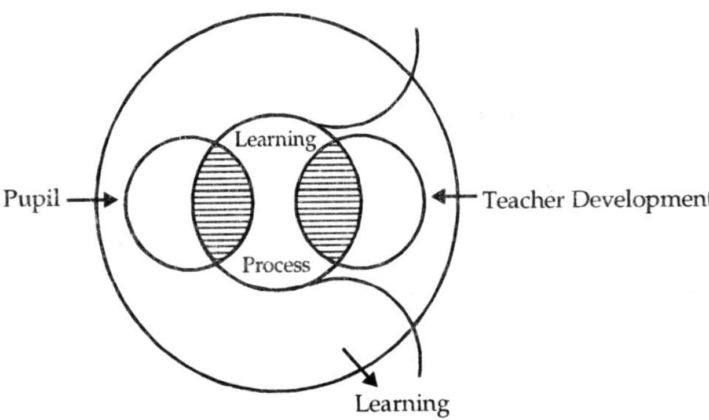

Learning Process and Teacher-taught Interaction

The most distinctive feature of modern society is its science-based technology which has been making a profound impact not only on the economic and political life of a country but also on its educational system. The changes that occur as a result of this impact are broadly described as 'Modernisation'. This modernisation has affected the teaching-learning process in many ways. The recent changes in the concept of teaching-learning process have led to the development of newer areas of educational endeavour. In a traditional society the aim of teaching-learning was the preservation of the accumulated stock of knowledge. But in the modern society, the main aim of teaching-learning is not acquisition of knowledge alone. It is the awakening of curiosity, the stimulation of creativity, the development of proper interests, attitudes and values and the building of essential skills such as independent study. Teaching-learning process has to serve as a powerful instrument of social, economic and cultural transformation of the society. Teaching-learning process is conditioned by the nature and demands of society to which the learner should get adapted and attuned. One of the main aims of teaching-learning in the modern society is to keep pace with the advancement of knowledge and skills. In the modern society teaching-learning cannot be done passively.

For a Pretty Long Period: The teaching-learning process has been by and large, a process dominated by the institution of professional teachers. Now, the process is to be replaced to a great extent by a process in which the individual learner will take challenges through an inevitable intellectual revolution. This intellectual revolution will be set in by forces of hardware technologies at low-cost socialization process due to interdependence. Besides, projects, farms, factories, markets, excursions and playgrounds will become classrooms in the new teaching-learning process.

Elements of the Teaching-learning Process. These may be summed up as under:

1. Who is to learn or whom to teach? The child is to learn and therefore his interests, abilities and aptitudes have to be taken note of. It must be remembered that he is an

active being. Individual differences have to be attended to.

2. Who is to teach or from whom to learn? The teacher is to teach. He should, therefore, present a good model of teaching.
3. Why to teach or why to learn? Education should not be taken in terms of the traditional 3 Rs, i.e., reading, writing and arithmetic but in terms of 7 R's i.e., reading, writing, arithmetic, recreation, rights, responsibilities and relationships.
4. What to teach or what to learn? This includes the acquisition of knowledge, skills and behaviour.
5. How to teach? The teacher must be well-versed with the technology of teaching.
6. How to learn? The teacher and the learner must fully understand that learning takes place through mutual cooperation. A learner learns maximum, when he is motivated. The teacher, therefore, has to provide motivating situations so that the learner is at his best. He has to be fully conversant with learning theories and teaching strategies.
7. When to teach or when to learn? This is concerned with creating motivational situations for the learner.

Operations and Stages

Three Definite Stages. Teaching is not a simple task to analyse. Jackson trunks that if we are to obtain a complete description of the teaching activity, we must consider what the teacher does before and after class also.

1. Pre-active Stage,
2. Inter-active Stage, and
3. Post-active Stage.

Pre-active Stage. Before actual classroom leaching or what Jackson calls "calm" part of teaching, a teacher has to perform many tasks. These tasks include such as preparing lesson plans, arranging furniture and equipment within the classroom, making papers, studying test reports, reading sections of a textbook and thinking about the aberrant behaviour of a particular student. These activities are very crucial to the teacher's performance doing regular teaching session.

Pre-active behaviour is, more or less deliberative. The teacher at this stage hypotheses about the possible outcome of his action. As the teacher decides what textbooks to use or how to group the children for reading or whether to notify students' parents of their poor performance, his behaviour is at least analyzable.

At moments like this, concepts such as evaluation, production and feedback have real meaning for understanding what the teacher is doing.

Inter-active Stage. This is actual classroom teaching. At this stage, the teacher uses a number of strategies for achieving the goal already set. In the inter-active setting, the behaviour of the teacher is more or less spontaneous. Research suggests that things happen quickly during the teaching session. For example, the elementary teacher may change the focus of his concern as many as 100 times daily. Amid all this hustle and bustle the teacher often has little to think.

The differences in the teaching behaviour with and without students have relevance for conceptualizing the teaching task, for justifying certain training requirements and for identifying the criteria for good teaching.

Many teachers try to devote sometime alone with individual students but the teacher-student dialogue is usually public rather than private. When a teacher is alone with a student, he is not faced with the problem of control and management that frequently absorbs a major portion of his energies in a group setting. There is a greater sense of physical and psychological intimacy between the teacher and the student during individual sessions than when the teacher is responding to the class as a group.

The task of keeping pupils involved may entail explanation, demonstration, definition, and other logical operations that have come to be thought of as the heart of teaching.

Post-active Stage. The post-active stage arises when the teacher has left the class and tries to have a look back into what happened in the class.

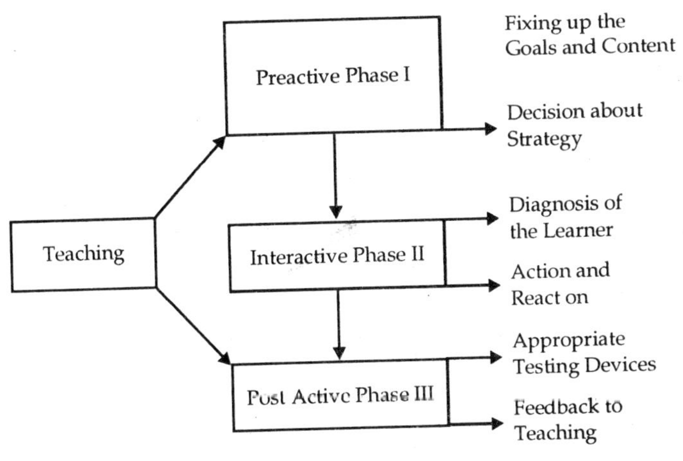

Diagrammatic View of Teaching Operations

Anatomy of Teaching—Three Variables. Structure of teaching comprises three variables which operate in the process of teaching and creating learning conditions or situations.

Teacher as Independent Variable—The teacher does the planning, organizing, leading and controlling of teaching. He is free to perform various activities for providing learning experiences to the learners.

Student as the Dependent Variable—The student is required to act according to the planning and organization of the teacher. Teaching activities of the teacher influence the learning of the students.

Content and the Strategy of Presentation as Intervening Variables—The intervening variables lead to the interaction between the teachers and the students. The content determines the mode of presentation—telling, showing and doing.

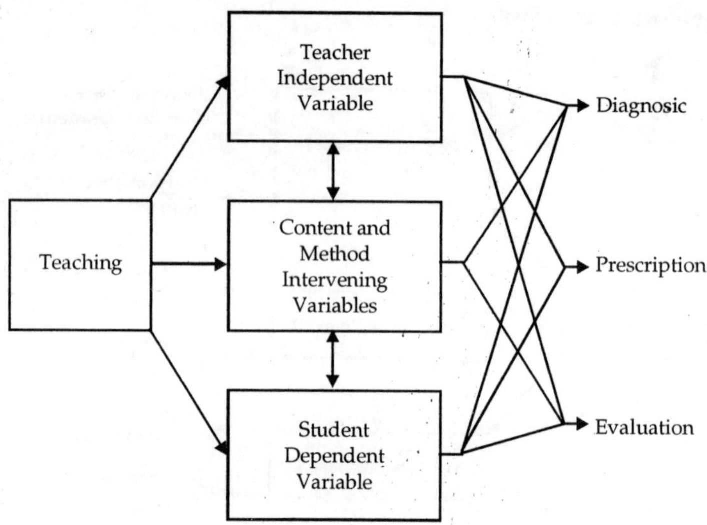

Anatomy or Structure of Teaching

Dynamic and Progressive Skills

The effect of recent developments in educational psychology upon the nature of methods of teaching has been quite revolutionary. A central place for the child has been envisaged. It is widely held that any method that is not based upon 'student activity' is not in accord with sound educational theory.

There is no doubt that even the best curriculum will remain dead unless quickened into life by the right methods of teaching.

Progressive methods of teaching provide opportunities for 'learning by doing', for observation, for experimentation and for co-operation.

Eminent Educators on Progressive Methods

The new teaching recognises the right of the pupil to do things in his own way, within reasonable limits.

Adams

The first principle of true teaching is that nothing can be taught. The teacher is a helper and a guide. His business is to suggest and not to impose.

Sri Aurobindo

Effectiveness in learning lies not in reading and listening but in action, performance and experience.

Cladwell Cook

Impression must be ensured by expression and what has to be done must be learnt by doing.

Comenius

(a) Where there is experience, there is the living being. (b) Action must precede knowledge. (c) Education is by experience. (d) The teacher is a guide and director, he steers the boat but the energy that propels it must come from those who are learning.

Dewey

(a) Play is the highest phase of child development. Play is the purest, most spiritual activity of man at this stage. (b) To learn a thing in life through doing is much more developing, cultivating and strengthening, than to learn it merely through the verbal communication of ideas.

Froebel

(a) I want, the whole process of education to be imparted through some handicraft or industry. (b) The core of my suggestion is that handicrafts, are taught not merely for production work but for developing the intellect of the pupils. (c) I do not want to teach the village children only handicrafts. I want to teach through handicrafts all the subjects like History, Geography, Arithmetic, Science, Language, Painting etc.

Gandhiji

We have buried the tedious and stupid ABC Primer side by side with the useless copy books.

Montessori

I have fixed the highest supreme principle of instruction in the recognition of sense impression as the absolute foundation of all knowledge.

Pestallozzi

Children are restless and then curious. Instead of making the child stick to his books, I keep him busy in workshop; his hands will work to the profit of his mind.

Rousseau

To the child, the environment will provide an ever ready background for its spontaneous activity.

Tagore

You cannot teach a child more than you can grow a plant. The plant develops its own nature. The child also teaches itself.

Vivekananda (Swami)

THE CHARACTERISTICS

1. The methods of teaching in schools should aim not merely at the imparting of knowledge in an efficient manner, but also at inculcating desirable values and proper attitudes and habits of work in the students.
2. They should, in particular, endeavour to create in the students a genuine attachment to work and a desire to do it as efficiently, honestly and thoroughly as possible.
3. The emphasis in teaching should shift from verbalism and memorisation to learning through purposeful, concrete and realistic situations. For this purpose, the principles of 'Activity Method' and 'Project Method' should be assimilated in practice.
4. Teaching methods should provide opportunities for students to learn actively and to apply practically the knowledge that they have acquired in the class-room.

Expression work of different kinds must, therefore, form part of the programme in every school subject.

5. In the teaching of all subjects special stress should be placed on clear thinking and clear expression both in speech and writing.
6. Teaching methods should aim less at imparting the maximum quantum of knowledge possible and more on training students in the techniques of study and methods of acquiring knowledge through personal effort and initiative.
7. A well-thought out attempt should be made to adopt methods of instruction to the needs of individual students as much as possible so that dull, average and bright students—all may have a chance to progress at their own pace.
8. Students should be given adequate opportunity to work in groups and to carry out group projects and activities so as to develop in them the qualities necessary for group life and cooperative work.

Children differ in their basic intelligence, aptitudes, interests and habits. Therefore, no single method of teaching will suit quite appropriately all the children of a group. Various methods are needed for catering to the diverse needs of the children.

Principles of Teaching

Teaching is a science as well as an art. Teaching to be effective must be based on certain principles and maxims of teaching.

Principle of Self-education Activity and Stimulation. Children, we are told, must be left free to express themselves, for effective education is self-education.

Children are by nature curious, assertive and creative. The two important aspects of teaching are stimulation and inspiration. The teachers must fire the enthusiasm of their pupils. They must encourage them in the development of their natural desire to work and to be active and guide their desires into worthwhile channels.

Principle of Individual Differences. Teaching must take into consideration the individual differences of children in various aspects.

Principles of Motivation. Teaching must be based on various techniques which appeal to motives of students.

Principle of Stimulation. Best learning takes place when the teacher is successful in arousing the interest of the student. "The guidance of the teacher is mainly a matter of giving the right kind of stimulus to help him to learn the right things in the right way", writes Ryburn.

Principle of Goal Setting. A definite goal should be set before each child according to the standard expected of him. Immediate goals should be set before small children and distant goals for older ones. It must be remembered that the goals should be very clear and the children must understand these goals.

Principle of Association. Thorndike points out that things which we want to go together should be put together. Many different things should be brought together as a part of one process. Then it becomes easier to make the students understand. We have discussed at various places that things can be associated in a number of ways.

Principle of Emotional Development. Children should be praised when they show good results. This gives them encouragement to show all the more better results and they develop confidence, hope, self-reliance and self-respect. Sympathetic attitude on the part of the teachers gives stimulus and a sense of security to the students. We should discard our habit of fault-finding. This develops fear and feelings of insecurity and of inferiority.

The Principle or Law of Readiness. The law is indicative of learner's state to participate in the learning process. According to Thorndike, readiness is preparation for action. Readiness does not come automatically with maturation. According to this law, for a conduction unit ready to conduct, to do is satisfying and for it not to do so is annoying. A teacher must be alive to this.

The Principle or Law of Effect. It states that a response is strengthened if it is followed by pleasure and weakened if followed by displeasure.

The Law or Principle of Exercise or Repetition. According to it the more a stimulus induced response is repeated, the longer it will be retained. Other things beings equal, exercise strengthens the bond between situation and response. Conversely a bond is weakened through failure to exercise it. Thus the law has two sub-parts, (i) law of use, and (ii) law of disuse.

Principle or Law of Multiple Response. Confronted with a new situation the organism responds in a variety of ways before arriving at the correct response.

Principle of Attitude. The learner performs the task well if he has his attitude set in the task.

Principle of Prepotency of Elements. The learner reacts to the learning situation in a selective manner. He uses his insight, selects the prepotent element in a situation and bases his responses upon those elements.

Principle of Analogy. The organism responds to a new situation on the basis of the responses made by him in similar situations in the past. He makes responses by comparison or analogy.

Principle of Associative Shifting. According to it we get any response, from the learner of which he is capable, associated with any situation to which he is sensitive.

Principle of Polarity. It states that connections act more easily in the direction in which they were first formed than in opposite directions.

The Principle or Law of Similarity. This law states that "other things being equal" the stimuli that are more similar to one another will have greater tendency to be grouped. Thus learning similar things is easier than learning dissimilar things.

The Principle or Law of Proximity. According to this law, "perceptual groups are favoured according to the nearness of parts." This means that we perceive all closely situated or located things as groups.

The Principle or Law of Closure. This law states that "closed" areas are more stable than unclosed ones and therefore move readily from figures perception." It is similar to the Thorndike's law of effect. Unless the work is finished the individual does not feel satisfied. He is under tension which is over only when the work is completed.

The Principle or Law of Good Continuation. This law states that "organization is perception which appears to go in a particular direction appears to be going infinitely in the same direction."

Maxims of Teaching

They make learning inspirational, interesting, effective and meaningful. They keep the students attentive to their work. They bring clarity, comprehensiveness and totality to the teaching-learning process. They make the students active participants in the work.

From Known to Unknown— This means that the teacher should arouse interest in a lesson by putting questions on the subject matter already known to the pupils. The teacher is to proceed step by step to connect the new matter to the old one. New knowledge cannot be grasped in a vacuum. A lesson on profit and loss in arithmetic can easily be taught to the pupils by referring to the shopkeepers who make profit. A history lesson on Shri Ram may be taken up with the celebration of Ram Lila. A civic lesson on the powers of the President of India may start from the powers of the President of Municipal Board or the President of Village Panchayat.

Proceed from Easy to Difficult—Our lessons must be graded in order of difficulty to suit the pupil's standard. This will help in sustaining the interest of the students. In determining what is easy and what is difficult we have to take into account the psychological make-up of the child.

Proceed from Simple to Complex—The terms 'simple and complex' are used here to denote 'what is simple and not what is complex from the point of view of the child and not from adult's point of view.

Proceed from Concrete to Abstract—"Things first and words after" is the common saying. Small children learn first from things they can handle and see. They cannot think in abstractions and hence the necessity of concrete things and illustrations. Very young pupils cannot give the sum of six plus seven all at once. They would either need concrete things like pebbles to count or fingers to calculate the total. Thus by concrete things they will give out sums immediately. Similarly, a child cannot understand what an aeroplane is. Small models will enable him to have correct notions of different types of aeroplanes. Actual visits to canals and rivers may be planned to give a clear idea about these things. The geography lesson should be made interesting with pictures and illustrations of mountains, rivers, bridges, etc. In the same way, concrete things and illustrations give a vivid picture of the matter pertaining to other subjects.

The teacher must take care to see, however, that the students do not remain in the 'concrete stage' all the time. This is only the initial step lot children with a view to reach the higher one of 'abstractions' as they would advance in age. The limitation of this system should also be borne in mind by the teachers.

Proceed from Indefinite to Definite—Early ideas of children are very vague, indefinite and incoherent. These ideas have to be made precise, clear, definite and systematic. Mechanical memorising of rules, definitions and definite ideas should not be thrust upon the students. Children should be made interested in the lesson and made active in the learning process.

Proceed from Particular to General—The study of general rules should be undertaken with the help of the particular examples. Particular is more definite to the child than the general. Children have no notion of truth, honesty or bravery. Definitions and wordy classifications will not be of any help. The stories of Harishchandra, Netaji Subhash and Gandhiji should be told to the students to give them these ideas.

The study of particular facts should enable the children themselves to frame general rules.

Proceed from Empirical to Rational—Empirical knowledge is based only on observation or experience and for which any reasonable account, cannot be given. Rational knowledge is that for which we have got scientific explanation. Sometimes we have to start from less general to more general laws. To reach the rational type of knowledge, empirical observations have to be collected, analysed and rationalised.

Proceed Inductively—It practically includes all the maxims explained above. In this method, we start from particular examples and try to establish general rules from them. The deductive procedure is quite contrary to it. In it we start from general to particular. The students accept theories, generalisations and definitions discovered by others and learn them by rote. They may apply the same to examples afterward. Both of these methods have their own importance.

An example will make the distinction very clear. 'The farmers in India are very poor' is a general statement in the deductive type of reasoning. The inductive will follow thus: Ram is a farmer/He is very poor. Shyam is a farmer. He is very poor, and so from various such examples it will be quite evident that, farmers are poor.

In this way generalisations are derived at. This maxim is more important than the deductive one.

Proceed from Psychological to Logical—Logical approach is concerned with the systematic exposition of the subject-matter. It is also concerned with the arrangement of the subject-matter. The psychological approach looks at the child's interests, needs, reactions and mental make up.

Thus we find that there is a radical difference in these two view-points. The function of the teacher is to combine these two in such a way that the child learns easily and quickly.

When we treat a subject logically we are usually thinking of it from our own point of view and not from the point of view of the child. We start reading by teaching the child to read a whole sentence as for him the unit is the sentence, not the word or the letter, as it is for the adult. This is psychological approach. In a lesson of drawing, we have seen that the child has no sense in lines and curves. Logically we start with simple lines and curves but psychologically we start with drawing a whole animal.

The process of teaching involves a complex behaviour which is not easy to analyse. It is very difficult to give an exact number of skills involved in the teaching process. Commonly identified skills in the teaching process may be listed as under:

Planning Stage

1. Writing instructional objectives.
2. Selecting the content.
3. Organising the content.
4. Selecting of audio-visual aids.

Introductory Stage

5. Creating setting for introducing the lesson.
6. Introducing the lesson.

Presentation Stage

Skills in Questioning

7. Structuring classroom questions.
8. Fluency in questioning.
9. Probing questions.
10. Distributing questions.
11. Managing student response.

Skills in Presentation

12. Pacing of the lesson.
13. Lecturing.
14. Narration.
15. Explaining.

16. Discussing.
17. Demonstrating.
18. Illustrating with example.

Skills in the Use of Aids

19. Using blackboard.
20. Using various teaching aids.
21. Stimulus variation.
22. Silence and non-verbal cues.
23. Reinforcement.

Management Skills

24. Promoting pupil participation.
25. Recognising attending behaviour.
26. Class management discipline.

Closing Stage

27. Achieving effective closure.
28. Planned repetition.
29. Giving assignments.
30. Evaluating pupil's progress.
31. Diagnosing learning difficulties of pupils and taking remedial measures.

SKILLS OF NARRATION

Skills in narration consist of the following four components:

1. Using appropriate beginning and concluding statements.
2. Using explaining links in the form of words and phrases like: as a result of, due to, in order to, on the other hand, write etc.
3. Covering essential points leading to clear understanding of the desired concept or principle.

4. Testing pupil's understanding by asking appropriate questions from the students to ascertain, whether the purpose of narration has been served.

Testing Skills

The skill of probing questions consists of the following components

1. Prompting which refers to the use of some clues or hints provided by the teacher through framed questions to pupils.
2. Seeking further information from the responding pupil to bring his initial incomplete or partially correct response to the desired response.
3. Refocussing implies asking the pupil to give an example in support of answer.
4. Increasing critical awareness by asking 'how' and 'why' of the correct response.

Questions in Order of Difficulty and Importance. These may be categorized as:

(a) Lower Order Questions (L.O.Q.)

(b) Middle Order Questions (M.O.Q.)

(c) High Order Questions (H.O.Q.)

Stimulus Variation. It has been generally observed that children especially up to the age of 10 years are not able to attend to one thing for a very long period. The effectiveness of the teaching learning process in such a situation depends to a great extent on the stimulus variations used by the teacher behaviour. Some of the common teacher behaviours in the classroom which fall under variation are:

(i) Teacher movement.

(ii) Teacher gestures.

(iii) Changes in speech pattern.

(iv) Changes in sensory focus.

(v) Changes in postures.

Teaching Learning Activities

Sl. No.	*Activity*	*Best Suited for*	*Limitations / Not Suitable*
1.	Lecturing by the teacher and listening by the pupil	Presenting facts	Passivity on the part of the learner
2.	Demonstration	1. Teaching principles and phenomena. 2. Showing manipulative operation of any equipment. 3. Explaining a process.	Lack of suitable equipment
3.	Individual Practical Work	1. Providing direct experience 2. Making students fully understand principles, phenomena and process by investigation.	1. Overcrowding classes 2. Lack of equipment
4.	Individual Work in Workshop	1. Developing specific skills 2. Learning about operations of machines. 3. Enabling pupils to undertake any project. 4. Preparation of any article.	Requires huge funds
5.	Field Trips	1. Providing direct experience in natural setting. 2. Highlighting pragmatic application of knowledge.	1. For merely going out for seeing places 2. Needs elaborate planning

Contd.

Sl. No.	Activity	Best Suited for	Limitations / Not Suitable
6.	Projects	1. Providing purposeful activity. 2. Relating practical use of knowledge. 3. Making pupils comprehend fully what they learn.	1. Adequate guidance and planning is needed 2. For show work 3. Lack of expertise
7.	Discussion	1. Motivating pupils to think. 2. Reviewing topics already dealt with individuals. 3. Promoting better comprehension.	1. Danger of discussion going on off the track 2. Dominance of a few
8.	Conference Seminar	1. Sharing of experiences and knowledge 2. Encouraging group thinking 3. Developing understanding	Discussions become futile if background and agenda papers are not sent well in advance
9.	Class and Home Assignments	1. Consolidating knowledge 2. Understanding applications 3. Practising skills	Unchecked and too heavy assignments fail to serve any purpose.
10.	Tutorial (Individual)	Meeting the needs of individual students	There is very little time for teachers
11.	Programmed Instruction	1. Individual learning 2. Scope for self-evaluation	1. Not possible to cover the entire content 2. Expensive
12.	Teaching Machines	1. Individual learning 2. Scope for self-correction	1. Expensive. 2. One way communition

Reinforcements. These may be classified as:

Positive Verbal Reinforcement—Following a pupil's answer, the teacher verbally indicates pleasures at the pupil's response by the use of words like 'Good', 'Fair', 'Excellent', 'Correct' etc.

Positive Non-verbal Reinforcement—These include:

Nods and smiles.

Teachers' friendly movements towards pupils.

Teacher's friendly look.

Teacher writing student's response on the blackboard.

Negative Non-verbal—This comprises gestures—sneering, frowning, expression of annoyance, impatience etc.

Negative Verbal—This includes comments like 'No', 'Wrong', 'No good', 'Poor', 'of course not' etc.

MANAGING CLASSROOM

I.K. Davies introduced the concept in this field of education. This concept includes four steps which manage teaching learning. The relationship has been illustrated diagrammatically. The teacher is the manager of the teaching learning process.

Four Steps of Managing Teaching Learning System

Sl. No.	*Step*	*Activities*
I.	Planning	1. System analysis
		2. Task analysis
		3. Engineering behaviour
		4. Specification of knowledge, skills and attitudes
		5. Identification of needs
		6. Formulation of objectives
		7. Criterion test
		8. Construction of criterion test
II.	Organising	9. Organising learning resources
		10. Implementing teaching activities
III.	Leading	11. Selecting communication strategies
		12. Motivation and reinforcement
IV.	Controlling	13. Evaluation of teaching system
		14. Observing learning system
		15. Modification in teaching system on the basis of feedback.

Educational Technology

A very remarkable trend in the field of education during the last forty years in the advanced countries like the U.S.A., and the U.K., has been the tremendous use of educational technology in making education more productive, relating it to the individual, providing instruction on more scientific bases, making learning more powerful and more lasting, making up the cultural handicaps of certain categories of pupils and for extending educational services in the remote areas.

Eric Ashley (1967) talks of four revolutions in education: (i) shifting the task of educating the young ones from parents to teachers and from home to school; (ii) Adoption of the written word as a tool of education; (iii) Invention of printing and availability of books; (iv) Development in electronics, chiefly involving radio, television, cassette recorder and computer, and development systems concept.

Audio-Visual Aids

Before the sixties, the term audio-visual aids was very popular in teaching-learning. Generally audio-visual aids are used to make lesson interesting and to involve more senses in learning process. Educational technology on the other hand is a wider term and audio-visual a part of technology. Scientific inventions have greatly influenced every aspect of human life. Our education process could not remain untouched with these innovations. The advent of teaching machines, radio, television, tape recorder, computer and language laboratory gave a new dimension to the role of audio-visual aids.

'Audio-Visual Aids', 'Educational Technology', 'Communication Technology', 'Audio-Visual Media', 'Learning Resources' and Instructional or Educational Media'. All these terms mean the same thing. Earlier the term used was audio-visual aids in education. With the advancement in the means of communication and that of technology, educators coined new terms. More specifically media refers to films, filmstrips, recordings etc. The use of the newer terms Educational Technology or Instructional Technology is primarily due to the dynamic expansion of programmed learning, computer assisted instruction and educational TV. This revolution in the field of audio-visual education is the outcome of the development in electronics, notably those involving the radio, television, tape recorder and computer.

The replacement of the older and perhaps more familiar term 'Audio-Visual Material' in education by the newer term Educational Technology or Instructional Technology is primarily due to the dynamic use and expansion of TV, and other exciting new developments in the field of audio-visual education that promise much more for the future.

The Significance

1. Helpful in introducing new contents into the educational system.
2. Using improved basic methods in the educational system.
3. Meeting the needs of the individual student.
4. Covering new sectors of the public who could not be reached by the traditional institutions.
5. Eliminating the cultural handicaps of certain categories of pupils and equalising educational opportunity.
6. Providing continuing education to the vocational and other workers with the help of TV lesson and self-instructional programmed material.
7. Raising the individual teacher's qualifications.
8. Offering greater opportunities for independent study.
9. Serving as models.
10. Making instruction more inspirational.

Projected and Non-projected Aids

	Graphic Aids	*Display Boards*	*3-Dimensional Aids*	*Audio Aids*	*Activity Aids*
1. Films	1. Cartoons	Blackboard	Dioramas	Radio	1. Computer Assisted Instruction
2. Filmstrips	2. Charts	Bulletin Board	Models	Recordings	2. Demonstration
3. Opaque Projection	3. Comics	Flannel Board	Mock-ups	Television	3. Dramatic
4. Overhead Projection	4. Diagrams	Magnetic Board	Objects		4. Experimentation
5. Slides	5. Flash Cards	Peg Board	Puppets-		5. Field Work
	6. Graphs		Specimens		6. Programmed Instruction
	7. Maps				7. Teaching Machines
	8. Photographs				
	9. Pictures				
	10. Posters.				

A Word of Caution, New instructional technology cannot he 'heralded' as the 'panacea' for educational ills. The hardware of educational technology should not be looked upon as a convenient substitute for professional competency and planning. A teacher cannot relinquish his responsibility and say 'let multi-media do it'. These media are servants and not the masters. The effectiveness of aids depends not only on the materials provided but also on the techniques used. The ability and resourcefulness of the teacher is equally important. It also must be remembered that different media are suitable for realising different learning outcomes. A chalk-board may suffice in the realisation of some instructional objectives while in others simple demonstration may be enough and still some may require projector and so on. It remains with the teacher to decide which aid can easily and quickly serve his purpose.

Hardware and Software

A group of educationists categorise the concept of educational technology into two approaches—

1. The Hardware Approach.
2. The Software Approach.

The Hardware Approach. This is based on the application of engineering principles for developing electro-mechanical equipments like motion pictures, tape recorders, teaching machines, computers, video-tapes, closed circuit television etc. (used in class-room instruction). This approach of educational technology is a bye-product of the scientific and technological developments of 20th century.

Davies (1971) thinks that the hardware approach is based on the application of physical science to the education and training system which mechanizes the process of teaching gradually so that teachers would be able to deal with more students, resulting in less costs and economy in finances.

In this context Marilym Nickson (1971) has observed that educational technology deals with the application of the many fields of science to the educational needs of the individual as well as of the equipment.

It is said that good teachers have always used visual aids to assist their teaching. Ancient Greek geometers were drawing diagrams on the earth; even the Gzeh Comenious suggested teachers to use illustrations and models to increase the interests of their students. Today educational technology is stressing modern audio-visual equipment.

The Software Approach. It uses the principles of psychology for behaviour modification purposes. It originates from the pioneer efforts of Skinner and other behaviourists. Arthur Melton (1959) says that this teaching technology is directly related to the psychology of learning which comprises behavioural changes resulting from experience.

Davies (1971) observes, "This view of educational technology is closely associated with the modern principles of programmed learning and is characterized by task analysis; writing precise objectives, selection of appropriate learning strategies, reinforcement or correct responses and constant evaluation."

According to Leith, "Educational technology is the application of scientific knowledge about learning and the conditions of learning, to improve the effectiveness and efficiency of teaching and training."

The so-called software and hardware approaches cannot be separated from each other. In a manner, both are interlinked to plant the seed of educational technology which is developing with other essential ingredients of other varieties (like system engineering, educational planning, management).

CREATIVE READING AND TEACHING

Before understanding the significance of creative reading and creative teaching it is of utmost importance to understand the term creativity. According to Albert Baez creative people exhibit the following behaviours:

- Challenge assumptions
- See in a new way
- Recognise new patterns

- Make new connections
- Construct new networks
- Take risks
- Take advantage of chance

Creative individual is also seen as one who—

- exhibits-high level curiosity;
- thinks originally, flexibly, divergently, and imaginatively;
- is able to elaborate;
- is able to improvise, innovate and invent;
- is sensitive to situations.

Creativity in reading usually implies the use of talents in composing poems and constructing pieces of literature. It also involves writing articles.

The creative teacher will suggest various themes to the children to exhibit creative talents. He would also make references to literary figures in various fields. After spotting out creative students the teacher will organise special clubs or group for the benefit of such children. He will provide individual guidance to such students. He will ensure that appropriate reading literature is made available in the library. Suitable reading habits must be developed in the students for fostering creativity. Creative persons in difficult fields may be invited to inspire creative students.

LESSON PLANNING

Daily Lesson Planning

Planning is essential not only in teaching but in all spheres of human activity. Probably there is no type of work where the results of poor planning are so devastating as in teaching. R.L. Stevenson said, ' To every teacher I would say, "Always plan out your lesson before hand but do not be slave to it." Bagley has put it thus, "However able and experienced the teacher he could do never without his preliminary preparation." To be effective, every intelligent worker plans out his work. A surgeon diagnoses the case, prepares his surgical instruments before he puts the patient on the operation table, a lawyer makes attempts to anticipate and prepare for every move in the court, an engineer prepares his blue-print before he actually starts the construction work of a bridge or a building, the house mistress plans the details of the daily meals, the sales manager gives careful attention to every step in a proposed selling campaign. So must a teacher plan and prepare his work. I.K. Davies observes "Lesson must be prepared for there is nothing so fatal to a teacher's progress as un-preparedness". Ryburn states the importance of this concept as, "To teach we must use experience already gained as starting point of work."

Definition of Lesson Plan. L.N Bossing has given a comprehensive definition of a lesson plan; "Lesson plan is the title given to a statement of the achievements to be realized and the specific meaning by which these are to be attained as a result of the activities engaged during the period."

Structure of a Lesson Plan. Bining and Bining observe, "Daily lesson planning involves defining the objectives, selecting and arranging the subject matter and determining the method of procedure."

What a Good Lesson Plan Should Include. A lesson plan indicates the aims to be realised by teaching a lesson, the methods to be employed and the activities to be undertaken in the class so that it is engaged for the realisation of the aim.

A lesson plan is the programme of the teacher which indicates class and also the method of doing it well. The lesson plan reflects the teacher's skill, intelligence, ability and his personality.

Essentials of a Good Lesson Plan. Generally speaking the following are the characteristics of a good lesson plan:

1. It should be written- A lesson plan preferably be written and should not remain at the oral or mental stage. Panton writes, "The teacher is strongly advised, at least in the early stages, to make a written note of his preparation.

Memory sometimes proves a treacherous servant, especially when his attention is divided. "It is advisable, however, not to teach from notes, "Excessive reliance upon these may undermine the teacher's confidence so that he can never do without them. If, however, the teacher has occasion while teaching to refer to his notes, it is better for him to do so openly than to take a suspicious look at them. He loses nothing in the eye of the children by the former method whereas by the second he is likely to be misjudged by his pupils." Writing helps in clarifying thoughts and concentration.

2. It should have clear aims. The lesson plan should clearly state the objectives, general and specific, to be achieved.
3. It should be linked with the previous knowledge. The plan should not let the lesson remain an isolated one. It should have its basis on the background of the class. It should grow out of what the pupils have already learnt.
4. It should show techniques of teaching. It should state clearly the various steps that the teacher is going to take, and also various questions that he will ask.
5. It should show illustrative aids. The illustrative aids to be used should be shown in the lesson plan.
6. It should contain suitable subject matter. The materials of instruction or subject matter should be carefully selected or organised.
7. It should provide for audio-visual aids. To motivate the lesson, there must be a provision for audio-visual aids.
8. It should be divided into units. The plan should be divided into units; but care should be taken to see that the lesson remains an integrated whole and every unit develops from the previous and submerges into the next one.
9. It should provide for activity. The children must be given enough scope to be active. It should not make them mere passive listeners.

10. It should provide for individual differences. The plan should be prepared in such a way as it does full justice to all the students of varied capacities.
11. It should show certain routine things. The plan should indicate the duration of the period, the period itself, average age of the students, subject and the class.
12. It should be flexible. The plan is a means and not an end. It is wrong to follow it slavishly. It is an instrument and should be used as such. The teacher should be prepared to change his teaching methods from those as referred to in the plan, if need be.
13. It should include the summary. The lesson plan should include the summary of the whole lesson which is to be built up on the blackboard with the help of the students.
14. It should refer to reference books. The plan becomes more useful if it refers to references or other reading material. This will encourage the bright students to read extra books. Care should be taken to suggest only those books which are available in the library.
15. It should include assignment for children. A good lesson plan cannot be thought of without any assignments for the children. The assignments may be in the form of recapitulatory questions or home task.
16. It should provide for self-criticism. A good lesson plan must have some plan for self-criticism. The teacher should put some questions to himself and find out the answer and judge thereby the effectiveness of the lesson or otherwise.

The Advantages

1. Lesson planning provides the guidelines to the teachers and especially the pupil-teachers for the teaching-learning process.
2. Lesson planning provides awareness of teaching objectives.

3. Lesson planning provides awareness of the structure and content with which teacher is involved in the direction to achieve the objectives.
4. Task analysis in lesson planning enables the teacher to finalise the sequence of content to be presented.
5. Lesson planning relates the learning structures with teaching activities.
6. Lesson planning enables the teacher to maintain the sequence of content presentation and prevents him deviating from the topic.
7. Lesson planning enables the teacher to organise classroom teaching activities by considering the individual differences of students.
8. Lesson planning enables the teacher to develop apperceptive mass of the students by linking the new knowledge with the previous knowledge of the students.
9. Lesson planning enables the teacher to determine appropriate teaching aids, strategies and tactics in the presentation of the content to make it more relevant, lively, meaningful, effective and inspirational.
10. Lesson planning enables the teacher to relate the learning structures with teaching activities.
11. Lesson planning develops the reasoning, imagination and decision making ability of the teachers.
12. Lesson planning facilitates micro teaching.
13. Lesson planning develops confidence in the teacher.

VARIOUS APPROACHES

The Herbartian Approach. This is based on the apperceptive mass theory of learning which regards the learner as a 'clean slate' and that all the knowledge is given from outside. New knowledge is imparted by linking with old knowledge. The teaching content is presented into units. Famous Herbartian steps are- - introduction, presentation, organisation, comparison and evaluation. The main emphasis is on content presentation.

Evaluation Approach. B.S. Bloom is the originator of this approach. According to this approach, teaching activities must be objectives centred. Bloom considers education as a tripolar process, educational objectives; learning experiences and change of behaviour. This approach is 'objective centred' rather than 'content centred'.

Evaluation Approach

1. Education is a purposeful process.
2. Teaching activities are objective centred.
3. Evaluation includes all activities of teaching and not only student's performance.
4. It is not confined to the academic achievement of the student but covers the total behavioural changes.
5. Evaluation approach takes into consideration the learning objectives, methods and devices of providing learning experiences.
6. Student's performances are evaluated and measured in terms of learning objectives and not achievement of the content. It may cover cognitive, affective and psychomotor learning outcomes.

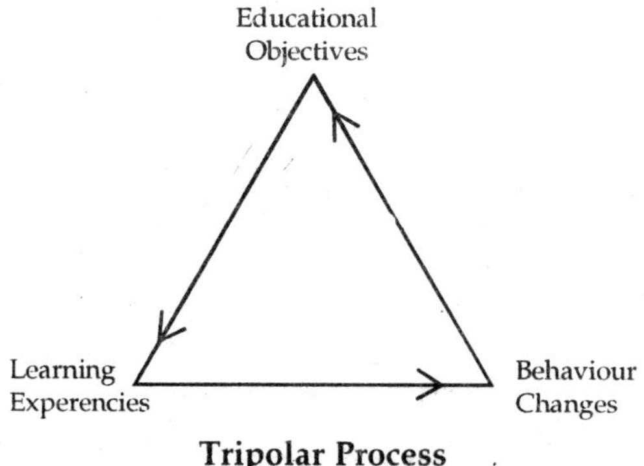

Tripolar Process

Steps in Evaluation Approach to Lesson Planning—Following are the three steps:

a. Formulating Educational Objectives.

b. Creating Learning Experiences.

c. Evaluating the change in behaviour.

Project Approach to Lesson Planning. This approach developed by W.H. Kilpatrick and John Dewey stresses on self-activity, social activity and real activities of life.

Morrison's Approach. Henry C. Morrison has based this approach on Units. He has given five steps for his 'cycle plan of teaching.' These steps are Exploration, Presentation Assimilation, Organization and Recitation. Morrison gives main stress on assimilation aspects whereas Herbart stresses the presentation aspects of teaching.

Blackboard. The blackboard plays a significant role in making the teaching efficient and effective. It is a necessary equipment in a class-room and a handy apparatus at the hands of a teacher.

The Types

(i) Fixed blackboard.

(ii) Easel or removable.

(iii) Roller blackboard.

The Uses

Blackboard should be placed at a place from where the writing on the blackboard could be seen very easily. It should never be placed between windows. Its back should not be towards the light as in this position its surface would be in the dark and the eyes of the students in trying to read what is written on the blackboard. It should be either black or green in colour and should not be glossy, otherwise it will adversely affect the eyesight of the pupils. Its height from the floor should vary from 26 to 39 inches according to the height of the students. It should be four feet wide.

Easel blackboard is better as its both sides can be used and it can be raised or lowered. It is also easily removable. Damp duster should be used to clean it so as to avoid the inhalation of chalk dust which leads to consumption. Blackboard should not be used at its extreme lower bottom as the students sitting on the last rows would not be able to see the writing on it. Summary may be developed on the blackboard. Salient points of the lesson may be written. Sufficient time should be given to the students to copy from it. While writing on the blackboard, it should be ensured that the students remain attentive. The teacher, therefore should take appropriate position and occasionally look at the class while making use of the blackboard. Before leaving the class, the teacher should make it a point to rub off the writing on the blackboard.

Exercise

1. Explain the teaching-learning process. What is interactive approach?
2. What are the important elements in the teaching-learning process?
3. State skills in teaching. Describe any three teaching skills.
4. What is the importance of a lesson plan? What points will you mind in preparing a lesson plan?
5. "Lesson plan is a servant and not a master." Explain this statement.
6. Elucidate the factors involved in the classroom management.
7. Write short notes on:
   (i) Questioning,
   (ii) Stimulation,
   (iii) Reinforcement,
   (iv) Blackboard.
8. What are hardware and software in education. Explain their utility.
9. What is the place of audio-visual aids in education? Explain one aid in detail.
10. State the characteristics of creative writing. How can a teacher foster creativity?

13

Observation Techniques

Observation is one of the oldest techniques that man has made use of. Even today it is our common experience to notice the farmers feel the breeze, watch the sky, sun, moon and stars—all to determine what the weather is likely to be and what season is approaching.

The physician and the educational psychologist depend heavily on what they observe. The teachers in the school also make judgement after observing children's gestures, talks and various movements.

Rousseau wrote, "Watch nature long and observe your pupil carefully before you say a word to him."

Observation has been defined as "measurement without instruments."

Two Types of Observation

Participant Observation. Here the observer plays a double role. He becomes by and large a member of the group under observation and shares the situation as a visiting stranger, an eager learner and an attentive listener.

The Advantages

1. It is more reliable.
2. It is very flexible.
3. It is more searching.
4. It discloses the minute and hidden facts.
5. Its cost is relatively less.

The Demerits

1. It is time consuming.
2. The observer's presence is likely to modify the behaviour of the subjects under study.
3. It becomes more subjective.

Non-participant Observation. This is used with such groups as infants, children or abnormal persons. The observer takes such a position as he is able to observe in detail the behaviour of the individual under observation. The position of the observer is least disturbing to the subject under study.

Non-participant observation permits the use of recording instruments.

Non-participant observation permits the gathering of larger quantity of data.

Structured Observation. Structured observation starts with relatively specific formulations. The observer in advance sets up categories in terms of which he wishes to analyse the problem. The observer always keeps in view:

(i) A frame of reference.

(ii) Time units,

(iii) Limits of an act.

Unstructured Observation. It mainly takes the form of participant observation. The observer takes the role of a member of the group.

The Principles

1. One student should be selected at a time for observation.

2. The student should be observed in a 'whole' situation.
3. Students should be observed over a reasonable period.
4. Students should be observed in different situations—in the classroom, on the playground, in the assembly, in going from class to class etc.
5. Reliance should be made on a large number of observations.

The Requisites

- Proper planning.
- Proper execution.
- Proper recording.
- Proper interpretation.
- Secrecy.

Cumulative Record Card

Meaning and Significance of a Cumulative Record Card. It is a school document which contains cumulatively the relevant information about a particular pupil, at one place, preferably covering a period of three years, thus presenting a complete and growing picture of the child concerned.

The cumulative record is needed because in presenting a developmental picture of the child, it helps teachers and counsellors to understand him and thereby assist him in the solution of the manifold problems which confront him during his stay at school and the time of leaving it.

The Secondary Education Commission 1952-53 has made the following observation regarding the need for school records: "Neither the external examination nor the internal examination, singly or together, can give a correct and complete picture of a pupil's all-round progress at any particular stage of his education: yet it is important for us to assess this, in order to determine his future course of study or his future vocation. For this purpose, a proper system of school records should be maintained for every pupil indicating the work done by him in the school from day today, month to month, term to term, and year to year. Such a school record will present a clear and continuous statement of the attainment of the child in different intellectual pursuits throughout the successive stages of the education. It will also contain a progressive evaluation of development in other directions of no less importance such as the growth of his interest, aptitudes, and personality traits, his social adjustments, the practical and social activities in which he takes part, in other words, it will give a complete career."

General Uses

1. It helps teachers and counsellors to identify the needs of individual pupils and understand their manifold problems.
2. It helps both counsellors and teachers know the strengths and weaknesses of individual pupils and to deal with them accordingly.
3. It aids teachers and counsellors to discover special abilities in pupils which should be developed.
4. It furnishes suggestions as to reasons why certain pupils are not adjusted to the school situation.
5. It contains data which may be useful in conferring with certain pupils about behaviour problems.
6. It provides information which is helpful in talking with pupils about their achievement in school.
7. It contains data of use in conferring with teachers about individual pupils.
8. It furnishes assistance to counsellors in aiding pupils to plan their high and post-high school courses of study intelligently.
9. It is valuable in assessing pupils' occupational insight and in aiding them to become realistic in their vocational planning.
10. It provides much of the raw material which is used in the making of case studies of certain problem pupils.

11. It is of great use in conferences with parents about the achievement and school adjustment of their children.
12. It forms an excellent basis for reports to colleges, school and prospective employers.

Classroom Uses

The cumulative record is used:

1. When a teacher wants to make a systematic appraisal of a student for the purpose of seeing trends in his physical, intellectual, social and emotional development.
2. When a teacher wants to confer with parents about their child's progress.
3. When a teacher wants to understand a behaviour of discipline problem in the class.
4. When a teacher wants to understand the problem of failure of a boy in a particular subject.
5. When a teacher wants to group his pupils for instruction within a class and aims at more individualized instruction.
6. When a teacher wants to single out children with special abilities and/or handicaps to provide instruction which accords with their individual needs.
7. When a teacher wants to identify pupils who need special diagnostic study and remedial instruction.
8. When a teacher wonders about discrepancies between potentiality and achievement.
9. When a teacher wants to make a report to parents.
10. In fact, whenever a teacher wants to help an individual pupil in his manifold educational, vocational and personal problems.

Important Points for Teachers

(1) Information which presents a child in unfavourable light and is likely to prejudice a person against him should, as a rule, not be made on the record card. If any confi-

dential material has to be maintained it should be kept in a separate file.

(2) While filling in information about a particular child the teacher should be conscious of what is known as the 'halo effect', and should try that his judgment about the child is not distorted on that account.

(3) No information which is doubtful should be entered on the cumulative record card. It is better to leave certain entries blank if objective and reliable information is not available than to fill them in by unreliable information.

(4) Recording should be easy if it is done for small groups of pupils at different sittings rather than for the entire group at one sitting.

INTERPRETING AND USING RECORDS

A school record has to be used as a unified account of the child's personality. The different items of information have not to be read and interpreted in isolation. Taken together they should aid in understanding and interpreting any particular aspect of the child's behaviour and personality make-up.

Common Ways in which Teachers Generally Go Wrong in Interpreting Records

(i) Teachers make too sweeping generalisations and draw inferences which are not warranted by data.

(ii) They fail to note important relationships.

(iii) They are influenced by their own prejudices or by previous impressions of the individual.

(iv) They give too much weight and authority to test (examination) results.

(v) They seldom make the distinction between what the records show and what they suggest.

Three Things to be Kept in View While Using Records

1. That a student is growing and changing. What was true of him last year is not necessarily true this year.

2. That record represents only a small sampling of his behaviour. There is much that is unknown about him.
3. That the record often reflects the bias of the person recording.

Mathewson (1955) has rightly pointed out "less attention has been paid to the functional uses of records than to their content and format, and as a consequence there is much more clerical work done upon them than there is professional use of the facts gleaned." More attention has, therefore, to be paid to the pupil rather than to the paper.

It may be pointed out there that objectives will not be automatically served unless a continuous effort is made by teachers to improve their understanding of pupils, to interpret pupil characteristics to parents, to motivate learning and adjustment and to adapt curriculum and instruction to the individual and group needs.

It may be mentioned that the development of a good recording system in schools requires: (i) close cooperation among the members of the staff, (ii) some budgetary provision for clerical work, and (iii) provision of adequate time to teachers for filling in the record cards. A head who is convinced of the utility of such records should be resourceful enough to get all that he needs for organizing a good record system in his school.

Methods of Popularising this System. The use of the cumulative record in our educational institutions is still in its infancy. It cannot be imposed upon the teachers. The teachers must be familiarized with the advantages of this system. Talks and refresher courses should be organised for this purpose. Faculty meetings should be organised to discuss the nature of the information that these cards should contain. It must be remembered that the maintenance of cumulative records is a co-operative affair in which administrators, counsellors, teachers, clerical staff, students and their parents must participate and all of these must be convinced of the importance of such records.

In order to maintain these cards properly, the teachers will have to be given some training. The Secondary Education Commission suggests that the State Department of Education should provide such training in the Training Colleges for teachers. The

Commission feels that with such training and certain amount of practice and with an occasional check-up by the head of the institute and by the inspectors, the teachers will be able to discharge their duties to the satisfaction of all. The Commission is of the opinion that in his sense of responsibility, the average Indian teacher does not yield to any teacher in any other country; "what he needs is clear direction, eucouragement and sympathy."

Sources of Collection of Information

Parents/Guardians Data Form. Family background and the personal history of the child may be gathered from the parents who are asked to fill in a form.

Personal Data Form. In order to obtain information regarding the pupil's interests and participation in extra-curricular activities and his vocational preferences, the personal data is of great use. The pupil may be asked to give details of himself. This will supplement the information obtained from the parents data form.

School Records. These include:

(i) Records of achievement tests.

(ii) Records of other tests.

(iii) Admission and withdrawal record.

Other Sources. These include:

(i) Personal visits by the teacher.

(ii) Observations made by the teacher.

Types of Information

- Identification Data
- Environment and Background Data
- Family History
- Physical Data
- Psychological Data
- Scholastic Achievement Data
- Achievement in Co-curricular Data
- Personality Data
- Vocational Data

Forms of Cumulative Record Card

It is used in various forms such as cards or sheets contained in an envelope, booklet or some combination of these forms.

A Specimen of the Cumulative Record Card

School Cumulative Record Card

IDENTIFICATION DATA

Name of Pupil .... Date of Birth ....
Father's Name .... Occupation ....
Guardian's Name .... Occupation ....
Relationship with the child .... Address ....
Schools Attended ....

Sl. No.	*Name of School year of joining*	*Month and which joined*	*Class in year of leaving*	*Month and which left*	*Class from leaving*	*Reasons for*
1.						
2.						
3.						

Family History

	Year	*200....*	*200....*	*200....*
Type of family (whether joint or unitary)				
No. of members in the family				
Economic status of the family				
Child's position in the family (whether only child, eldest or youngest child, his number among the siblings)				
Any other significant factor				

Physical Data

Year	Height	Weight	Chest Measurement Normal	Expd.	Contnd.	General Condition

Medical Report

	Any Serious Illness
200...	
200...	
200...	

Attendance

Year	Possible	Actual	Nature of long absence, if any, with reasons
200...			
200...			
200...			

Scholastic Achievement

Subject	Class .... Year......... Half Annual Yearly	Class......... Year......... Half Annual Yearly	Class......... Year......... Half Annual Yearly
Hindi			
....			
....			
....			
Total			
Position in the Class			
No. of students in the class			

Psychological Report if Any and Results of Intelligence and Aptitude Tests

200...

200...

200...

Performance in Co-Curr1cular Activities

Activities	*Average grade of the child for each performance throughout the year* 200...	200...	200...
Sports and Games			
Personal Hygiene			
Literary Activities			
Cultural Activities			
Social Service			

Position of Responsibility Held Or Merits Obtained, If Any

Activities	*Year...*	*Year...*	*Year...*
Studies			
Games			
Bal Sabha			
Scouting			
Social Service			
Any other			

Vocational Information

Year	*Vocational ambitions*	*Counsellor's Report of the student*
200......		
200......		
200......		

Personality Tracts

Trait	200......	200.....	200....
Truthfulness			
Honesty			
Courtesy			
Co-operativeness			
Industry			
Self-confidence			
Emotional stability			
Initiative			
Sociability			
Reliability			
Signature of the class teacher			
Signature of the Head			

National Policy on Education (1986)

Process and Examination Reform

Assessment of performance is an integral part of any process of learning and teaching. As part of sound educational strategy, examinations should be employed to bring about qualitative improvements in education.

The objective will be to re-cast the examination system so as to ensure a method of assessment that is a valid and reliable measure of student development and a powerful instrument for improving teaching and learning. In functional terms, this would mean:

(i) The elimination of excessive element of chance and subjectivity;

(ii) The de-emphasis on memorisation;

(iii) Continuous and comprehensive evaluation that incorporates both scholastic and non-scholastic aspects of education, spread over the total span of instructional time;

(iv) Effective use of the evaluation process by teachers, students and parents.

(v) Improvement in the conduct of examinations;

(vi) The introduction of concomitant changes in instructional materials and methodology;

(vii) Introduction of the semester system from the secondary stage in a phased manner; and

(viii) The use of grades in place of marks.

The above goals are relevant both for external examinations and evaluation within educational institutions. Evaluation at the institutional level will be streamlined and the predominance of external examinations reduced.

Exercise

1. "The term evaluation tends to replace the term examination." Explain the significance of this statement.
2. What is evaluation? What are its cognitive and non-cognitive aspects?
3. What should be the contents of comprehensive evaluation? What are its purposes and principles?
4. Why do we need examinations? State their shortcomings and limitations. How can we improve upon examinations?
5. Explain the significance of a cumulative record card. In what way is it useful in evaluation? What are the difficulties in its maintenance?
6. What is the present concept of evaluation?

14

Curriculum Development

The Significance

Curriculum is the base on which the subjects, activities and experiences of the students are planned. It is more than the textbook, more than the subject matter or course of studies. It is the totality of all the learning to which students are exposed during their study in the school; in the classroom, in the laboratory, in the library and the playground.

The child of today is the builder of tomorrow. It is only through a well designed and effectively implemented curriculum that the child could be equipped to realise his inner potential and to contribute meaningfully to nation-building. Curriculum is basic to the aesthetic, emotional, ethical, intellectual, physical, social, spiritual and vocational development of the child.

As observed by William J. Bennet (1984), "If the teacher is the guide, the curriculum is the patl. A good curriculum marks the points of significance so that the student does not wander aimlessly over the terrain, dependent solely on chance to discover the landmarks of human achievement."

The Functions

'National Curriculum for Primary and Secondary Education' (1985) has observed, "School curriculum, on the whole, should aim at enabling the learners to acquire knowledge, develop concepts, and inculcate skills, attitudes, values and habits conducive to the all round development of their personality and commensurate with the social, cultural, economic and environmental realities at national and international levels".

School curriculum should, therefore, help to promote development in the learner of:

Language abilities and communication skills needed for social living and further learning;

Competencies that facilitate mathematical operations and their applications in day-today life and learning;

Knowledge, attitudes and habits necessary for keeping physically fit and strong in conformity with normal developmental pattern;

A proper understanding about the role and importance of sex in human life, and healthy aptitude towards sex and members of opposite sex;

Qualities that make a man socially effective and happy in various social settings such as friendliness, cooperativeness, compassion, self-discipline, self-criticism, self-control, humour, courage, love for social justice, self-control, etc.

Moral and character values such as honesty, truthfulness, dependability, courtesy, fearlessness, compassion, etc.

Pre-vocational/vocational skills, willingness to work hard, entrepreneurship and dignity of manual work necessary for increased productivity and job satisfaction;

Ability to appreciate and discover beauty in various life situations and integrate it into one's own personality.

Understanding of the environment and its limited resources and the need for conservation of natural resources and energy.

Appreciation of various consequences of large families and over population and need of checking population growth;

Understanding of the diverse cultural and social systems of people living in different parts of the country and the country's composite cultural heritage;

Appreciation for the need of a balanced synthesis between the change-oriented technologies and the continuity of country's cultural heritage;

Knowledge of national symbols and desire and determination to uphold the ideals of national identity and unity;

Capability of appreciating and tolerating differences and diversities of various sorts and the capacity to choose between alternative value systems;

An awareness of the inherent equality of all and need of global fraternity with a strong commitment to humane values and to social justice;

Scientific temper characterised by spirit of inquiry, courage to question and objectivity leading to elimination of obscurantism, superstition and fatalism;

Knowledge of scientific methods of inquiry and its use in solving problems;

Appreciation of sacrifices and contributions made by the freedom fighters and social workers in the country's freedom struggle and social regeneration, and readiness to follow their idea is;

Appreciation of and readiness to practise in life the national goals of socialism, secularism, democracy and non-violence;

Divergent and independent thinking and ability to discover new relationships and combinations;

Qualities and characteristics necessary for self-learning and for life-long learning leading to creation of a learning society.

Important Definitions

The term 'Curriculum' is defined in many ways by educators. Some use the term in very limited and specific contexts while others attach very broad and general meanings. Some define it in descriptive terms, i.e., what curriculum is and others in prescribed terms, i.e., what curriculum ought to be. Again curriculum is defined in terms of subjects, activities and experiences.

Following are some of the important definitions of curriculum:

Alberty A, and Alberty E. (1959) define curriculum 'as the sum total of student activities which the school sponsors for the purpose of achieving its objectives."

In the words of H. Robert Beck and W. Walter Cook, "Curriculum is the sum of the educational experiences that children have in school."

Blond's Encyclopedia of Education (1969) defines "Curriculum as all the experiences a pupil has under the guidance of the school."

F. Bobbit in 'The Curriculum' (1918) has observed that "Curriculum is that series of things which children and youth must do and experience by way of developing abilities to do things well that make up the affairs of adult life; and to be in all respects what adults should do."

Derek Rowntree in 'A Dictionary of Education' (1981) has defined curriculum in these words, "Curriculum can refer to the total structure of ideas and activities, developed by an educational institution to meet the needs of students and to achieve desired educational aims."

R. Doll, in 'Curriculum Improvement: Decision Making' (1982) has stated; "Curriculum embodies all the experiences which are offered to learners under the auspices or direction of the school."

In the words of K.G. Saiyidain, "The curriculum is primarily an aid in the process of adjusting the child to the environment in which he functions from day-today and in the environment in which he will have to organise his activities later."

According to Cunnigham it is a tool in the hands of the artist (the teacher), to mould his material (the pupil), in accordance with his ideal, in his studio (the school).

Brubacher writes that the word 'curriculum' has Latin origin. "It is a runway, a course which one runs to reach a goal, a course of study."

According to the Secondary Education Commission 1952-53, "It includes the totality of experiences that a pupil receives through the manifold activities that go on in the school—in the class-room, library, laboratory, workshop, playgrounds and in the numerous informal contacts between teachers and pupils. In this case the whole life of the school becomes the curriculum which can touch the life of the students at all points and help in the evolution of balanced personality."

Thus broadly speaking curriculum is the blue print or plan of the school that includes experiences for the learners to have. It is a means to achieve the ends of education. Guidance of the school staff plays an important part in providing suitable experiences to the learners.

Broad Components and Dimensions

The components of curriculum according to Agnes, S. Robinson (1971) are the goals, objectives, content, processes, resources and means of evaluation of all the learning experiences planned for pupils both in and out of school and community through classroom instruction and related programmes (for example, field trips, library programmes, work experience, education, guidance and extra classroom activities).

According to K.A. Leithwood (1981), curriculum encompasses educational philosophy, values, objectives, organizational structures, materials, teaching strategies, student experiences, assessment and learning outcomes.

Three main components of the curriculum are as under:

1. Programme of Studies.
2. Programme of Activities.
3. Programme of Guidance.

Programme of Studies. This refers to the various subjects like History, Languages, Mathematics, Science etc. Emphasis on the study of a subject/subjects has changed from time to time in accordance with the philosophical and sociological ideals. Conservation and promotion of culture has been an important determinant in the selection of the contents of the subjects. In view of the vastness of culture, principle of selection is followed. The level of information to be imparted at a particular stage or class is graded suitably.

The methods of imparting knowledge are determined on the basis of psychological findings especially regarding learning.

Programme of Activities. With the changing concepts of education and consequently curriculum, an increasing emphasis is being laid on the organisation of various activities in the schools. In view of the importance of activities in the promotion of ideals of citizenship, cooperative living and democracy many educators advocate that curriculum should be envisaged in terms of activities rather than subjects. The principles of learning emphasise that participation in activities goes a long way in sublimating the instincts of children and making teaching learning more enjoyable as well as effective.

Programme of Guidance. A comprehensive programme of guidance includes helping students solve their educational, vocational and personal problems. With the rapid changes in the society in various fields, it has become very necessary to include the guidance programme in curriculum.

Curriculum and Syllabus

A UNESCO publication entitled "Preparing Textbook Manuscripts' (1970) has differentiated the curriculum and syllabus as: "The curriculum sets out the subjects to be studied, their order and sequence, and so ensures some balance between humanities and science and consistency in the study of subjects, thus facilitating inter subject links. It follows that the curriculum determines the amount of school time allotted to each subject, the aim of teaching each subject, the place of the motor skills which take time to acquire and, possibly, the variations between rural and urban school teaching. The curriculum in the schools of developing countries is often directly related to the requirements for development.

The syllabus determines the basic content of instructions in a given subject and the range of knowledge and skills which the pupils must acquire and establish in detail the themes and individual points to be studied in each school year the syllabus is a refined detail of the curriculum at a particular stage of learning for a particular subject."

CURRICULUM ORGANISATION

1. Subject-centred Pattern of Curriculum.
2. Student Centred Pattern of Curriculum.
3. Activity/Experience Centred Pattern of Curriculum.
4. Work Centred Pattern of Curriculum.
5. Correlated Pattern of Curriculum.
6. Integrated Pattern of Curriculum.
7. Core Pattern of Curriculum.

Subject-centred Pattern of Curriculum. As the title indicates this type of curriculum is organised in terms of subjects. The subject-centred organisation of curriculum is traditional and a large number of schools follow this pattern. The curriculum includes different branches of knowledge, known as subjects like history, language and mathematics etc. Subjects are included in accordance with the level of various stages. For instance economics, psychology and sociology are introduced at the secondary and senior secondary stages of schooling. The contents of the subjects are also included in accordance with level of understanding at various stages. Following assumptions are made while organising the subject-centred curriculum.

1. It is believed that the school has a major role in transmitting cultural heritage from one generation to another through the medium of various subjects.
2. The child's cognitive functioning pattern follows the adult's functioning.
3. It is envisaged that various disciplines or subjects would allow for the accommodation of the expansion of knowledge.

What, Why, How, Who, Where and When of Curriculum According to Different Approaches

	Intellectual Traditionalist	*Social Behaviourist*	*Experimentalist*
What	The curriculum should consist of the liberal arts tradition.	The curriculum should consist of operationally designed skills and knowledge warranted by scientific studies as useful to society in the modern age.	What is most worthwhile to know, be and do? must be asked and acted upon by all members of society in the consequences that their action has on others.
Why	1. To develop the mind. 2. To become acquainted with life's great ideas.	To meet the needs of the society built on Industrial Revolution.	To make all persons not just expert agents of their own experience.
How	1. Serious reading 2. Contemplation 3. Discussion	By making use of technologies of instructional engineering.	To begin with learner's genuine interests.
Who	1. Everybody 2. The Children 3. Liberally educated teacher	This relates to several categories of professional educators.	Involvement of teachers, students,community members and curriculum leaders.
Where	1. Self-education 2. Formal education in schools and tutorials.	Curriculum to be built by schools and technical institutions.	Anywhere so that human beings can genuinely reflect on their experience and to construct their personal perspective.
When	1. Education throughout life. 2. Especially education through kindergarten to graduation.	Formal education should begin earlier. Retraining people who need new skills and technical abilities throughout life.	

(Adapted from Curriculum: Perspective Paradigm, and Possibility. William H. Schubert. New York: Macmillan Publishing Company. (1986).

4. Each subject has an internal order and it can be presented in a sequence.
5. The vast amount of knowledge in the world can be grouped into various subjects.
6. Subjects can be presented in suitable units or branches.

Historically the curriculum was first conceived in terms of subject-matter materials and even today many people view it as materials or textbooks that are used in schools.

This has dominated the Indian school system for a very long time. It has represented the mastery over certain types of knowledge and skills, as the main objective of the educational programme at school. It has meant that the teacher has focussed his effort and attention on making students learn the items in subjects and courses of study according to fixed syllabi, in a rigid, set pattern to enable them to pass a set of examinations. The pupil was given knowledge and skills which would fit him to become a mature and successful adult according to the criteria of adults. He was prepared to live in the future as foreseen by the teacher and the parents. The present needs of the child or growing youth were hardly kept in mind.

Dewey denounces the subject-centred curriculum in these words:

"We violate the child's nature and render difficult the best ethical results by introducing the child too abruptly to a number of special studies, of reading, writing, geography, etc.

The beginning is made with child's expressive activities in dealing with the fundamental social material —housing (carpentry), clothing (sewing), food (cooking). These direct modes of expression bring out the factors of social communication—speech, writing, reading, drawing, modelling, etc."

Student or Child or Learner Centred Curriculum. The student centred curriculum considers student a 'hero' in the drama of education and places more emphasis on the student rather than the subjects.

Here, the programme has the students and not the subjects in view. In its more extreme form, this concept holds that education is life, and since life is ever changing, there could be no fixed curriculum. Under this interpretation, we find out what the students are interested in and build the curriculum upon that. The student would want something, perceive something, do something, and get satisfaction from the resulting experience. The whole learning process would become vivid and, hence, more valuable.

In his 'Pedagogic Creed', Prof. Dewey has laid emphasis on the child's own social activities which according to him constitute curriculum. He states: "The social life of the child is the basis of concentration, or correlation, in all his training or growth. The social life gives the unconscious unity and the background of all his attainments.

We violate the child's nature and render difficult the best ethical results by introducing the child too abruptly to a number of special studies, of reading, writing, geography, etc., out of relation to this social life.

The true centre of correlation in the school is neither science nor literature, nor history, nor geography, but the child's own social activities.

Characteristics of the Student-centred Curriculum

(1) The interests of the pupils facilitate their learning. Most of the young pupil's interests are socially derived; hence it makes the programme more life-related.

(2) In terms of the highly developed Indian social organization, co-operation is important. Therefore finding common interests and working together in terms of unifying element bring about growth in life-related skills.

(3) A very flexible school curriculum is needed. In these rapidly changing times, and the different backgrounds of pupils, too much structuring of courses and syllabi has resulted in the student's lack of real participation in the learning process. Hence many unstructured, free and flexible areas of learning according to the pupils interests and individual needs, are essential.

(4) Flexibility can be brought about not only in the content and areas of learning, but also in the use of instructional materials. The text-book has dominated the classroom too long. There must be multiple and varied resources suitable for pupils of different interests, abilities and stages of growth — reference books, newspapers, journals, excursions to museums, libraries, films, audiotapes, television and others.

(5) To teach in a classroom characterized by the student-centred approach requires that teachers must know a great deal about the growth and development of children and youth.

Comparison between Subject-centred and Student-centred Curriculum

Subject-centred Curriculum	*Student-centred Curriculum*
1. It is structured around subjects.	1. It is centred around learners.
2. It aims at increasing the knowledge of subjects.	2. It aims at promotion of knowledge of the learners.
3. Subject matter is selected and organised before the actual teaching-learning situations.	3. Subject matter is selected and organised according to teaching-learning situations.
4. The teacher is the controller and director of curriculum structure.	4. Curriculum is initiated and organised by the learners.
5. Emphasis is on teaching facts and presenting information for the sake of possible future use.	5. Emphasis is on matters which are useful for the present and future also.
6. Stress is on the teaching of specific habits and skills as separate aspects of learning.	6. Stress is on integrated learning of habits and skills.
7. There is uniformity with respect to learning situations.	7. Variability of exposure is advocated.
8. Education is viewed as schooling.	8. Education is viewed as an all round growth of the learner.

Subject Curriculum and Activity/Experience. Herbert Read gives the definition of the curriculum in his book, Education Throughout as."The curriculum should not be conceived as a collection of subjects. At the secondary stage, as at the primary stage, it should be a field of creative activities, with instruction as incidental or instrumental to the aim of these activities. If at the infant stage these activities may be described as 'play' activities and at the primary stage as 'projects', then at the secondary stage, they merge into constructive work."

Subject Curriculum	*Activity/Experience Curriculum*
1. It is in terms of subjects.	1. It is in terms of activities and experiences.
2. It is centred in subjects.	2. It is centred in learners.
3. The subject-matter is selected and organised before the teaching situations.	3. All learners during the learning-teaching situation select and organise co-operatively the subject-matter.
4. It stresses the teaching of facts, imparting information for its own sake or for the possible future.	4. It stresses the practical aspects of life.
5. It is isolated from life.	5. Emphasis is on correlation with life.
6. There is no correlation of subjects.	6. It stresses correlated knowledge.
7. It is rigid and uniform.	7. It is flexible. It caters to individual needs.

Limitations of the Subject

1. It is bookish.
2. It is narrowly conceived.
3. It stresses knowledge aspect.
4. It does not adequately reflect life activities.

Limitations of the Experience

1. It is very difficult to break through the logical arrangement of the various aspects of the subject arrangement of human experience.
2. Correlation of subjects will be only casual and teaching cannot be sufficient to integrate human experience.

3. There is a likelihood of the attempts at correlation being largely forced with little reference to real sequence in human experience.
4. Attempts at correlation usually come from the teachers.
5. There is a limit beyond which it is not possible to provide all experiences.

The Principles

Curriculum is a tool in the hands of the teachers to give training to children in the art of living together in the community. It is a tool which considerably helps to inculcate those standards of moral action which are essential for successful living in society and for getting true satisfaction out of life. It is, therefore, very essential that the curriculum should be based on sound principles.

The following principles should be kept in mind when framing a curriculum:

The Conservative Principle. It has been stated that 'nations live in the present, on the past and for the future.' This means that the present, the past and the future needs of the community should be taken into consideration. The past is a great guide for the present as it helps us to decide what has been useful to those who have gone before and what will be useful to those who are going through now.

The Forward-looking Principle. While discussing the first principle, we have pointed out that in the present, future needs and requirements of the community should be given their due place. Children of today are the future citizens of tomorrow. Therefore, their education should be such as it enables them to be progressive-minded persons. Education should give them a foundation of knowledge, feeling and competence that will enable them to change the environment where change is needed.

The Creative Principle. In the curriculum those activities should be included which enable the child to exercise his creative and constructive powers. The objective of education is to discover and to develop special interests, tastes and aptitudes. None of the child's native gifts should escape our notice. In a curriculum that is suited to the needs of today and of the future, there must be a definite bias towards definitely creative activities.

The Activity Principle. The curriculum should be thought in terms of activity and experience, rather than of knowledge to be acquired and facts to be stored. Growth and learning take place only where there is activity. 'Experience' rather than 'instruction' is to meet the needs of the various stages of growth. In the words of John Dewey, "The general movement is away from the old over-reliance and verbal instruction, formulated subjects and learning from books, and in the direction of more varied and many-sided individual activities in keeping with child's real interests."

Play-grounds, shops, workrooms and laboratories not only direct the natural active tendencies of youth, but they also involve intercourse, communication and co-operation.

The curriculum must ensure the activity of body and mind. It should be the centre of the curriculum. All modern methods of teaching, i.e., Kindergarten, Montessori, Project, Basic, etc., are based on this principle of activity.

Principle of Preparation for Life. This is the most important principle in the construction of the curriculum. Curriculum must include those activities which enable the child to take his part effectively and amicably in the activities of the community when he becomes an adult. We have to prepare him in such a way as he is capable of facing the various challenges of the complex problems of the future.

Child Centred Curriculum. It is true that the child is to be prepared for life. But this does not mean that his immediate interests should be sacrificed for the sake of the future which is indefinite. As Ryburn puts, "The best preparation for life that we can give a child is to help him to live fully and richly his life at that stage at which he is." The child automatically prepares himself for the next stage by living well and truly at one stage. Smith and Harrison also observe, "Education......regards the child as an individual growing by his own activity, living in his own environment, and preparing himself for adult life, not by imitating the adult, but by living as fully as possible in the environment of childhood."

Principle of Maturity. Curriculum should be adapted to the grade of the pupils and to their stage of mental and physical development. In the early childhood 'wonder' and 'romance' predominate. So subjects and activities which present the elements of 'wonder' and 'romance' should be included at this stage. At a later stage they are interested in practical things. So at the Junior Secondary Stage the curriculum should provide for practical problems. At the next stage, that is the Senior Secondary Stage, students are interested in generalisations and accordingly curriculum should provide such activities. The child at this stage is keep to discover, to find out and discuss new facts. The curriculum should harness the adventurous spirit of the growing child.

The experiences provided should be within the comprehension of the students.

Principle of Individual Differences. Individuals differ in taste, temperament, skill, experience, aptitude, innate ability and in sex. Therefore, the curriculum should be adapted to individual differences. It should not be rigid.

Vertical and Horizontal Articulation. on the one hand each year's course should be built on what has been done in previous years and at the same time should serve as basis for subsequent work. It is absolutely essential that the entire curriculum should be coordinated.

Principle of Linking with Life. The community needs and characteristics should be kept in view while framing the curriculum.

Principle of Comprehensiveness and Balance. The curriculum should be framed in such a way as every aspect of life i.e., economic relationships, social activities, occupations and spiritual life, is given due emphasis.

Principle of Loyalties. The curriculum should be planned in such a manner that it teaches a true sense of loyalty to the family of the school, the community, the town, the province, the country and the world at large. It should enable the child to understand that there is unity in diversity.

Flexibility. Curriculum should take into consideration the special needs and circumstances of the pupils. Curriculum of the girls may not always be identical with that of boys. The special needs of both the sexes should be given their due consideration.

In general the curriculum of the village and the urban school will be the same but there might be variation according to the specific needs of the locality.

Principle of Core or Common Subjects. There are certain broad areas of knowledge, skill and appreciation with which all the children must be made conversant and these should find a place in the curriculum. This is more important at higher secondary stage where there are diversified courses. These subjects are to be common to all groups. They are known as core subjects. Mother tongue or regional language, social studies (general course), general science including mathematics and one craft are expected to be the core subjects.

Principle of Leisure. The curriculum should prepare the child for the use of leisure time. According to Herbert Spencer, Literature, Music and Art occupy the leisure part of life and should, therefore, occupy the leisure part of education. The capacity to enjoy leisure greatly determines a man's capacity to work. If leisure is spent in gambling, drinking and reading obscene literature, it will hamper progress not only of an individual but also the nation as a whole. The school curriculum should therefore, prepare the would-be-citizens to use effectively their leisure time.

Principle of All-round Development of Body, Mind and Spirit. All kinds of experiences should be provided to the students so that they may develop their all powers.

Curriculum Reconstruction

Drawbacks and Limitations of the Traditional Curriculum

1. There is very little choice for students.

2. Emphasis is on rote memory and there is lack of provision for activities and experiences.
3. Laboratory and library facilities are very meagre.
4. Play ground is generally non-existent.
5. Provision for vocational courses exists in a few selected schools only,
6. Very little provision is made for practical work related to work experience and socially useful productive work.
7. Very little stress is laid on the provision of co-curricular activities.

Important Issues and Curriculum Development in India

Important issues and problems of curriculum development in India may be listed as:

1. Centralised or decentralised curriculum.
2. Curriculum for rural and urban areas.
3. Curriculum for the slow as well as for the fast learner.
4. Curriculum for the handicapped.
5. Curriculum for the disadvantaged children—slum areas and backward areas.
6. Change in methods of instruction, processes of learning and instructional materials.
7. Claims of various pressure groups.
8. Setting minimum standards of learning at the end of each stage and in every subject.
9. Cycle of curriculum change period after which curriculum should be changed.
10. Curriculum load.
11. Relating general education with some sort of vocational education.
12. Tradition versus modernization.

National Curriculum for Elementary and Secondary Education

In accordance with the directions contained in the National Policy on Education 1986, the National Council of Educational Research and Training (NCERT) has prepared the national curriculum. This curriculum contains broad outlines and provides sufficient flexibility to the States to develop their own curricula.

Basic Features of the National Curriculum. These are as under.

(i) Emphasis on the attainment of the personal and social goals and propagation of values enshrined in the constitution.

(ii) The development of human resources for the realisation of the national goals of development.

(iii) Broad-based general education to all learners at the primary and secondary stages.

(iv) Learner-centred approach rather than the teacher-centred approach to the transition of the curriculum.

(v) Provision for flexibility in terms of selection of content and learning experiences which would facilitate the attainment of the expected learning outcomes.

(vi) Applicability of the curriculum to all learners, irrespective of their modes of learning.

(vii) Provision of the threshold resources (physical and academic) necessary for effective transaction of the curriculum in all schools and non-formal learning centres.

SCHEME OF STUDIES

Pre-primary Education

The basic mode of upbringing of children at this stage should be through group activities and play-way techniques, language games, number games and activities directed to promote environmental awareness, etc. These should be used to make the learning experience joyful to the children. No formal teaching of subjects be undertaken at this stage.

Lower Primary Stage (5 years)

(i)	One language—the mother tongue or the regional language.	30% Time
(ii)	Environmental Studies I and II	15%
(iii)	Mathematics	15%
(iv)	Work Experience	20%
(v)	Art Education	10%
(vi)	Health and Physical Education	10%

Upper Primary Stage (3 years)

(i)	Three languages	32%
(ii)	Science	12%
(iii)	Mathematics	12%
(iv)	Social Sciences	12%
(v)	Work Experience	12%
(vi)	Art Education	10%
(vii)	Health and Physical Education	10%

Secondary Stage (2 years)

(i)	Three languages	30%
(ii)	Science	13%
(iii)	Mathematics	13%
(iv)	Social Sciences	13%
(v)	Work Experience	13%
(vi)	Art Education	9%
(vii)	Health and Physical Education	9%

CORE COMPONENTS

The National Curriculum envisages certain areas which will be common at all stages. However, these areas will not be included as separate subjects. They are integrated into the content of various subjects of the curriculum. It is believed that the inclusion of the core areas is very conducive to the ideals of emotional and national integration. They are also very helpful in promoting the values as enshrined in our constitution. Indian identity will also be strengthened. Core-curriculum is the general education aspect of all teaching.

The National Policy on Education 1986 has given an important place to Core Curriculum in the National System of Education. It observed, "The National System of Education will be based on a national curricular framework which contains a common core along with other components that are flexible." The National Policy visualised the concept of the core programme as, "The common core will include the history of India's freedom movement, the constitutional obligations and other content essential to nurture national identity." "These elements," according to Policy "will cut across subject areas and will be designed to promote values such as India's common cultural heritage, egalitarianism, democracy and secularism, equality of the sexes, protection of the environment, removal of social barriers, observance of the small family norm and inculcation of the scientific temper."

The Programme of Action 1986, on the National Policy of Education listed the following ten core curricular areas:

1. History of India's Freedom Movement.
2. Constitutional Obligations.
3. Content Essential to Nurture National Identity.
4. India's Common Cultural Heritage.
5. Egalitarianism, Democracy and Secularism.
6. Equality of the Sexes.
7. Protection of the Environment.
8. Removal of Social Barriers.
9. Observance of Small Family Norm.
10. Inculcation of the Scientific Temper.

Levels of Learning

The National Policy on Education 1986 has observed in Part 3 and para 7 as "Minimum levels of learning will be laid down for each stage of education." This concept has been explained in the 'National Curriculum for Elementary and Secondary Education: A Frame Work' (1988), prepared by NCERT. More details about Minimum Levels of Learning are available in ' Minimum Levels of Learning at the Primary Stage: Syllabi Including Common Core Components' (1988), NCERT.

The main focus in prescribing minimum levels of learning is on learning (development) of the child as against on evaluation (assessment of the child). With a view to bringing about a broad uniformity in the standard of education throughout the country, emphasis has been laid on prescribing minimum levels of learning at each stage so that each learner or the student attains these. The minimum learning levels are prescribed on the mental ability of the learners at different stages of their development and the academic and physical resources available in the school for the implementation of the curriculum.

'Minimum learning outcomes (MLOs) help to define in concrete terms the level or standard at which teaching-learning should be directed to and the extent to which the topic should be dealt with. Learning outcomes are in terms of numbers, quantum, quality, etc. For instance, a learner should acquire a total vocabulary of 5000 words at the primary stage in the first language. In classes I and II the learner should recognise and recall the sounds of about 1200-1700 (class 1) and 1700-2000 words in class II in Hindi, where it is the mother tongue. The words may comprise single or combined letters. He should pronounce correctly the same number of words. The number of words prescribed for class III is between 2000 to 2500. For class IV the suggestive number is about 1000 new words. In class V the learner should be able to recognise, recall and pronounce about 5000 words.

The Languages

In the first two years of primary stage (classes I and II), the objective would be to the development of child's ability for creative self-expression. Language learning should be used as a potential instrument for encouraging independent thinking among the learners from the very beginning. Therefore, efforts should be made to help the learner acquire the basic skills in reading and writing in his mother-tongue or regional language. The learner's pronunciation is also to be improved. The total vocabulary of the child at the end of the primary stage should be about 5000 words in the first language.

At the upper primary stage (classes VI to VIII) main objective of language teaching would be to strengthen further the competencies achieved at the primary stage. The learners should be able to use the language effectively in their day-today life. Special stress is to be laid on the applied side of the mother tongue/ regional language. Oral form of language should be given an important place. Encouragement is to be given to creative expression of the learners and their ability to think independently. Learners at this stage are also required to be introduced to the second and third languages.

At the secondary stage (classes IX and X) students should achieve maturity in oral and written expression. Students should be introduced to the teaching of literature.

While teaching English as second language only functional grammar should be taught.

THE MATHEMATICS

Mathematics should be seen as a vehicle of training the learner to think, reason, analyse and articulate logically. Relevance of mathematics in relation to learner's environment and day-today living should also be kept in view. The role of modern technology like the use of computer is also to be emphasised.

At the primary stage, the objective of learning mathematics should be to lay foundation for mathematical thinking about the numerical and spatial aspects of the activities and objects of the learner's environment. Learning through concrete material should be the basis.

The main objective of teaching mathematics at the upper stage (classes VI to VIII) is to enable the students acquire knowledge and understanding of facts, concepts, principles, etc., related to the functional aspects of commercial mathematics, mensuration, descriptive statistics, practical geometry and algebra.

At the secondary stage (classes IX and X), a beginning is to be made to study mathematics as a discipline in the appropriate form.

Environmental Studies

At the primary stage, during the first two years (classes I and II), the child should be introduced to the environment as a whole. There should be no clear-cut distinction between natural sciences and social sciences that go into the making of the environment. The child should mainly learn through concrete situations. The major thrust of environmental studies at this stage should be to sharpen the senses of the students, to encourage them to observe and explore their environment and to explore their environment. Emphasis should be to enrich their experiences related to different aspects of their immediate environment. Imparting of information to students should occupy the second place.

In classes III to V, science as a component of environmental studies should be made more structured. It should expose the children to a variety of objects, events and phenomenon in the environment. Towards the later years of this state the child should be guided and assisted to discover and understand the scientific facts, concepts, principles and processes underlying various phenomenon around them. Science education should promote in children attitudes and values like objectivity, open-mindedness and precision.

Social studies, the other component of the environment studies in classes III to V should widen the child's horizon from his home, school and neighbourhood to the state, country and the world. It should also develop in the children love and appreciation of the cultural history of India. It should also enable the students to understand the contribution of great personalities to the enrichment of the culture.

Social Sciences

At the secondary stage (classes IX and X), the objectives would be to promote an understanding of contemporary India and of India's role in relation to problems like world peace and international understanding. Elements of history, geography, civics and economics will constitute the contents of social sciences.

Science

The secondary stage (classes IX and X) is the terminal stage of general education. After this stage, a large number of students enter life. The main objective of teaching science, therefore, at this stage would be directed towards problem-solving and decision making through the learning of key concepts which cut across all the disciplines of science. The teaching of science should enable the learners grasp the basic nature, structure, principles and processes of science with special reference to the relation of science with agriculture, industry and contemporary technology.

Work Experience

Work experience is introduced with a view to inculcate in the learners a respect for manual labour and work ethics. The learners are also to be helped through work experience to make their entry in the work force.

Work experience at the primary stage should help the learners in preparing a strong foundation. Activities and programmes in work experience at this stage are intended to develop in the child neuro-muscular control and coordination, basic motor skills and habits of community living.

At the primary stage, emphasis in work experience should be on the development of desirable healthy living. The learners are to be made aware of the world of work and work ethics.

At the upper primary stage, work experience should emphasise agricultural and technological processes. Work experience is visualised to be helpful to the learners to enter into the work force.

At the secondary stage, work experience should assume a clear pre-vocational orientation. The nature of work experience activities will remain more or less the same as during the upper primary stage.

The Arts

The main objective of art education should be to sensitize the learners to respond to the beauty in line, colour, form, movement and sound.

At the primary stage, art education should enable the learner make aware of the good and beautiful in his environment. The learner should also be enabled to express his feelings through simple activities in arts like music, dance, drama, drawing and painting etc.

At the upper primary stage the learner should be enabled to develop a sense of organisation and design.

The secondary stage should be treated as a transitional stage between the creative expression of childhood and vocation biased education for later period.

Physical Education

Health, physical education and sports should enable the learner to understand that the harmonious development of the body and mind is essential for good health. The learner should be helped to develop desirable attitudes and practices with regard to nutrition, health and sanitation.

At the primary stage, health and physical education would aim at the development in the child adequate personal hygiene habits, emotional health and healthy community living.

At the upper primary stage vigorous developmental exercises, rhythmics, gymnastics, drill, yoga and various team games are provided for neuro-muscular co-ordination and social development.

The learner at the secondary stage is more adventurous. Rapid changes occur in the functioning of body. This period is associated with the onset of puberty. Interests during this period narrow down to fewer games and sports. Major games should be introduced at this stage. Students should be encouraged to take an active part in NCC and social service.

Exercise

1. "The entire programme of the school constitutes curriculum." Explain this statement and bring out the meaning and significance of curriculum.
2. Compare and contrast subject-centred and activity/experience centred curriculum. State the merits and demerits of each type of curriculum.
3. Write brief notes on:
   (i) Minimum Learning Level or Outcome.
   (ii) Core-curriculum.
   (iii) Learner-centred curriculum.
   (iv) Dimensions of the curriculum.
4. What are the drawbacks of the traditional curriculum? Explain the principles on which curriculum should be constructed.
5. What is the meaning of national curriculum? State the subjects which should be included in the curriculum?
6. List the subjects that are included in the curriculum at the primary and middle (elementary) stages. Give reasons for the inclusion of each subject.

15

Reconstruction of Curriculum

A Continuous Process

It is widely accepted that curriculum is an on going process. Carefully designed, sincerely and vigorously implemented, it is the most powerful instrument of achieving national goals and the maximum and to development of the future citizens.

Over the 1990-2000 decade, changes in every area of human endeavour had been much greater in magnitude as compared to those during the earlier five or six decades. Curriculum must reflect all these developments.

With a view to make education relevant to new demands, the NCERT, as an apex body has been taking suitable steps to reconstruct the curriculum. Accordingly after a good deal of debate and discussion on a nation-wide scale, it formulated the 'National Curriculum Framework for Social Education' in November 2000 and in November 2001. it published detailed guidelines and syllabi for different stages of school education.

IMPORTANT OBJECTIVES

The National Curriculum Framework (2000) has listed the following objectives and thrusts:

- Inculcation and sustenance of personal, social, national and spiritual values like cleanliness and punctuality, good conduct, tolerance and justice; a sense of national identity and respect for law and order and truthfulness.
- Elimination of poverty, ignorance, ill-health, casteism, dowry, untouchability, and violence, and ensuring equity, health, peace and prosperity.
- Thinking, experiences and innovations which are rooted in the Indian tradition and ethos and relating these with global thinking.
- Establishing uniformity of structure of school education, i.e., 10+2+3 throughout the country.
- Broad-based general education to all learners up to the end of the secondary stage to help them become life long learners and acquire basic life skills and high standards of Intelligence Quotient (IQ), Emotional Quotient (EQ). and Spiritual Quotient (SQ).
- A common scheme of studies for the elementary and secondary stages with emphasis on the skill of learning 'how to learn' with flexibility of content and mode of learning to suit all learners including those with special needs.
- Inclusion of Fundamental Duties and the core curricular areas at all the stages of school education.
- Human Rights including the rights of the child, especially those of the girl child.
- Ensuring the minimum essential level of the acquisition of knowledge, understanding and skill at all stages, commensurate with the learners' abilities and the societal context.

- Freedom, flexibility, relevance and transparency in the selection of content, transaction and procedures at different stages of school education.
- Nurturance and sustenance of multiple talents and creativity among all learners in various domains of knowledge.
- Shift of emphasis from information-based and teacher centred education to process centred and learner friendly education.
- Development of a responsive and supportive system of evaluation.

Curriculum in 21st Century

The school curriculum must develop and promote

- language abilities of listening, speaking, reading, writing and thinking and communication skills—verbal and visual-needed for social living and effective participation in the day today activities;
- mathematical abilities to develop a logical mind that would help learners perform mathematical operations and apply them in every day life;
- scientific temper characterised by the spirit of enquiry, problem-solving, courage to question and objectivity leading to elimination of obscurantism, superstition and fatalism, while at the same time, sustaining and emphasising the indigenous knowledge ingrained in the Indian tradition;
- understanding of the environment in its totality both natural and social, and their interactive processes, the environmental problems and the ways and means to preserve the environment.
- understanding of the diversity in lands and people living in different parts of the country and the country's composite cultural heritage;

- appreciation of the sacrifices and contributions made by the freedom fighters and social workers from rural, tribal and weaker sections from all the regions of the Indian society, particularly from the North-East and the Andaman and Nicobar Islands, in India's freedom struggle and social regeneration, and readiness to follow their ideals;
- appreciation for the need of a balanced synthesis between the change oriented technologies and the continuity of the country's traditions and heritage;
- knowledge of and respect for the national symbols and the desire and determination to uphold the ideals of national identity and unity;
- deep sense of patriotism and nationalism tempered with the spirit of Vasudhaiva Kutumbukam;
- understanding of the positive and the negative impact of the processes of globalisation, liberalisation and localisation in the context of the country;
- qualities clustered around the personal, social, moral, national and spiritual values that make a person humane and socially effective, giving meaning and direction to life;
- knowledge, attitude and habits necessary for keeping physically and mentally fit and strong in perfect harmony with the earth, water, air, fire and the sky;
- qualities and characteristics necessary for self-learning, self-directed learning and life-long learning leading to the creation of a learning society;
- capacity not only to process information but also to understand, reflect and internalise and develop insight;
- willingness to work hard, enterpreneurship and dignity of manual work necessary for increasing productivity, obtaining job-satisfaction and creating wealth generating systems;

- acquisition of pre-vocational/vocational skills: and
- appreciation of the various consequences of large families and over population and need for checking population growth.

Value Education

Since India is the most ennobling experiment in spiritual co-existence, education about social, moral and spiritual values and religions cannot be left entirely to home and the community. School education in the country seems to have developed some kind of neutrality toward the basic values and the community in general has little time or inclination to know about religions in the right spirit. This makes it imperative for the Indian school curriculum to include inculcation of the basic values and an awareness of all the major religions of the country as one of the central components.

Value education and education about religions would not form a separate subject of study or examination at any stage. These would be so judiciously integrated with all the subjects of study in the scholastic areas and all the activities and programmes in the co-scholastic areas that the objectives thereof would be directly and indirectly achieved in the classrooms, at the school assembly places, play-grounds, cultural centres and such other places.

National Needs and Curriculum

The NCERT 'Curriculum Framework for School Education' (2000) observed that the curriculum should stand on three pillars—(i) relevance, (ii) equity and (iii) excellence.

It pointed out that the national curriculum should take into account the following concerns:

1. Education for a cohesive society—provision of 'equality of access to education and opportunity.'
2. Education of children with special needs.
3. Education of children from disadvantaged groups.

4. Education of the girl child.
5. Strengthening national identity and preserving cultural heritage.
6. Integrating indigenous knowledge and India's contribution to mankind.
7. Responding to the impact of globalisation.
8. Meeting the challenge of information and communication technologies.
9. Linking education with skills.
10. Education for value development.
11. Non-formal/alternative schooling.
12. Integrating diverse curricular concerns.
13. Relating education to world of work.
14. Reducing the curriculum load.
15. Child as a constructor of knowledge.
16. Recognising interface between cognition and emotion.
17. Using culture specific pedagogies.
18. Education and development of aesthetic sensibilities.
19. Continuous and comprehensive evaluation.
20. Education as a life-long process.
21. Towards curriculum of the unknown.
22. The approach to curriculum development process-coordinated decentralisation.

Role of Teacher

Teacher is usually the implementor only in the entire curriculum transaction. He has very little say in determining the subjects and experiences to be included in the curriculum. It is true that sometimes, agencies and authorities charged with the framing of the curriculum include teacher representatives also in various committees formed for this purpose. However, there are several pressure groups which dominate these committees. In general, it can be said that the teachers are required to implement the curriculum prescribed. of course, they have some freedom as to the means and methods to be employed to carry out the programmes. 'Grassroots approach' to curriculum planning is not being followed.

All the States and Union Territories of India have their own mechanism of curriculum development. The National Council of Educational Research and Training prepares a model curriculum which serves as a guide.

The Central Board of Secondary Education (CBSE) Delhi, is the premier board in India which prescribes curriculum for its more than 5000 schools, affiliated to it. It organises seminars and workshops etc. for teachers to get feed-back as well as for improving the implementation of the curriculum.

Major Concerns

Some major developments in primary education also resulted in concerns that demanded immediate attention. Some of them are:

1. The unprecedented increase in enrolment at the primary stage caused by efforts in the field of Universalisation of Elementary Education. A vast majority of these children are still first generation learners. Lack of any support from their homes necessitates changes in school programmes to provide opportunities to these children for getting 'ready for formal education';
2. Pedagogical implications emerging from the implementation of the scheme of Minimum Levels of Learning (MLLs);
3. The issue of curriculum load in terms of both the physical load and that of non-comprehension, and the recommendations made by Yashpal Committee in this context;
4. Relating school to community in terms of providing flexibility in the curriculum with a view to addressing the diverse needs and contexts specific to different communities and the immediate environment and also involving community in the education of children;

5. The need to refocus on value-based education in view of the noticeable erosion of basic values witnessed during the past few decades.

Scheme of Studies

1. For Classes I and II
   - (a) One language—the Mother Tongue/the Regional Language
   - (b) Mathematics
   - (c) Art of Healthy and Productive Living (AHPL)
2. For Classes III to V
   - (a) One language—the Mother Tongue/the Regional Language
   - (b) Mathematics
   - (c) Environmental Studies
   - (d) Art of Healthy and Productive Living (AHPL)

Salient Features

The salient features of this curriculum are summarised below.

1. There is emphasis on school readiness programmes to constitute an essential input for qualitative improvement of primary education.
2. Reduction in curriculum load has been ensured not only in terms of the number of areas of learning but also by making all learning relevant to the needs and requirements of individual learners, the society and the country at large.
3. The erstwhile areas under Environmental Studies, that is Environmental Studies-I (Social Sciences) and Environmental Studies-II (Natural Science) for Classes III to V have been integrated. The new integrated subject is expected to be more relevant for children. Besides, promoting healthy habits among children, it is in perfect

harmony with their developmental characteristics. The content is to be drawn from their immediate environment and the strategies to be adopted would help enhance their skills of observation, collection, classification, experimentation, estimation, prediction and drawing of inferences. In Classes I and II. environmental concerns are being integrated with the learning of language and mathematics.

4. Focus on the all-round development of children's personality especially in the affective and psychomotor domains has been ensured, through the introduction of a new area of Art of Healthy and Productive Living (AHPL) wherein opportunities would be provided for the nurturance of free and creative expression of children's skills, habits, attitudes and values necessary for becoming successful and useful citizens. No textbooks for students would be prescribed for this area of learning. However, teachers will be encouraged to organise activities for children with their active involvement

5. Adequate emphasis has been laid on promoting oral skills particularly in the areas of language and mathematics.

6. Activities within and outside school to make the experiences of learners realistic and permanent have been encouraged and supported. Evaluation at this stage would be both formal and informal. It is envisaged to be conducted on a continuous basis, and would ensure comprehensiveness and transparency. It would also be learner friendly in character.

7. The content and processes are recommended to be geared to local traditions and culture and gradually link them to modern developments. Children will be encouraged to acquire skills for lifelong learning for which suitable activities would be planned and organised in and outside school.

8. Linkages between different curricular areas have been recommended to be strengthened by drawing concrete examples from the learners' immediate environment. Involvement of all children in a variety of activities is to be ensured. The language used in the teaching-learning materials will facilitate smooth understanding of the concepts besides encouraging children for self-learning.
9. Alternative strategies for teachers to handle content have been suggested. Due emphasis has been put on acquiring mastery level learning for which necessary diagnosis and remediation activities have to be devised. Enrichment activities for fast learners also find place in the scheme of things. Suitable orientation programmes including action research are envisaged for teacher education.

Working Hours

A minimum of one hundred and eighty days in a year have been stipulated for effective instructions in school. A primary school should function for five hours a day out of which four hours may be set aside for instruction. Some time is spent in activities like evaluation/test, school functions etc., but it is expected that inspite of this, adequate time for effective instruction should be given for completing the prescribed quantum of the subject areas in this syllabus.

Mother Tongue

Rationale. The mother tongue of the child is what develops and shapes her/his basic personality, besides being a natural expression of what she/he is thinking and experiencing. From the time the child is born, she/he gets exposed to the language being spoken by her/his parents and siblings. She/he hears this language in the neighbourhood, on the streets, and also over the radio and television, if these are available. The child thus learns to speak the same language that she/he hears in the environment. A small child looks at the world around him/her, names objects and persons in the environment and starts to talk about them. In this way she/he begins to gradually build up her/his knowledge of the world around her/him. As the child's store of language develops, her/his world also grows and expands. This language that a child grows up with is known as the child's mother tongue.

General Objectives of Teaching

The objectives of teaching-learning of the mother-tongue at the primary level are to enable the child:

- to listen with understanding and to comprehend ideas through listening;
- to speak effectively in both informal and formal transactions;
- to read with comprehension and enjoy reading various kinds of instructional materials;
- to write neatly, grammatically, logically and creatively;
- to think independently and differentiate between fact and opinion.

Approach of Teaching Learning

The approach of teaching-learning of mother tongue at the primary level would focus on:

- Relating language teaching to themes pertaining to the life and immediate environment of the child.
- Developing language abilities in children, through teaching-learning processes that are contextualised.
- Enhancing the child's lexical repertoire and speaking ability through planned activities for language development selected from their immediate environment.
- Providing opportunities to the children to narrate incidents, stories, anecdotes from their own experience.

Language Learning

A small area in the classroom can be earmarked Language Learning Corner. This could be used for display of reading and writing materials, colourful pictures, library books, materials provided under Operation Blackboard, old magazines, newspapers, etc. Short stories, poems, pictures and other literary creations produced by the children themselves could be displayed here. All the children should have easy access to this corner.

Language Teaching

A flexible and eclectic methodology of language teaching needs to be explored for optimal results. The two methods of language teaching namely; Word Method and the Whole Language Development Method should be tried in an integrated form. The Word Method is useful for meaningful reading, reducing burden of memorisation by providing words as units of teaching-learning. These words are taken from the children's vocabulary and familiar surroundings. The child is gradually led from the known to the unknown (Word to Letter) and from the whole to the part (Word to Letter).

Language Approach

In the Whole Language Approach teaching and learning of reading and writing is undertaken through description of events, narration of stories and activities from real life situations. The teaching-learning process is built upon the pre-knowledge of the child around which classroom activities are organised. Since it is the sentence which is the meaningful unit of language, the sentence-approach is adopted. There is a need to provide a comfortable environment in the classroom and opportunities for easy peer group interaction. Children would first be encouraged to select those activities which they find interesting followed by undertaking of, as many activities as possible by them individually as well as in groups. These could be in the form of reading an advertisement, reading maps of the locality, finding out the rules for crossing the road and following them, making charts, having a conversation, etc.

An ideal classroom situation would be one in which useful aspects of both the methods are harmoniously blended. The teaching-learning processes should be undertaken keeping in mind the learning pace and style of the individual child.

Methodology for Teaching Functional Grammar. At the primary level the effort would be to reduce the structuralism and prescriptivism of teaching theoretical grammar. As the child already possesses the basic grammatical structures of the mother tongue, formal grammar teaching needs to be reduced to a minimum. Language should be taught essentially for functional and communicative purposes.

Development of Skills

The basic purpose of language is meaningful communication. For the development of this faculty it is necessary that the child be provided opportunities in the classroom for purposeful and meaningful language use. A contextual approach for language teaching needs to be followed. All language activities, be it for development of listening, speaking, reading or writing skill, should be undertaken by relating it to the child's environment.

Evaluation Procedures

Evaluating the child's proficiency in the mother tongue at the primary level needs to be extremely child-friendly and stress-free. Constant evaluation of the children's progress at short intervals, followed by appropriate remedial work should be the hallmarks of evaluation. Performance tests, which could include creative work, group discussion, recitation of poems, etc. could be taken up. Continuous assessment should be taken up through oral and written tests. Oral tests should evaluate the skills of both listening and speaking.

The purpose of evaluation at the primary level should not be on highlighting the weaknesses of the child. Positive evaluation should be aimed at. Diagnostic tests should be administered followed by remedial teaching.

Teaching English

Objectives of Teaching English at the Primary Stage To help the child to:

- develop the abilities of listening, speaking, reading and writing English
- communicate in English with appropriateness and with right pronunciation
- think independently, to differentiate between fact and opinion and to use language intelligently and creatively (understand emotion/intention behind words)
- appreciate the melody of the spoken word and to enjoy learning English

Learning Outcomes

LEVEL I

Class I and II

By the end of level I, the child should be able to acquire the skills of:

Listening

- to be able to listen to simple, familiar popular rhymes, poems and stories in English
- to understand simple 'Yes' - 'No' type questions
- to understand and follow oral requests and simple instructions in familiar situations
- to understand oral commands and questions in familiar situations
- to understand simple expressions of greetings, introduction, gratitude, etc. in familiar social situations.

Speaking

- to recite simple rhymes and songs in groups with appropriate gestures/actions
- to answer simple questions with 'Yes' - 'No' and one word/short answers
- to talk about oneself, members of the family and immediate environment

- to convey expressions of greetings, introduction, gratitude ('thank you'), requests, etc. in normal social situations.

Reading

- to recognise the letters of the alphabet from A-Z both capital and small
- to read simple words and short sentences with the help of pictures and understand them.

Writing

- to perform simple - pre-writing functions like drawing lines and figures, semi-circles and circles
- to write letters of the alphabets (both capital and small)
- to write simple words and short sentences in English related to their immediate environment as well as those that are commonly used in the learner's mother tongue. Vocabulary
- to develop a vocabulary of about 250-300 words, related to the immediate environment.

LEVEL II

Class III

By the end of class III, the child should be able to acquire the skills of:

Listening

- to understand simple questions, requests and suggestions
- to follow oral instructions for playing games, performing tasks and activities
- to listen to and understand short narration and descriptions.

Speaking

- to speak simple sentences with ease and fluency using appropriate sound, stress and intonation
- to recite poems and songs effectively
- to describe simple familiar things and objects and situations
- to use accepted formulae in English in inter-personal interaction.

Reading

- to read with understanding connected text containing simple statements questions and instructions
- to read and enjoy simple poems
- to develop correct reading habits
- to acquire a reasonable speed in reading.

Writing

- to practise copy writing from the blackboard and the textbook
- to write using correct shape, sequence and spacing of letters and words
- to take dictation of simple familiar words
- to write simple connected sentences to describe and narrate an experience/event, etc.
- to learn the use of common punctuation marks.

Vocabulary

- to develop an active vocabulary of over 450-500 words.

Class IV

By the end of Class IV, the child should be able to acquire the skills of:

Listening

- to understand simple conversation and dialogues in familial and unfamiliar situations
- to follow directions given orally
- to follow narration and descriptions.

Speaking

- to respond to questions, suggestions, instructions
- to describe objects and situations using appropriate language
- to describe, report and narrate incidents and experiences
- to recite poems with appropriate stress and intonation.

Reading

- to read texts appropriate to the level
- to read with understanding simple short stories and descriptive pieces
- to acquire a reasonable speed in reading
- to learn to use a suitable dictionary.

Writing

- to write short connected paragraphs
- to take dictation of connected sentences
- to write short descriptive and narrative pieces
- to write short notes containing information, requests, instructions, etc.
- to organise jumbled sentences in the right order.

Vocabulary

- to develop an active vocabulary control of over 750-800 words

Class V

By the end of class V, the child should be able to acquire the skills of:

Listening

- to listen and understand short pieces of conversation in different life situations
- to understand and enjoy poems recited effectively
- to listen with sustained attention and interest to short stories, talks and descriptions
- to listen to radio/TV newscasts and other programmes and audio cassettes.

Speaking

- to speak intelligibly with reasonable fluency
- to speak on simple familiar themes
- to describe simple situations and events
- to take part in group activity, role play, dramatization, etc.
- to interact with the peer group
- to perform certain language functions such as apologizing, agreeing/disagreeing, giving directions.

Reading

- to read and understand instructions on sign boards, names of places, headlines in newspapers, advertisements, etc.
- to practise silent reading with comprehension of short passages
- to infer meanings of words and sentences from the context
- to locate significant details
- to follow sequence of ideas and facts.

Writing

- to write answers to questions based on the text in complete sentences
- to write personal letters, leave application and short personal notes
- to write a short composition based on pictures
- to write short comments giving reasons
- to complete incomplete stories and paragraphs.

Vocabulary

- to develop a vocabulary of about a 800-1100 words.

Techniques and Teaching of English. At Level I, an oral-aural approach would be followed with less focus on reading and writing skills. No formal textbooks will be introduced for children of Classes I and II. Only a Teacher Resource Book would be used for initiating teaching-learning processes at Level I (Classes I and II).

At Level I, there would be an Activity Book for children containing plenty of illustrations and some exercises for drawing/colouring and developing pre-writing skills and the mechanics of writing. Activities would also be provided for initiating reading skills.

Situational and communicative language teaching methodologies would be followed.

Linkage with sound pedagogical principles at primary level would be ensured, in commensuration with the profile of the primary child.

Learner-centred methodologies would be followed.

Activity based teaching-learning processes would be evolved.

Integration of key environmental and arithmetical concepts would be undertaken.

Cartoons and comic strips would be used in the teaching-learning process to arouse the interest of the child.

Teaching of English would focus on learning of the language for communicative purposes. Functional grammar would be underscored.

Instructional Materials

There would be no formal textbook for classes I and II. A Teacher Resource Book would be developed containing activities for facilitating oral-aural as well as some pre-writing and reading/recognition skills in children. There would be one Teacher Resource Book for each year, i.e. classes I and II.

Language kits for use of teachers would be developed which would serve as a model for development of other similar kits using local specific materials. It would contain the following materials;

- Pocket board
- Flash cards
- Language games
- Quiz/puzzle exercises
- Audio Package, etc.

An Activity Book would be developed for the children for Classes I and II each. They would contain illustrations, exercises for drawing/colouring, for developing pre-writing skills and the mechanics of writing. Activities would also be provided for initiating reading/recognition skills in the children, with the help of illustrations and drawing and colouring exercises.

Audio media would be used extensively at level I. It would also be used in the other classes as well.

From Level II, i.e., from Class III onwards a language Reader along with an Activity Book would be introduced.

The Reader would have grammatical as well as literary pieces.

Child-friendly textual materials would be prepared with a plenitude of illustrations, poems, stories and rhymes.

There would be heavy reliance on Educational Technology and media for preparation of supplementary materials.

The textbooks/course book would contain about 90 pages.

The workbook/activity book would contain about 60 pages.

The Textbook/Course book would contain 'Instructions for Teachers' as footnotes, wherever necessary.

Evaluation Processes

At Level I (Classes I and II), informal evaluation with focus on oral-aural competencies would be taken up. There would be no formal evaluation of reading and writing skills.

The child's responses in different situations would be observed to enable the teacher to assess the strengths of the child.

The weightage to various skills in Classes III, IV and V would be as under:

Listening	30%
Speaking	30%
Reading	20%
Writing	20%

Appropriate testing devices would be used—

Formative evaluation would be undertaken to evolve corrective measures

Summative evaluation in terms of class end would be taken up and remedial measures identified from Class III onwards.

Assessment of reading comprehension, elements of language (both grammar and vocabulary) and composition would be undertaken.

Child-friendly evaluation processes would need to be evolved. Continuous comprehensive evaluation would be followed.

At the entire primary level, the base of evaluation would focus on the oral-aural approach.

Time Allocation

There are about 180 working days available for classroom interaction.

One period per day would be allotted for the teaching of English—

- A total of 180 periods per year would be available for teaching-learning English in the classroom
- Periods available for actual teaching would be about 150 (excluding 30 periods for continuous comprehensive evaluation).

Objectives of Teaching Mathematics

The major objectives of teaching mathematics at the Primary Stage are to enable the learner to:

- develop an understanding of the number concepts
- develop understanding of four fundamental operations of addition, subtraction, multiplication and division and perform them with speed and accuracy in solving problems of day-today life
- develop understanding of various kinds of measures such as length, mass, capacity, time, money, temperature, area and volume and use these measures in situations arising in the learner's immediate environment
- develop understanding and appreciation of geometrical shapes and their characteristics and discuss, describe and draw two/three dimensional shapes
- develop power of interpretation and representation of given information
- develop and exhibit creativity
- develop power of thinking and reasoning
- develop scientific temper

Learning Areas

The following five learning areas have been identified for the curriculum in mathematics at primary stage.

- Number and Numeration

- Four Fundamental Operations
- Measures
- Geometrical Shapes
- Pictorial Representation of Data

Teaching-learning Strategy

With a view to making learning of mathematics interesting for the learner, the following, strategies are suggested.

(a) Ensuring readiness for learning mathematics.

(b) Planning and sequencing experiences to suit the process of learning.

(c) Relating new learning to learner's previous learning, both in and out-of-school situations.

(d) Ensuring active involvement of children in the learning process.

(e) Providing opportunities for spiral learning.

(f) Providing opportunities for peer group learning.

(g) Adopting a combined approach of both teacher-centred and learner-centred activities depending on the learning objective.

(h) Creating a democratic and joyful learning environment.

Integrating Mathematics with other Subjects

Mathematics can really be enjoyable provided the curriculum and its transactional strategies are designed properly. Let stories, drama, poetry, puzzles, riddles, games, drawings, painting, dance, music flow into the mathematics period and before long we will find a highly motivated and keen mathematics learner! Let children colour their geometrical figures, make patterns in them, write stories on fractions or shapes, write dialogues between two numbers and role play it, solve puzzles, riddles, create games and their roles, write their experiences of mathematical activities, create bulletin boards and carry out innumerable such activities. If all these fun filled activities become a part of mathematics learning, children will look forward to the mathematics period as eagerly as they do to their language, environmental studies of arts' periods. For example, when talking about 'Means of Transport' or 'Kinds of Food' in Environmental Studies, let children survey and represent their data pictorially, which is one of the learning experiences of mathematics. When doing a topic on 'water' in Environmental Studies, relate it to measures in mathematics. In Arts, let learners make geometrical shapes, patterns, paper craft (folding½, ¼), etc. Let them use their compass, protractor or other geometrical instruments outside the mathematics periods as well. The more creative the activities, the more enthused will the children be. The activities need to be planned in such a manner that the children appreciate mathematical concepts in their surroundings, nature and real life situations and begin to think systematically and logically for solving day-today problems.

Teaching-learning Materials

The following teaching-learning materials are recommended for use in different classes:

Class I

- A Text-cum-Workbook containing instructions/notes for teachers/parents;
- Teaching aids in the form of concrete materials, games, puzzles, mathematics kit, etc.

Class II

- A Text-cum-Workbook with illustrations and worksheets for giving practice to students;
- Teaching aids in the form of concrete materials, games, puzzles, mathematics kit, etc.

Class III

- A Text-cum-Workbook, containing instructional notes for teachers/parents;
- Suitable Teaching aids.

Classes IV and V

- A Textbook with graded exercises with sufficient number of questions, for each class along with instructions/ notes for teachers/parents;
- Suitable Teaching aids.

Assessment of Learning

Assessment is a process of collecting evidences of learning, analysing evidences, interpreting and improving the level of learning. It is an essential and integral part of the teaching-learning process. Assessment is not a one-time activity to simply label children good or average etc. but aims at improving levels of learning by assessing the learning on a continual basis. It is not an end in itself but a means of providing information, which can form the basis for future action in the form of remedial measures and enrichment activities. Assessment is aimed at ensuring attainment of the desired learning by all and not only on grading.

General Objectives of Teaching Environmental Studies

The objectives of Environmental Studies at Primary Stage are to help the child to be:

- physically, emotionally, socially and mentally healthy
- able to function effectively as a member of the social groups (family, community) she/he belongs to
- able to develop skills, attitudes, and values for improving the quality of life of self and that of the community
- able to appreciate the need to live in harmony with nature.

Expected Learning Outcomes (ELO)

An attempt has been made to define the Expected Learning Outcomes (ELOs) in terms of processes rather than focusing on the end products. To emphasise the significance of processes in the all round development of child's personality the terminology used in Delore's Report for defining the ELOs in terms of four pillars has been used to detail out the objectives in the context of the child in India at the primary stage. These ELOs are aimed at helping the child to construct knowledge herself/himself and learning from the personal experiences.

Learning to Know

The child will:

- develop an understanding of basic structure and functions of various parts of human body and the need to take care of these parts.
- develop an understanding of social, cultural, natural and man-made environment and their inter-relationships.
- develop awareness and understanding about her/his personal well-being, belongings and surroundings and ways to keep them clean.
- demonstrate an understanding for conservation of natural resources and protection of the environment and also take action for protecting it and proper utilisation of resources.
- demonstrate an understanding of distance in space and time and the relationship between them.

Learning to Do

The child will:

- develop competencies and skills for life-long learning (for quality of life), i.e., skills of observation, reporting, collecting information, discrimination, classification, experimentation, making predictions and estimations, drawing inferences, etc.
- interpret and report observations in a variety of ways—oral, written, pictorial (graphs, charts, tables).
- practise healthy habits such as cleanliness, discipline, punctuality, proper care of belongings, etc.
- develop healthy attitude towards dignity of labour and prepare adequately to face life.

- develop skills of reading a map and locating places in the map.
- develop skills of using the globe.
- develop skills of using standard and non-standard units of measurement.
- plan and canyon! simple and safe experiments/activities on her/his own/under the guidance of the teacher.

Learning to Live Together

The child will:

- develop social skills and values, such as sharing, caring/helping others (including differently abled children) tolerance, team-spirit, cooperation, working together for common good, waiting for ones turn, etc.
- learn to live in harmony with the environment and people of different communities and having different faiths.
- recognise and appreciate the contributions made by people in the past and in the present for the well-being of the community.
- respect rules made for the benefit of the community and follow them.

Learning to Be

The child will:

- understand and play her/his role as an individual in home, at school, and the community (neighbourhood).
- express herself/himself freely in creative activities.
- acquire habits of self-learning through creative/productive activities.
- develop ability to ask simple questions relating to natural and social environment.
- practise some positive values specific to her/his own context, e.g. truthfulness, honesty, brotherhood, patriotism, etc.

- appreciate beauty in the environment and show a sense of aesthetic appreciation through expression in varied forms of art.
- appreciate culture and traditions and take pride in being an Indian.
- show and promote respect and concern for others and for the environment.
- develop abilities to process information and take independent decisions in simple situations in day-today life.
- develop scientific temper.

The Approach

The curricular area perceives the environment as an integrated whole taking into its fold the natural, the man-made, the social and the cultural environment.

The approach to curriculum development takes into account the principle of moving from oneself to immediate environment and extending it gradually to wider environment limiting it to our country and its people and their linkages with the life of the child, directly or indirectly.

The curricular area of Environmental Studies assumes provision of experiences to children that are locally relevant and specific to the needs of the community and physical environment. At the same time it lays stress on the global values of brotherhood, national identity and development of pride in being a citizen of this country and its cultural heritage.

Environmental Studies presumes a shift in teaching-learning strategies from teacher-centred, subject-based and classroom-oriented approach to child-centred, learning-based and community-oriented approach. It would require concerted efforts in shifting the emphasis from communication through written word to visual communication, i.e., changing from content-based learning to process-based and outcome-oriented learning.

Healthy and Productive Living

Rationale. The Art of Healthy and Productive Living (AHPL) has been included as one of the areas of study at the Primary Stage. The area has been conceived through a meaningful merger of the earlier curricular areas—'Art Education', 'Work Experience' and 'Health and Physical Education'. The major purpose of including this area is to provide meaningful opportunities for the all around development of the child's personality. The area perceives 'living' as an 'art', as all forms of art have originated from the life of human beings over the ages. Creative expression through the different art forms is a sign of a healthy mind for which a healthy body is a must. There is a need, therefore, to provide suitable opportunities to children to develop desirable habits, skills and abilities to appreciate and internalize the beauty in life and nature and also to express their feelings through different forms of art. AHPL envisages provision of such opportunities through day-today life experiences. In brief, this curricular area aims at adopting an approach that will reduce the information load and help children to develop and grow in an effortless and natural manner.

The Scope. The scope of this area of study is not only confined to the development of mechanical skills but goes much beyond to include meaningful experiences that will promote values like dignity of labour, respect for people, appreciating and understanding the need for good physical and mental health as well as positive attitudes. The National Curriculum Framework for School Education 2000, describes its scope for Classes I and II, as follows:

Experiences to be provided for art of healthy and productive living will further contribute toward all-round development of the personality of the child. These will be organised keeping child in central focus involving students in activities commensurate with their developmental stage. Activities related to health will get a prominent place so that children acquire necessary skills, attitudes and habits to keep themselves healthy and participate in games and sports suitable for their age. Children will be initiated into preliminary yogic exercises and will be exposed to various soothing experiences in the field of music, drama, drawing and painting and clay modelling. In organising these activities local factors may be given due importance. They will be encouraged to participate in creative activities such as free hand drawing and painting. Besides this, children will be involved in the activities related to work education so as to enable them to be free from inhibitions and like to work. For value inculcation stories and anecdotes would play an effective role. These will also generate and strengthen the element of curiosity, imagination and a sense of wonder. All the experiences will need to be presented in an integrated manner for which themes will be identified and teachers will make use of locally available resources and harness community support wherever necessary.

Scope in Classes III and V

In addition, for Classes III to V the National Curriculum Framework for School Education suggests as under:

The experiences gained earlier will be further strengthened by ensuring participation of all children in the activities related to music, dance, drama, drawing and painting, puppetry, health and physical education, games and sports, yoga and productive work. Integrated approach will be used. Autonomy and flexibility incorporating the locally developed curriculum and materials will be encouraged. Concerted efforts will be made to ensure proper value orientation among children.

The Objectives. The following specific objectives will enable children to:

- develop regular habits and attitudes to meet the natural needs of the body.
- know and understand the functions of the different parts/organs of the body and develop habits to keep them clean and healthy.
- develop awareness and sensitivity towards the immediate environment and understand the inter-dependence between humans and the environment.

- develop respect for manual work, dignity of labour and hard work.
- develop values such as cooperation, tolerance, caring and sharing.
- develop physical, mental and emotional well-being through yoga and games.
- nurture the inherent abilities of self-expression and creativity through the visual and performing arts and to enable children to appreciate and develop aesthetic sensitivity towards these arts.
- develop human values like honesty, truthfulness, respect for others, punctuality, regularity and appreciating the good qualities in others.
- appreciate the cultural heritage both local and national.
- develop a feeling of oneness with the culture of the country.
- develop qualities of leadership.
- take care and protect public property.
- know about the existing public facilities in their surroundings and how to use them properly.
- develop feelings of patriotism, nationalism and pride in being an Indian.
- develop an awareness towards the need to protect and conserve India's historical and cultural heritage.

Teaching-learning Strategies

Participation of each child in meaningful activities is the focus of this curricular area. While planning activities, the following considerations may be kept in mind. All activities should be:

- joyful, that the child should find it interesting
- related to the child's background and immediate environment
- providing scope for creative expression through various art forms

These activities should be varied in nature. Participation of each child would be ensured and opportunities would be provided to help develop her/his interest in the activities of her/his own liking. Both individual and group activities will be so organised that children imbibe values of cooperative living with better understanding of each other, practising tolerance, humility, mutual respect, dutifulness, selflessness and above all commitment to social and national integration. It should provide training in good citizenship.

While evolving activities it should be ensured that some activities would be core activities common in all schools, for all children. Whereas, other activities would be specific to the needs of the individual child, school environment and local community. Since the scope of the subject goes beyond classroom activities, parents too will play a very significant role in assessing the behavioural changes in their child from time to time. Their observations should also be taken into consideration before planning of further activities by teachers.

Teaching-learning Material

In this curricular area no textbook is prescribed. The themes for developing various activities would be drawn from the curricular areas of Environmental Studies, Language and Mathematics. Only a Teachers' Handbook containing exemplar activities for reference purposes by the teacher will be developed.

Curriculum at the Upper Primary Stage (Class VI to VIII)

Introduction: The Emerging Context. The existing curriculum and the syllabi of different subject areas, for the upper primary stage, had been in use for the last twelve years or even more (Since 1988). During this period, not only numerous changes had taken place in different subject areas but many new constitutional, societal, cultural and pedagogical issues had also emerged. The National Policy on Education. 1986 added a few more educational dimensions in its subsequent review in 1992 and fixed responsibilities in clear terms for their implementation through its Programme of Action, 1992. This made it imperative to consider the various issues and concerns in education and relate them to societal, economic and cultural issues along with numerous other issues related to environment, industry, agriculture, conservation of natural resources, defence, health, nutrition and population and give a fresh look to these issues while designing syllabi in an integrated manner. There was also an urgent need to address some other educational concerns like eliminating imbalances and biases in the society and making education an instrument for building a cohesive society, strengthening national identity, preserving cultural heritage, integrating indigenous and contemporary knowledge, making India's contributions to world civilisation known, facing the impact of globalisation, meeting the challenges of information and communication technology, linking education with life-skills and harnessing education for value development.

The constitutional obligation of the state for providing free and compulsory education upto the age of fourteen years has yet to be fulfilled through the Universalisation of Elementary Education. In this context, expanding access, arresting drop-outs, raising learning achievements to an acceptable level of quality, making it relevant to life and reducing gaps in educational outcomes across states and among groups are the major challenges.

Integrating diverse curricular concerns, relating education to the world of work, reducing the curriculum load, making a case for culture specific pedagogy, and nurturing aesthetic sensibilities are some of the other concerns which have been addressed adequately while developing the syllabi at the upper primary stage.

Scheme of Studies

This scheme of studies is as follows:

1. Three Languages-the mother tongue/regional language, Modern Indian language, and English
2. Mathematics
3. Science and Technology
4. Social Sciences
5. Work Education

6. Art Education-Fine Arts: Visual and Performing
7. Health and Physical Education (including Games and Sports, Yoga, NCC, Scouting and Guiding)

Instructional Time

Regarding instructional time, it has been stipulated that a minimum of one hundred and eighty days in a year will be available for instructional activities. It is expected that the loss of instructional time due to unspecified reasons would be prevented or minimised through better educational management. After taking into account, the activities like evaluation/test, school functions, etc. schools will be getting adequate time for effective instruction and it is hoped that the prescribed quantum of the subject areas in syllabus will be properly completed. At the upper primary stage, the duration of school days will be six hours out of which five hours will be fixed for instruction and the rest for other routine activities. The duration of a class period may be around forty minutes.

Learning outcomes in English

At the end of Class VIII the learner would have further developed the abilities of listening, speaking, reading, writing and thinking with reference to a certain quantum of language spelt out in terms of grammatical and vocabulary items. The various competencies of the language abilities are listed below.

Understands English when it is spoken

- understands and responds appropriately to instructions, requests, questions, suggestions and proposals
- comprehends narrations and descriptions
- understands, appreciates and enjoys poems, anecdotes, jokes and riddles

Participates in a conversation/discussion in English on a topic within the range of her/his experience and interests

- produces English speech sounds which are intelligible

- speaks with accuracy following the overall rhythm of spoken English, i.e., proper pauses and sentence stress
- converses in familiar social situations » asks and responds to questions, gives instructions, narrates simple experiences, describes things and reports happenings

Reads texts in English with ease and understanding

- locates details in texts both prescribed and non-prescribed
- understands the central ideas
- follows the sequence of ideas and events
- analyses, compares, contrasts ideas in the text
- relates ideas to her/his own experience
- uses his/her thinking faculty to read between the lines and beyond the lines
- interprets tablets, charts, diagrams, graphs and maps
- learns to use a suitable dictionary
- develops a taste for reading

Expresses herself/himself with ease and felicity using appropriate vocabulary and sentence structures

- masters the mechanics of writing
- writes neatly with proper speed
- writes simple notices for the school notice board
- writes short paragraphs, letters, and simple narrative and descriptive pieces
- writes accurate descriptions of people, places and things
- writes compositions on events and processes
- develops the skill of making notices

Uses her/his proficiency in English

- as a spring board to explore and study other areas of knowledge

- as a vehicle to keep herself/himself abreast of the latest developments in different fields of knowledge

Social Sciences

Rationale. Social Sciences is an integral component of general education up to secondary stage of school education. Its study is crucial because it helps the young learners to understand the society and the world in which they live, and view the socio-economic developments and changes in the context of time and space and also in relation to each other. It thus widens their mental horizons. Evolution of human society is a dynamic process having continuity. The present forms a small part of this continuum and cannot be understood independently or in isolation. In fact, the changes and development of today are linked to the past as also to the contemporary developments in other parts of the world. As such, temporal (historical) and spatial (geographical) dimensions together help the learners in developing a comprehensive picture of the present-day society and the world at large. Besides providing essential knowledge and understanding, the social science education aims at developing skills and attitudes necessary for self-development and for becoming effective and contributing members of society.

The curriculum of Social Sciences in schools draws its content mainly from History, Geography. Civics and Economics.

At the primary school stage, the children are introduced to 'Environmental Studies', which comprises natural and social elements of the environment. Starting from the immediate environment, the children get familiarised gradually with distant places, state and country.

At the upper primary stage, for the first time Social Sciences is introduced as an independent area of study and continues to enjoy the same position at the secondary stage.

The Objectives. The major objectives of the Social Sciences course at the upper primary stage are to:

- develop an understanding about the earth as the habitat of humankind;

- develop an understanding of the evolution of human societies and civilisations in India and other parts of the world with their interconnections;
- inculcate an appreciation of the contributions made by different societies and civilisations to the progress of humankind as a whole—with special reference to the contribution of India to world civilisation and vice versa;
- develop an appreciation of the growth of various components of Indian culture and take legitimate pride in the achievements of Indians in different periods and in different parts of the country and the world;
- understand and appreciate the diversities in lands and peoples of India and the world, and the interdependence of regions and countries;
- understand contemporary India and the world; become aware of current processes of change and related issues and challenges;
- develop an understanding of natural and human resources and their potentialities for a better tomorrow:
- acquire a positive attitude towards conservation and preservation of environment, its resources and heritage;
- develop an understanding of the structure and functioning of civic, political and economic institutions;
- develop an awareness of the various social and economic challenges before the country;
- acquire necessary abilities and skills, both academic and social, which would enable the learner to differentiate between fact and fiction, and would help her/him to think critically and creatively, communicate effectively, cooperate with others and respond to the needs of others;
- develop a scientific temper and a pro-active attitude enabling the learner to face challenges with confidence and to adjust to unfamiliar situations.

The Evaluation. Evaluation needs to be exploited profitably for the development of cognitive and non-cognitive capacities of pupils. Hence, adequate emphasis must be given on both formative and summative forms of evaluation. While formative evaluation should be used for designing and providing remedial measures for slow learners and enrichment materials for the fast learners, summative evaluation needs to be used for classification of placement and promotion to higher classes. Only school based evaluation in the form of continuous and comprehensive evaluation is recommended at this stage i.e., from Classes VI to VIII. Criterion-references tests will be employed periodically for ensuring the acquisition of competencies upto the mastery level. The evaluation of co-scholastic attributes needs to be carried out continuously using observation, rating scale and check lists and must be reported quarterly. It would be useful in monitoring the progress of the learner.

Mathematics

Objectives of Teaching Mathematics. To enable the pupil to:

- consolidate her/his mathematical knowledge acquired at the Primary Stage;
- acquire knowledge and understanding of concepts, facts-principles, etc. related to commercial mathematics, mensuration, elementary statistics;
- develop abilities to solve simple problems from commercial mathematics, mensuration and elementary statistics;
- acquire knowledge and understanding of properties of geometrical figures through activities, experimentation, verification, etc. in the mathematics corner;
- develop abilities to solve geometrical problems by identifying relationships between different parts of the problem and applying logical reasoning;
- acquire knowledge and understanding of the fundamentals of elementary algebra;

- develop drawing, model making and measuring skills;
- develop abilities to read and interpret data from statistical graphs;
- develop awareness of the need for national unity, national integration, protection of the environment, observance of small family norms, removal of social barriers, elimination of sex biases;
- appreciate the great contribution made by ancient mathematicians with special reference to Indian mathematicians;

The Evaluation

Evaluation should be built in with the teaching-learning process and use for better learning by the pupil and for better teaching by the teacher. Mastery learning tests should be administered and timely remedial instructions should be provided, wherever necessary. Thus, remediation and proper evaluation should constitute an integral component of teaching-learning of mathematics at this stage. Some enrichment material for brighter students should also be provided on the basis of these tests. Evaluation has to be comprehensive and continuous. Chapter tests/unit tests should be administered regularly. These tests may include: (i) oral tests, (ii) written tests and (iii) practical work. Development of drawing skills, model making skills, measuring skills, etc. are equally important. Their assessment should also be a part of evaluation. Regularity in home assignment should also be included in the total evaluation. In addition to the evaluation by the teachers, opportunities may also be provided for peer evaluation and evaluation by the pupil herself/himself. The final evaluation should be the sum-total of all the above periodical and continuous evaluations.

Science and Technology

Objectives of Teaching Science and Technology. The objectives of Science and Technology education at the upper primary stage are to:

- expose the children to basic processes of science;
- understand the processes that underlie simple scientific and technological activities;
- develop an understanding of some basic principles and laws of science;
- make the children understand applications of basic scientific principles to solve problems related to daily-life;
- develop the ability to apply appropriate concepts of Science to Technology;
- develop measurement and manipulative skills and to encourage use of locally available resources;
- familiarise the children with life processes, health, nutrition and human diseases;
- acquaint the children with the technology that abounds in their immediate surroundings:
- create an awareness of the immediate environment and a need for its protection;
- make the children recognise the relationship of Science, Technology and Society;
- inculcate in children some of the Science and Technology related values; and
- to provide scientific and technological literacy to the learners.

Selection and Organisation of the Content

The syllabus in Science and Technology has been developed in order to translate the curricular concerns into an appropriate content. A thematic approach has been adopted to organise the syllabus. The themes are the Universe, Our Environment, Matter, Measurement, the Living World, Energy. Nutrition and Health and Agriculture. Most of these themes continue throughout the upper primary stage and continue even up to the secondary stage.

An attempt has been made to grade the concepts and the subject matter across the classes VI-VIII. These themes have been further divided into chapters that contain suitable subject-areas and also indicate extent of coverage. The activities envisaged in the textual materials are likely to help the children in learning science more meaningfully. The experiences of the upper primary stage are also likely to inculcate in the learner Science and Technology related values and also help them in improving their quality of life.

This syllabus is aimed at presenting "Science" as a single discipline, avoiding its conventional compartmentalisation, but emphasising the use of some of the scientific principles in Technology. It is also envisaged that a study of the topics such as nutrition and health, adolescence and common diseases will not only develop an understanding of the subject matter but will also help in removing myths and prevailing superstitions.

Some of the salient features of the syllabus are:

(i) A fresh look has been given to various concepts at this stage and an effort has been made to present Science as a single discipline. The syllabus has been so designed as to impart scientific and technological literacy to learners.

(ii) Inclusion of the life and experiences of some scientists, including Indian scientists, has been envisaged to inspire the children to pursue the study of science.

(iii) While translating the syllabus into textual material, efforts will be made to ensure that Science and Technology education at the upper primary stage has something of value to offer to learners of varying abilities and socio-cultural background.

(iv) Another noteworthy feature of the present syllabus is an attempt to impress upon the young minds the relationship between science, technology and society and a focussed emphasis on the various processes of science.

(v) Component of technological applications of some of the scientific principles appropriate at the upper primary stage has been included.

The Evaluation

Evaluation has to be a built-in component to assess the achievement of the learners. A multipronged strategy is to be adopted for the (i) assessment of the learning of scientific concept; (ii) assessment of the experimental skills and; (iii) assessment of the abilities of the children to understand the technological applications of scientific principles and laws. All these would require situation/experiment-based tests. The teachers would have to apply their ingenuity in framing them.

It is envisaged that evaluation in Science and Technology at the upper primary stage will be comprehensive and continuous. Evaluation will comprise tests, unit tests and practical work. Development of drawing skills and skills of measurement are also to be evaluated. The final evaluation at the year-end should be a cumulative total of the various class tests, unit tests and the tests administered periodically.

The Arts

Objectives of Art Education. The major objectives of Art Education at this stage are to:

- help the child identify feelings, thoughts, emotions and fantasies as an interaction to the environment;
- help the child organise thought processes and experiences and express them through a variety of media, namely — body movements, sound, graphic, plastic and locally available materials and words and movements, guided by experience activities and textual materials;
- help the child discover and identify his own potentials, experience the self and relate the same to the surroundings through different modes of expression:
- inculcate the habit and liking for self-dignity, originality, self-expression, individuality, initiative and being enterprising through creative experiences:
- help the child to develop a sense of expression, organisation and a sense of design;

- include the habit and liking for order in regard to his belongings pertaining to art activities;
- help the child to achieve a balanced growth as a social being in tune with our culture, through project work;
- develop team spirit through group activities;
- develop appreciation and understanding of the cultural heritage of one another.

The Content

What is taught at this stage has a particular significance, bearing in mind the rapidly changing physical and intellectual development of learners of this age and the mass culture to which they are extremely vulnerable. The aims and objectives of the art work need to be thought out very clearly and their realisation carefully planned in relation to the administrative support and physical resources that are locally available. The purpose of providing a wide variety of activities, which are to be offered as a means of reaching the objectives, is to provide opportunities to develop the ability to perceive, and interact with varied situations. The creative activities of the Art Curriculum should provide opportunities to children to come out with their day-today experiences, inner emotions and feelings. This leads them to be articulate in expression and presentation, which reflect the cultural, moral, social values of the time. Learning to handle art materials, understanding simple concept of visual and performing arts; theatrical arts, stories of great personalities in the field of art and stories connected with other countries, creating objects of aesthetic value through free, creative and original expression, playing simple musical instruments and sound producing objects, movement, mime and simple dance form; singing alone, in groups and community singing are the components through which this set objectives could be achieved.

Approach to Art Activities

At this stage, the learners have developed reasoning abilities, therefore, they look forward to help from the teachers. The children are to be encouraged to mobilise their own resources and to develop creative expression. A wide variety of media and techniques are to be provided at this stage for exploration and experimentation for various permutations and combinations. Indirect and inductive guidance in various art techniques through the discovery, exploration, improvisation and experimentation methods are to be provided. Through these methods gradual awareness of aesthetic and expressive qualities of various art media and techniques could be developed. Some preliminary rudiments for formal art forms, music, dance and visuals arts may be introduced indirectly.

Students need the opportunity to work collectively to foster team spirit and to build a sharing-caring society. Instead of selecting a few students with special talents, the interests of all students must be identified and they must be encouraged to participate in various art activities in one way or the other. The learner should be encouraged to take help from the community to acquaint themselves with the local folk and classical tradition and other skills.

Media Oriented Art Activities

- Two-dimensional pictorial experiences: drawing, painting, mask making, collage, applique, print making, etc.
- Three dimensional or sculptural experiences: clay, pottery, construction with paper, cardboard and cardboard boxes, soft wood, soft stone, etc.
- Performing Art education: learning rudiments of vocal music, playing simple regional musical instruments, body movements and facial expression in response to various situations of real and imaginary life experiences.
- Community singing and dancing.
- Dramatic activities.
- Projects like aesthetic organisation of the physical environment by enhancing the surrounding land, i.e.. landscaping (including plantation, playing with levels, rocks and junk) school museum, and mural and other display work.

Integrated Approach

Puppetry and drama are good examples of integrated art forms, which can later meet the varied interests of students. Within these forms, (here are aspects of script writing, music, movement, dramatisation, drawing, modelling and other stage crafts. Dramatic activities for schools must not be imitated from professional adult 'theatre' techniques with expensive lighting, stage setting, make-up, etc. All these should be improvised in the classroom situation. Students may discuss social and school issues and develop scripts. Students interested in modelling and drawing may make puppets or costumes. The materials for these may be drawn, as far as possible, from local resources. Those who are interested in music and movement may suggest such aspect of drama. If the play is related to some social issues, students can organise awareness programmes for the community at large.

Resources for Art Teaching

The basic resources are students, the teacher (who is considered to be resourceful and link personnel) and the cultural and natural environment in which they live. Simple charcoal, chalk and pencils are generally used by every child at home or in the school. And the child is able to scribble on paper, the ground and walls. There are many indigenous craft materials and wastes of village products and goods from the city: vegetation and its fibres, vegetables dyes and earth colour. which are easily available and already in use in villages and cities. Local songs of the community, lullabies, traditional folk-art works, festivals and associated colourful art and craftworks, painting and drawing on the walls and floors of the home are equally important. Sometimes, even family members of the children and other community members can be coordinated by the imaginative teacher for various creative art activities.

Physical Education

Rationale. Health is defined as "a state of physical, mental and social well-being and not merely the absence of disease or infirmity" (WHO). Thus, it assumes great importance in the all-round development of a child. Health and Physical Education enable the pupil to attain such a state of health, in fact, becomes education for man.

A rationale syllabus of Health and Physical Education in school must, therefore, enable the pupil to know and understand that harmonious development of body and mind is essential for good health and it should help the pupil to raise his own health status. The syllabus should also be such that, if transacted effectively, it enables the pupil to contribute meaningfully, in order to raise the health status of the self, family, community and also of the environment to which he belongs.

Objectives of Health and Physical Education

The objectives of Health and Physical Education are to help the students:

- understand the meaning and importance of being healthy;
- identify factors and conditions influencing his/her own health and that of others;
- recognise common, personal, family and community health problems and seek help from teachers and parents to solve them;
- acquire healthy practices relating to personal health; environmental health, exercise, rest, recreation, relaxation, sleep, posture, safety, eating and serving food; care of body-parts, especially the sense organs; consulting a physician: community living and getting along with others: and child care practices to help parents in the case of younger brothers and sisters, to protect and promote their health;
- learn about human body, changes that take place while growing up from a boy to a man and from a girl to a woman and take measures to stay healthy;
- develop skills in providing first-aid in athletic and other common childhood injuries that occur in the home, school and outside the home and school;

- know about qualified health functionaries operating practising in his/her community to seek help when needed;
- develop organic fitness, normal sense organs and efficient organic systems;
- cultivate habits of engaging in appropriate exercises so that immediate and future health needs will be met;
- develop neuro-muscular skills and promote the ability to perform work with ease and grace;
- develop attitudes of cooperation, good sportsmanship and fair-play;
- cultivate such traits of character as self-mastery, self-discipline, courage and confidence;
- develop a sense of patriotism, self-reliance, self-sacrifice, the desire to serve and tolerance;
- prepare herself/himself for making a worthwhile use of leisure time by acquiring knowledge of sports for the purpose of participating and observing, appreciating and enjoying them.

Organisation of Health and Physical Education

Some specific points which should be given proper thought in this area for classes VI to VIII are given below:

The term 'Health and Physical Education' includes knowledge of health, science and physical activities including games, sports, and other recreational activities.

All the programmes of Health and Physical Education are for all students. It should be incumbent on each and every student to participate in these programmes. The organisation of any such programme at the upper Primary Stage should, therefore, ensure general participation by all and this should get preference over competition.

The activities prescribed in the syllabus should cover a very wide range so that each and every pupil can participate according to her/his interest and needs, specially in physical activities.

Activities which do not involve much cost or no cost activities may be identified because most schools cannot afford high cost apparatus.

Facilities for physical education should be increasingly developed in rural as well as in urban schools. In this regard, special attention should be paid to socially and economically under-developed areas, urban slums, remote/rural and tribal areas.

Content in health education syllabus should be meaningfullv related to the pupil's environment and life. There can be some overlapping between topics under health and science education. To avoid this, the science syllabus may be studied before syllabus formulation in health education.

Games and sports have to find a prominent place in the total scheme of things. Emphasis should be on acquisition of adequate neuromuscular coordination commensurate with their developmental stage. Yoga and meditation can be very well-organised under the regular school schedule to help children acquire concentration and relaxation.

The syllabus in physical education should be such that talent in sports and games is discovered. In upper primary classes, there should be provision for extra inputs of training/coaching for talented students. This will help to catch them young.

The syllabus should clearly indicate which programmes/activities are core in nature and which are elective. The core element should be for all students.

Community involvement should be initiated at all levels in providing various resources (e.g. facilities for coaching funds, monitoring, etc.) specially Panchayat and school education committees should be approached.

Work Education

Rationale of Introducing Work Education. One of the most important goals of education is to enable learners to acquire knowledge, develop understanding and inculcate skills, positive attitudes, values and habits conducive to the all-round development of their personality. The learners should learn to value and preserve the rich heritage of our composite culture, to develop the scientific temper, humanism and the spirit of inquiry and reform, to strive towards excellence in all spheres of individual and collective activity. Work Education is viewed as an essential component of education at all stages of education and should be provided through well-structured and graded programmes. Work Education helps in developing the intrinsic values and the emotional intelligence of the learner leading towards the spiritual upliftment of the learner.

Work Education is a conscious effort to bridge the gap between manual and intellectual work, thus, giving a meaning and purpose to the learning process. Work Education not only develops love for manual work and a sense of dignity of labour, but also promotes the creative faculties of the child. It inculcates desirable social and moral values and qualities among pupils and develops capabilities to achieve productive efficiency. It helps them identify their day-today needs and develop self-reliance and confidence in meeting them. It acquaints them with productive activities going on in the society, the principles and processes involved in work and the tools and materials used for production. Thus, the principal aim of Work Education is to prepare children for life, equipping them with the proper attitudes, knowledge and skills in respect of work, which will lead to their personal-social and vocational development and, ultimately, to their smooth transition from the world of learning to the world of work.

Work Education helps in the all-round development of the child and aims at the inculcation of positive attitudes towards work as also desirable habits of health and hygiene, both personal and environmental, awareness of the world of work through exposure to different work situations and acquisition of elementary skills in handling simple tools and materials which may result in the production of simple articles.

Objectives of Work Education

The major objectives of Work Education at this stage are to develop among the young learners:

- understanding of the environment in its totality both natural and social, and their interactive processes, the environmental problems and the ways and means to preserve the environment;
- appreciation for the need of a balanced synthesis between the change oriented technologies and the continuity of the country's traditions and heritage;
- understanding of the positive and the negative impact of the processes of globalisation, liberalisation and localisation in the context of the country;
- qualities clustered around the personal, social, moral, national and spiritual values that make a person humane and socially effective, giving meaning and direction to life;
- capacity not only to process information but also to understand, reflect and internalise and develop insight;
- willingness to work hard, entrepreneurship and dignity of manual work necessary for increasing productivity, obtaining job satisfaction and creating wealth generating system; and
- pre-vocational/vocational skills.

Knowledge and Understanding

- identify her/his needs and those of his/her family and community for food, health and hygiene, clothing, shelter, recreation and social service;
- get acquainted with different aspects of productive activities around her/him;
- relate his knowledge of scientific facts and technological principles to various types of work;
- identify and use tools and raw materials scientifically and confidently.

The Skills

To help the child to:

- engage in suitable Work Education activities and thereby develop competence in meeting her/his day-today needs and those of his/her family and the community.
- participate intensively in production processes and thereby develop a reasonable level of work skills;
- develop his/her productive capacities sufficiently so that he/she can start earning while learning;
- apply the problem-solving method in work.

The Attitudes and Values

To help the child to:

- reinforce a sense of dignity of labour and desirable social qualities such as self-reliance, mutual helpfulness, cooperation, team work, sympathy and tolerance;
- develop proper work values and habits such as regularity, punctuality, discipline, honesty, efficiency, love of excellence and dedication to duty;
- develop a deeper concern for the environment and a sense of responsibility and commitment to the community;
- develop readiness for entry into the world of work or aptitude for pre-vocational courses at the secondary stage;
- enable the learner to have an in-depth understanding of the principles of various technologies.

Selection and Organisation of Content

The content of Work Education is to be based on the developmental level and needs of the child on the one hand and resources and facilities available in the school and the community on the other. Since all these factors differ from place to place, no fixed syllabus or single programme can be prescribed for all schools in any one area, let alone in a State or in the country as a whole. It is in keeping with this realisation that only a suggestive list of Work Education activities at the upper primary stage is being recommended at the national level. It must be emphasised that in order to ensure relevance Work Education should be local specific and therefore, the State syllabi should also ensure local variation. However, a great deal of commonality is possible in some Work Education activities which need to be performed by all pupils as they are basic to the satisfaction of every day needs of children, their families and communities. Accordingly, a programme of 'Essential Activities' has been visualised which must be undertaken by all the schools besides a programme of 'Elective Activities' for the production of goods and rendering of service to the community. The programme of Essential Activities is intended to result in life skills and basic attitudinal changes towards work and should by and large, lead to the enhancement of the nutritional, health, sanitation, productivity and economic status of the community. The nature of activities selected for this purpose is such that they can be performed by all the upper primary schools, which should ensure the regular participation of pupils. The programme of Elective Activities is aimed at the learning and mastery of work skills and habits which are much more important at this stage than at the lower primary stage. Under this programme a number of related activities arising out of pupil community needs and problems have been put in such a way that they can assume the form of a project to be completed in shorter or longer duration.

General Observations

The suggested curriculum seems to be an appropriate one. It duly takes note of the 'Information and Technology Revolution'. It is also based on national concerns. The approach is idealistic as well as pragmatic.

Exercise

1. What is Curriculum reconstruction ?
2. What are main objectives of education ?
3. What are national needs of education ?

16

Evaluation Techniques

Meaning of Evaluation

The word 'Evaluation' in place of the word 'Examination' is now being increasingly used in current educational literature. The evaluation process is not restricted to the result of tests and examinations, scales and inventories and such other gadgets as employed by the teacher, but it has a wider meaning. It includes the learner's own estimate also.

In traditional examinations, the emphasis is on the cognitive (knowledge of subjects) aspect only whereas evaluation includes non-cognitive (attitudes and values) aspects also. Evaluation is concerned with all the changes that take place in the development of a balanced personality. It measures the qualities of the head, the hand, and the heart. Evaluation takes into account the development or changes in 7 Rs, i.e., reading, writing, arithmetic, rights, responsibilities, relationships and recreation.

Evaluation is undertaken to find out 'how' a child is learning and 'how' learning can be improved rather than 'what' he has learnt. The primary purpose of evaluation should not be limited to declaring children 'pass' or 'fail' but to identify the strengths and weaknesses, and making good of deficiencies and making improvements.

Comprehensive evaluation includes changes in the following aspects:

1. Achievement in academic subjects.
2. Achievement in skills.
3. Achievement in attitudes and values which include: cultural, ethical, moral, physical and social.

According to Wrightstone, "Evaluation is a relatively new technical term introduced to design a more comprehensive concept of measurement that is implied in conventional tests and examinations."

In the words of Clara M. Brown, "Evaluation is essential in the never ending cycle of formulating goals, measuring progress towards them and determining the new goals which emerge as a result of new warning."

Aims of Evaluation. According to Reavis and others the evaluation should be effective in the following spheres in addition to the usual aims of classification and promotion :

1. Providing a periodic check that will direct along definite lines on the continued improvement of the programme of the school.
2. Giving everyone working with pupils the information that is necessary to provide guidance and counsel for boys and girls.
3. Securing help in validating the function and the goal that the school strives to attain in determining the programme upon which the school operates.
4. Providing a sound basis for good public relation to secure an understanding on the part of a community of the school and its effectiveness. Such an evaluation will meet many of the criticism of the school expressed by the parents, tax-payers and others because they do not know what the school is attempting to be.
5. Providing a sense of security to members of the school staff, to pupils, and to their parents so that they have

tangible evidence that the programme they are operating is an effective one.

Principles of Evaluation. Grim has suggested the following principles of evaluation:

1. In evaluation a complete picture may be taken into consideration as in learning the total personality is involved. Evaluation must take into consideration the difference in intelligence stage and rate of maturity, etc., and make proper allowance for these.
2. The effective appraisal demands that reliable, varied, and relatively evidence be gathered.
3. Evaluation should enable the pupil to appraise himself.
4. The teacher, the parents, the pupils, the community and the administration all must participate in evaluation
5. Evaluation to be effective must be continuous and cumulative.
6. Evaluation system must be closely related to the guidance programme.

Evaluation and Examination Compared. Examination measures academic achievement only. Evaluation endeavours to measures many-sided development of the personality of the child. Evaluation is concerned with the continuous growth and development of the individual whereas the sphere of examination is very limited. Examination depends for its data on achievement tests whereas evaluation uses many tools. Examination measures the knowledge acquired whereas evaluation is also concerned with the attitudes formed by the child.

Triangle of Objective, Learning Experience and Evaluation. There is an inter-relatedness between objectives (ends), learning experiences (means) and evaluation (evidence). Objectives remain central to both learning experience and evaluation. Learning experiences are also planned in terms of objectives. At every point of learning evaluation is an attempt to discover the extent of the effectiveness of the learning situation in bringing about desired changes in students.

Points to be Remembered in Evaluation: One cannot pass judgement on students by just testing them at the end of a course of instruction. The change occurs over a period of time and therefore no single appraisal can tell us completely of the change. It is necessary to determine the status of a student at the starting point. Then at periodical intervals evaluations have to be made and changes identified in comparison with his position at the starting point.

In Evaluation

1. One has to know where students were at the beginning if we are to determine what changes are occurring.
2. One has to obtain a record of the changes in pupils by using appropriate methods of appraisal.
3. One has to judge how good the changes are in the light of the evidence obtained.

What is a Good Evaluation Device? A good evaluation device or tool or method is one which can secure valid evidence of the desired change of behaviour. It is not synonymous with paper or pencil tests. It evaluates one specific performance of a student by rating his behaviour as it progresses and to sum up many casual observations of a student over a period of time.

Things that Teacher should Remember. In using a variety of evaluation techniques, the teacher must remember that :

1. The choice of the tool depends on the types of evidence sought.
2. Informal methods of evaluation are needed to supplement the evidence gained through formal paper pencil tests, and
3. The information secured through informal device is as important as that obtained by the use of formal written tests.

Useful in Many Ways

1. Evaluation appraises the status of and changes in pupil behaviour.

2. Evaluation discloses pupil's needs and possibilities.
3. Evaluation aids pupil-teacher planning.
4. Evaluation expands the concept of worthwhile goals beyond pure achievement.
5. Evaluation serves as a means of improving school-community relation.
6. Evaluation familiarizes the teacher with the nature of pupil learning, development and progress.
7. Evaluation relates measurement to the goals of the instructional programme.
8. Evaluation facilitates the selection and improvement of measuring instruments.
9. Evaluation appraises the teacher's competence.
10. Evaluation appraises the supervisor's competence.
11. Evaluation serves as a guiding principle for the selection of supervisory techniques.

Modern Evaluation Techniques

Fairly exhaustive techniques have been designed by educationists to evaluate the various aspects of child's growth. Following are the commonly used techniques:

1. Intelligence tests.
2. Achievement tests.
3. Aptitude tests.
4. Personality tests.
5. Tests of attitude and behaviour.
6. Rating scales.
7. Questionnaires and check lists.
8. Interview.
9. Anecdotal records.
10. Autobiographical method.
11. Pupils' diary.

12. Case history.
13. Sociometric techniques.
14. Protective techniques.

Formative and Summative Evaluation

Scriven (1967) has classified two types of evaluation on the bases of their roles—the formative and summative roles. Formative evaluation is described as evaluation used for the on-going improvement of a process. It is designed to enhance the teaching-learning process. The summative role of evaluation is described as evaluation of a finished product which has been refined by the use of formative evaluation Summative evaluation is concerned with making final judgment. Each situation needs to be examined to arrive at a proper balance between formative assessment and summative assessment.

Traditional Examination

Today, we hear a lot of talk of the abolition of the present system of examinations. There is no denying the fact that the present system of examinations is outmoded and outdated as it does not fit in the needs of present times. Still in the absence of any other system which may help us in evaluating the achievements of the child in a more systematic and scientific manner, it would not be wise to abolish the present system of examination.

Importance of the Examination. Its importance can hardly be minimised. The examinations have been in existence since times immemorial. "To close down examinations would be given to the signal for educational saturnalia", observed Sir Michael Sadler.

Similarly J.C. Mathur emphasises the value of examinations when he writes, "Even in the idealised picture of society portrayed in H.G. Well's Utopia, examinations find an important place."

The Secondary Education Commission has also observed, "Nevertheless examination—and especially external examinations—have a proper place in any scheme of education. External examinations have stimulating effect both on the pupils and on the teachers by providing well defined goals and objective standards of evaluation. To the pupil the examination gives a goal towards which he should strive and a stimulus urging him to attain that goal in a given time, thereby demanding steady and constant effort. This makes the purpose clear and the method of approach definite. He is judged by external and objective tests on which both he and others interested in him can depend. And finally it gives him a hallmark recognised by all." The Commission thinks that the examinations provide a goal and a stimulus to the teachers also. The external examination gives him standards common for all teachers and therefore, universal and uniform in character.

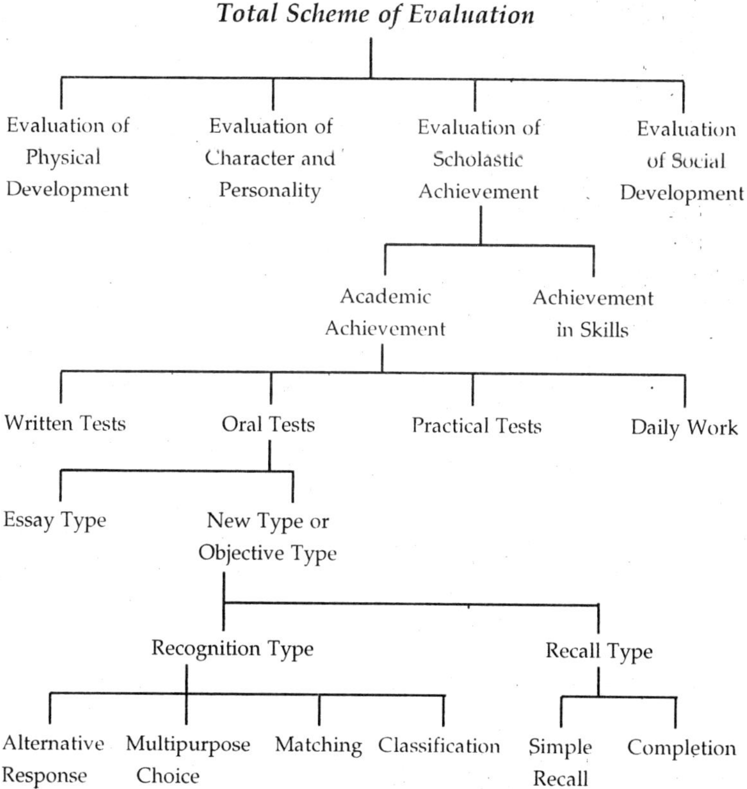

Functions of Examination

To Evaluate the Achievements of the Students. The abilities and the achievements of the students must be evaluated. Examinations are conducted to discover whether or not the child has been able to acquire a certain amount of knowledge or skill.

To Measure Personality. They are used to test the power of clear thinking, quickness of mind, calmness and perseverance.

To Measure the Efficiency of Teachers and of the School. They provide a suitable occasion for the authorities to measure the efficiency of the teachers. The efficiency of the institution is also measured through the examinations. They provide a proper occasion to the teachers to know whether or not their methods of teaching are appropriate.

To Help in Diagnosis. They help parents to know the progress of their children. They help to discover the specific weak points of an individual or class and thus give an opportunity to the teachers as well as to the taught to remove these defects.

To Act as Incentives. Stimulation to work hard is provided to the students through the institution of examinations. Some objectives are placed before the students and for the realisation of those objectives the students develop in them the habits of constant hard work.

To Help in Prognosis. The examinations have a prognostic value also. With this device the aptitude of the students are determined.

To give Uniformity of Standard. The external examinations facilitate the problem of uniformity of standards attained by the students of the different institutions.

To Help in Guidance. They facilitate the work of grouping individuals for the purpose of teaching by bringing those together who have more or less the same attainment.

To Measure Fitness for Admission to Higher Courses. They are designed to determine the capacity and fitness of the candidates to pursue higher courses of general or professional study or training. Examinations which serve this purpose are called Entrance or Qualifying Examinations.

To Help in Selection by Competition. The examinations are also conducted to select the best candidates for appointment to public services or for award to prizes and scholarships.

Defects of the Examinations

Examinations are bad masters when they begin to dominate our educational thoughts and practices. W.M. Ryburn strongly criticises them when he writes: "It goes without saying that examinations are the enemies of creative work at least as they are usually conducted.

Similar opinion has been expressed by the University Education Commission when it remarks, "For nearly half a century the examination has been recognised as one of the worst features of Indian Education."

Epithets Given to Examinations

1. An enemy of true education.
2. An incubus.
3. An obstacle to learning.
4. A blood sucker.
5. A bane of educational system.
6. A necessary evil.
7. A glorification of memory.
8. A begetter of rivalry and strife.
9. A dead hand of education.
10. A growing tyranny.
11. A presumptuous attempt to gauge the depth of human ignorance.

The main defects are as under:

Element of Chance. It decides the fate of a large number of students. It is often found that some students prepare a few selected questions and leave everything to chance. If per chance, the same questions are set in the examinations, they pass with credit. Have they actually attained the requisite standard? Perhaps not!

Now take another case of a student who has been regular in his work throughout the year but unfortunately falls sick near the examination. This may cost him one precious year.

Failure in one subject means a loss of one year, however brilliant student may be in other subjects. It is not appropriate and is not in conformity with the progressive view of education.

Lowering of Moral Standard. They adversely affect the moral standard of the students. They teach them different ways of becoming dishonest. Books are smuggled into the Examination Halls. False medical certificates are furnished. Sometimes the strength of the purse also plays its role in getting marks increased.

Lowering of Educational Standard. The efficiency of a teacher is judged by the pass percentage of the results. The teachers adopt the tricks for the trade to improve their results. 'Idea of exam', the sole aim and 'cram' the only method, dominates the entire educational system. According to the Secondary Education Commission, the examinations determine not only the contents of education but also the methods of teaching— in fact, the entire approach to education. They have so pervaded the entire atmosphere of school life that they have become the main motivating force of all effort on the part of pupils as well as teachers. "We are convinced that our system of education is very much examination ridden," writes the Commission.

Glorification of Memory. Examinations are a glorification of memory and do not test the real ability. The students are interested in only those methods which enable them to pass rather than in those which may be educationally more sound. They are more interested in notes and cribes than in next books and original works. They go in for cramming them rather for intelligent understanding. The examinations are in fact "an obstacle to learning'. W.M. Ryburn writes, "It goes without saying that examinations are the enemies of creative work at least as they are usually conducted.

Ignore Quality of Character. They do not provide any measure to test the originality, initiative, truthfulness, honesty, sociability of an individual and without these, true aim of education is not achieved. Our examinations are limited in their scope and do not test the many important aspects of the pupil's development.

Subjectivity. Subjective attitude of examiners influences the marks of individuals and leads to a great variability in marking. Dr. William called the examiner a 'mysterious person'. It is said that anything surprising may happen in his hands. A deserving candidate may fail and an undeserving candidate may pass. If it is asked to mark the same paper once more at a different time, there is every likelihood that he may get a different result. If another examiner is asked to mark the same paper, a different result may be arrived at. Results are influenced greatly by the moods, whims and fancies of the examiners. Vernon points out, "The same script might receive a different mark if read after instead of before dinner.

Heavy Mental Strain. They put a heavy mental strain on the students during the examination days. Moreover, they stimulate an unhealthy competitive spirit among children. They are known as 'a begetter of rivalry and strife.'

Frustration. Failures in examinations lead to frustration and to suicides in some cases.

Lack of any Definite Aim. Neither the examiners nor the examinees are aware of the purposes of the examinations. Mohiyuddin writes, "Business firms wanting employees look at the results of the examination, the high schools base their admission on it, and Government accepts it as a passport to all departments of service. There are no specific mental or moral traits and disabilities, that the ordinary examination seeks to discover and measure; and there is, therefore, no definite guidance it can offer to the professions, business houses, and higher educational institutions."

The Remedies

We have already discussed that these examinations are very important in the educational set-up. The only thing that is required is to reform them. They cannot be ended but can only be mended. To mitigate the shortcomings of the examinations, following reforms are recommended;

Introduction of New Types of Tests. Attempts should be made to minimise the subjective element. Essay type questions should be reduced and supplemented by new type of objective tests.

Thought-provoking Questions. Questions should be thought-provoking and evenly distributed over the entire course. Questions should be such as to discourage cramming.

Class Work. Due consideration should be given to the regularity of the students in class work.

Appointment of Examiners. The paper-setters and examiners for external examinations should be drawn from the teachers who actually teach subjects in schools.

Viva Voce Tests. External examinations may be supplemented by viva voce tests, if possible.

Standard of Marking. Standard of marking should be prescribed so as to minimise the variability in marking.

Balanced Questions. Difficult as well as easy questions should find a place in the question papers. These should not be either too difficult or too easy.

Monthly Tests. Instead of terminal examinations, a systems of monthly tests should exist. However, a recapitulatory test may be held at the end of the year.

Faith in the Teacher. The teacher should be trusted. He should be given a fair opportunity to know and study closely the pupils in his charge. His recommendations should find an important place while evaluating the achievements of the students through essay type or objective type tests. The Norwood Committee Report on Curriculum and Secondary Schools in England made the following observations, "No one can examine better than the teacher who knows the child."

Cumulative Record. The maintenance of cumulative record will be very helpful in evaluating the achievements of the students in different spheres, such as, social, literary, etc.

Reduction in the Number of Examinations. The number of external examinations should be reduced.

Symbolic Rather than Numerical Marking. The symbolic rather than numerical marking should be adoped for evaluating and grading the work of the pupil in external and internal examinations and in maintaining the school records. Instead of allotting marks, say, 50 or 70, five points scale of symbolic marking, i.e., 'A' for excellent, 'B' for good, 'C for fair and average, 'D' for poor and 'E' for very poor should be introduced.

Compartmental Examinations. The system of compartmental examinations at the final public examination is very helpful.

New Certificate. The certificate awarded by the examining authority to the pupils who complete the school courses and take the final examination should contain, besides the results of the school tests in subjects not included in this public examination as well as the gist of the school records.

No Compulsory Public Examination. The final public examination may not be compulsory for all, that is, if pupils so desire, they need not take it. However every pupil who completes the school course will get a school certificate based on school records testifying to his progress and attainments in different directions in school.

DIFFERENT TYPES

Essay Types. These may be classified into the undermentioned two categories:

External or Public Examinations—These are conducted by those outside teachers who have no direct hand in the preparation of the examinees.

Internal Examinations—These are conducted by those teachers who are teaching the examinees. These are held quarterly, half-yearly, yearly as the case may be.

Oral or Viva Voce. In an oral examination, evaluation regarding the capacities of the students is made at the spur of the moment. Most of the appointments to the various posts, public or private, are made through the oral examination. If sufficient time is devoted to these tests, there is every possibility that the evaluation may be a fair one. But in actual practice, not much attention is paid to this aspect. The subjective element also plays a dominant role. Chances of favouritism are quite high.

Practical. Practical tests are held to evaluate the progress made by individuals in certain skills. Tests in science practicals are the well-known examples of this type in school work. Driving licences are also issued after assessing the practical skill in driving a car, a bus or any vehicle of this kind.

Modern or Objective. Such tests are of recent origin. They may also be called by the name of short answer tests.

Systematic Observation by the Teachers. Teachers from time to time observe students.

Achievement Tests

The Meaning

By an achievement test, we mean the test of academic performance of a student such as in English or Hindi etc. An achievement test is a measure of learning itself and an intelligence test is a measure of learning capacity.

General Purposes of Achievement Tests. These can be used for the following purposes:

(i) To diagnose students' strengths and weaknesses,

(ii) To motivate students,

(iii) To predict future progress,

(iv) To report to the parents,

(v) To reflect teaching effectiveness,

(vi) To admit students,

(vii) To grant awards and scholarships.

Practical Uses

Administrator's Use

1. Tests help to evaluate the extent to which the objectives of education are being achieved.
2. Tests help to classify school objectives.
3. Tests discover the type of learning experiences that will achieve these objectives with the best possible results.
4. To evaluate, revise and improve the curriculum in the light of these results.
5. To discover backward children who need help and to plan for remedial instruction for such students.
6. To select talented pupils for special classes and courses.
7. To decide proper classification of students.
8. To get a better understanding of the needs and abilities of pupils.
9. To select students for the award of special merits or scholarships.
10. To group pupils in a class so that students are put in such a way that individual differences are as slight as possible.
11. To help the parents in recognising the strengths and weaknesses of their children so that they direct their energies on suitable goals only and do not put heavy demands on them.
12. To determine the efficiency of one school with others.
13. To determine the general level of achievement of a class and thus to judge the teaching efficiency of the teacher. The level of achievement of a class may be judged on the basis of the achievement of the class in the beginning and at the end of the school year.

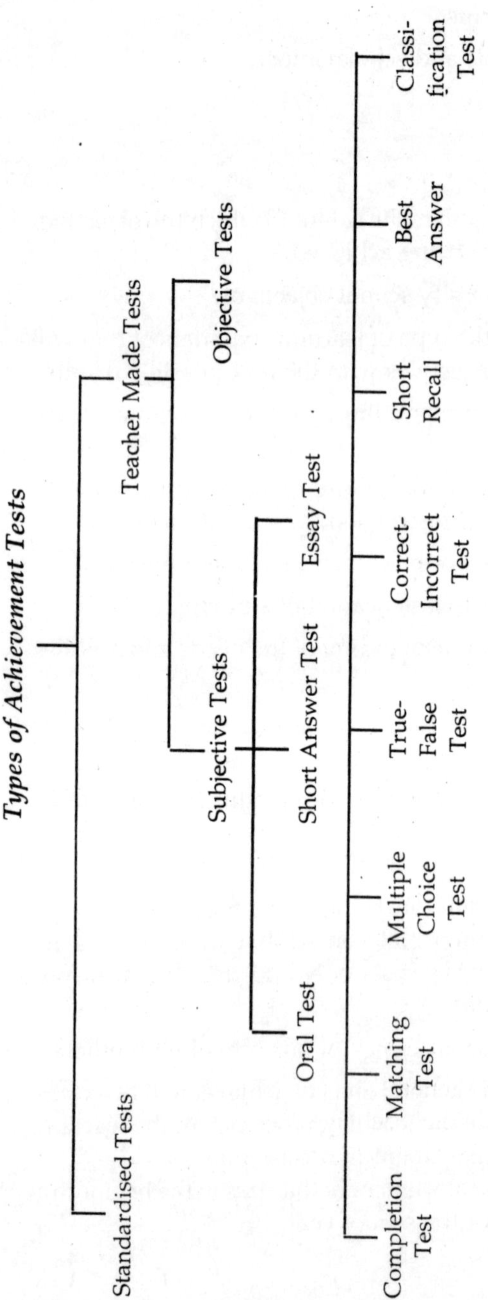
Types of Achievement Tests
Teacher Made Tests
Standardised Tests
Objective Tests
Subjective Tests
Essay Test
Short Answer Test
Oral Test
Classi-fication Test
Best Answer
Short Recall
Correct-Incorrect Test
True-False Test
Multiple Choice Test
Matching Test
Completion Test

The Teacher's Use

1. The teacher will come to know the general range of abilities of students in the class.
2. In the light of above, he will select appropriate materials of instruction so that all individuals benefit from instruction to the maximum.
3. The teacher will determine and diagnose the weakness of the students in various subjects.
4. The teacher will spot out brilliant and backward children.
5. He will determine the progress of the group in a particular subject over a period of time.
6. By studying the results of the students on achievement tests and intelligence tests, the teacher will determine whether or not the students are working at their maximum capacity.

Different Forms

Tests vary according to form, use and type. Yoakaya and Simpson give the following classification of tests:

Form

(a) Oral examinations, (b) Written examinations.

Purpose

(a) Prognostic, (b) Diagnostic, (c) Power, (d) Speed, (e) Accuracy, (f) Quality, (g) Range.

Organisation

(a) Essay, (b) Objective.

Period or Time of Administering

(a) Daily, (b) Weekly, (c) Monthly, (d) Term, (e) Yearly.

Duration

(a) Short, (b) Long.

Method of Scoring and Interpreting Results

(a) Non-standardized, (b) Standardized.

Abilities Involved

(a) Speed, (b) Comprehension, (c) Organization, (d) Judgement, (e) Retention, (f) Appreciation, etc.

Nature of Material Included

(a) Arithmetic, (b) Language, (c) Reading, (d) Spelling, (e) Writing etc.

Mental Functions Involved

(a) Association, (b) Memory, (c) Recall, (d) Recognition. (e) Problem-solving.

Types of Response Involved

(a) Alternate response: (1) True—False, (2) Yes—No, (3) Plus —Minus.

(b) Multiple response: (1) Best answer, (2) Correct answer.

(c) Completion, (d) Matching, (e) Identification, (f) Enumeration, (g) Essay.

OBJECTIVE TYPES

Objective tests are of a large variety. However, only seven or eight types of the objective tests are commonly employed.

Matching Test. Under column A, names of certain books and under B, names of certain authors are given. Write down the names of the right authors under column C.

	A	B	C
(i)	Meghaduta	Ashvaghosha	———
(ii)	Budha Charitam	Megasthenes	———
(iii)	Indica	Kalidasa	———

Multiple Choice Tests. Below are given a few questions. Against each are given a number of answers. One of these is correct. Underline the same.

Example—Who was Kalidas? King, Poet or Scientist.

True-False Tests. Certain statements are given below. Against each statement two words are mentioned, e.g., true and false. Underline the correct one:

Example—People used to lock their houses during the Mauryan Period. (True/False)

Correct/Incorrect Tests. Some sentences are given below. Against each are mentioned two words, i.e.. Correct and Incorrect. Underline the correct one.

Example—He has been absent from the school from last Saturday. (Correct/Incorrect)

I prefer English to French. (Correct/Incorrect)

Simple Recall Test. Write in one word the answer of the following:

Example—What is the per capita income in India? Best Answer Test. Put mark against the best answer.

Example—Alexander did not proceed further because:

(i) he did not know the route,

(ii) his forces refused to go further,

(iii) he was defeated by some king.

Completion Test. Fill in the blank by appropriate word(s) in the following:

To be wealth, a thing must have scarcity, utility and......

Classification Test. In each line, underline the word that does not belong there.

Example—Harbour, trade, export, import, mountain.

Limitations. Objective tests also have their limitations. They encourage guess work. They do not test ability to organise and discuss a problem.

THE PRINCIPLES

E.W. Menzel observes that whether old-type or new-type, we observe among others the following principles:

1. It will be general and comprehensive enough to test thoroughly the pupil's mastery of the desired skills or grasp of a subject-matter.
2. It will reliably grade the pupils into at least six to ten (or more) different classifications according to their ability.
3. It will be as objective as practicable. Some questions of a discussional nature can be given to advantage but there should also be some work which pins pupil and examiner down to answers which can be quite objectively scored. Even in the essay type of examination, the objectivity can be greatly increased with study and care.
4. Other things being equal, the test which examines most intensively or extensively in the least time and with the least fatigue on the part of the pupil is the best.
5. The test should encourage creative and self-reliant work and discourage mere mechanical rote-memory work.
6. The test should encourage the pupil to put forth his best effort.
7. The test should convincingly reveal to the pupil his deficiencies and encourage him to remove them.
8. The test should examine exactly what it pretends to examine.
9. The standard of a test should be based on actual performance and not upon mere opinion of what a standard should be or an arbitrary percentage work.
10. The more a test makes it possible to compare the performance of a certain groups of pupils to that of other pupils the more revealing it is.
11. No test is infallable. The daily work of the pupil and an observation of his habits of work are equally important in appraising the work and ability of a pupil.
12. Poor results on the part of a group of pupils indicate a faulty test or one that is not graded to the ability of the pupils or deals with matters the children have not been taught.

17

School System

A study of the elementary structure of education in the country will indicate that there is no uniformity as regards the age of entry and duration of this stage. This context the National Policy has observed in Para 3 of Part III as, "The National System of Education envisages a common educational structure. The 10+2+3 structure has now been accepted in all parts of the country. Regarding the further break-up of the first 10 years efforts will be made to move towards an elementary system comprising 5 years of primary education and 3 years of upper primary, followed by 2 years of High School.

A publication of the NCERT entitled National Curriculum of Elementary and Secondary Education; 'A Frame Work' (1988) has used the terms elementary education (8 years), divided into primary stage (5 years) and upper primary stage (3 years).

Earlier the Education Commission 1964-66 used the term lower primary school stage (classes I—IV/V) and the upper primary school stage (classes V/VI-VII/VIII).

The Article 45 of the Constitution does not mention any term. It states. "The State shall endeavour to provide, within a period of ten years from the commencement of the Constitution, for free and compulsory education for all children until they complete the age of fourteen years".

There has been a good deal of variation in the years of schoolings for the two stages. In 1986-87, there were six types of educational structures.

Six Types of Educational Structures

	State	Primary	Upper Primary
Pattern I	Andhra Pradesh	I—V	VI—VII
Pattern II	Arunachal, Bihar, Haryana, Himachal, Jammu and Kashmir, Madhya Pradesh, Manipur, Orissa, Punjab, Rajasthan, Tamil Nadu, Tripura, Uttar pradesh, West Bengal, A. and N. Islands, Chandigarh, Delhi, Pondicherry.	I —V	VI—VIII
Pattern III	Assam, Goa, Karnataka, Kerala, Gujarat, Maharashtra, Dadra and Nagar Haveli, Daman and Diu, Lakshadeep.	I—IV	VI—VII
		A B	
Pattern IV	Meghalaya	I—III	IV—VI
Pattern V	Mizoram	I—IV	V—VII
Pattern VI	Nagaland	I—IV	V—VIII

Generally speaking elementary school organisation refers to the combination of two stages of education—primary stage of education covering classes I to V (Age Group 6 to 11) and upper primary covering Classes VI to VIII (Age Group 11 to 14). Thus the elementary stage covers 8 classes from I to VIII and age group 6 to 14.

The Facilities

Among the primary schools, 71495 (13.50%) were without buildings, they were run in thatched huts, tents or in open space. of the rest, 385120 (72.75%) primary schools had pucca or partly pucca buildings. Others were in Kachha buildings. Among upper primary schools 121707 (86.79%) had pucca or partly pucca buildings and 11280 (8,13%) schools had Kachcha buildings."

Further among the primary schools, 40732 (7.69%), 200077 (37.79%), and 134551 (25.42%) had zero instructional room, one instructional room and two instructional rooms respectively. In case of upper primary schools, 3192 schools had no instructional room and 24909 had one or two instructional rooms.

73.70% of the upper primary schools were either run by the government or by local bodies. However more than 50% upper primary schools in the States of Kerala (65.77%), Maghalaya (85.56%), Mizoram (72.14%), Orissa (90.13%) and in West Bengal were private aided schools.

Percentage of primary schools with one teacher, two teachers, three teachers, four teachers and five or more teachers was 34.75%, 27.27%, 15.10%, 8.16% and 14.10% respectively.

Schools According to Management

Category	*Number of Schools*	*% of Total*
Primary Schools Government	219837	41.53
Local Body Schools	251699	47.54
Private Aided Schools	44701	8.44
Private Unaided Schools	13155	2.49

Note: 52.70% primary schools in Andhra Pradesh and 58.84% in Kerala were private aided schools. In other states, majority of the primary schools were government or local body schools.

Control and Support

Government schools are run by the State Governments and the Local Bodies Schools run by Municipal Corporation, Municipal Committee, Cantonment Boards or District Boards. Education is free in these schools. These schools have been established for fulfilling the obligation to provide for free and compulsory education to all children upto the age of 14 as stipulated under article 45 of the Constitution. Elementary education is also free in aided elementary schools. These schools have been set up primarily by specific sections of the society. Article 30 (1) of the Constitution provides for the setting up institutions by the minority groups, whether based on religion or language. Various voluntary organisations run these institutions.

Textbooks used in the government schools, local bodies schools and by and large in private aided elementary schools are prescribed by the Education Departments of the States.

Private schools which do not get any grant from the government or local bodies are usually called public schools or private non-aided schools. These schools charge fees and accept donations. They are governed by rules framed under Education Codes. The medium of instruction is generally English. Public schools enjoy a good deal of freedom in various matters. Many of the public schools are residential. These schools attract children from rich homes.

Single Teacher Schools—About one third of primary schools are single teacher schools. Such schools pose many organisational and academic problems. Because of the remote location of these schools, it is found difficult to provide a substitute teacher when the teacher proceeds on leave for a day or two. Frequent absence of the teacher adversely affects the working of the school and students and their parents lose interest in studies. Teachers working in these schools are not specifically trained to handle specific problems. In pursuance of the National Policy on Education, arrangements are being made to provide one additional teacher preferably a woman in single teacher schools.

Role of the Government

Prior to 1976, education was a state subject and thereafter all education became a concurrent subject. The Government of India has undertaken a few centrally sponsored schemes for the promotion of elementary education in the country. Nevertheless-elementary education is financed mainly through resources of the State Governments. Local bodies and voluntary organisations also work in this field.

Sixteen States and three Union Territories have passed legislation on compulsory education. These States are: Andhra Pradesh, Assam, Gujarat, Haryana, Himachal Pradesh, Jammu and Kashmir, Karnataka, Kerala, Madhya Pradesh, Maharashlra, Orissa, Punjab, Rajasthan, Tamil Nadu, Uttar Pradesh and West Bengal. The Union

Territories are: Andaman and Nicobar Islands, Chandigarh and Delhi.

The State prescribes the pay scales and other service conditions for teachers. It also provides for their training.

The State prescribes curricula and textbooks. Most of the States have nationalised textbook.

For inspection and supervision, State Governments maintain some staff even when the power to supervise is delegated to local bodies.

In addition to the above mentioned functions, State Government also performs functions in respect of its local bodies similar to those which the Government of India performs towards the State Governments, particularly in the context of allocation of resources and maintenance of standards and targets of achievement.

Each State maintains a Department or a Directorate of Education for administration of elementary education. The Director of Public Instruction or Director of Education (Various Nomenclatures) is the seniormost officer in the Directorate and is assisted by a number of other officers in the discharge of his duties. The Education Secretary or the Education Commissioner takes policy decisions in the field of school education. There is a growing tendency to post I.A.S. Officers as Secretary and Director of Education. There is a network of officers who run the administration at various levels — regional, district and block In some States, a separate cadre of Inspectors/Education Officers at the elementary level has been created.

As regards role of local bodies in elementary education, controversies have existed since 1882 when the Indian Education Commission first proposed the transfer of primary education to local bodies. The delegation of powers for administration of elementary education to local bodies varies from State to State. States like Maharashtra, Rajasthan and Andhra Pradesh have delegated large powers to local bodies for the administration of elementary education.

In inspection and supervision, emphasis has shifted from 'authoritarianism' to 'human relationships'. The inspectors and supervisors are expected to play the role of friends, guides and philosophers.

Exercise

1. Describe the elementary system of education of your State with reference to grant-in-aid and supervision.
2. Do you think it is desirable to allow public schools to run? Reflect on their role in the promotion of an egalitarian and socialist pattern of society.
3. Suggest measures for the efficient running of single teacher schools.

18

In House Cooperation

Importance of the Head

As is the Head, so is the School. The head occupies a very strategic position in the school. There is no doubt that schools are good or bad, in healthy or unhealthy mental, moral and physical conditions, flourishing or perishing as the headmaster is capable, energetic, and of high ideals or the reverse. Schools rise to fame or sink to obscurity as greater or lesser headmasters have charge of them. P. C. Wren thinks that the character of the school reflects and proclaims the character of the headmaster. The head is the seal and the school is the wax'. He is the nexus between the government and the school authorities; the management and the staff, the master and the pupils, and the parents and the teachers. He is the strategic centre of instructional inter-relationship—teacher-pupil, teacher-teacher, teacher-supervisor and teacher-parent. He is a link between internal and external administration. He is the keystone of the arch of school management and administration.

Will Flrench and others stress the role of a principal as, "If a teacher fails, the principal fails, if the teacher succeeds, the principal succeeds. To sum up, what the principal's job is, we may call him a referee—the captain of the ship—the boss of the firm—a juvenile judge before whose tribunal come not only the culprits but the adults who frequently contribute to the pupils' shortcoming. He is a promoter who must project the future of his institution and convert the public to his plan. He is a social physician to every parent who has a wayward son who needs attention. He is a friend in need to pupils and to all the homes in which misfortune comes. His power, his activities, even the good he does, cannot be measured by a measuring yardstick."

General Grant is said to have remarked that there are no poor regiments but poor colonels. Sultan Mohi-ud-din rightly states that no school can succeed if the teachers in it work only as individuals and not as a group. But just as every group needs a leader, so also a school must have a leader who would stimulate and direct its work. Such a leader is the Headmaster. And so is the case with the school. He is the hub of the education process. The success of the school system depends on his ability and skill as a sound and effective educational leader. The success or the failure of the school depends upon its Headmasters. "As is the Headmaster, so is the school." Great Headmasters make schools great. "The reputation of the school and position that it holds in the society depends in a large measure on the influence that he exercises over his colleagues, the pupils and their parents and the general public," observed the Secondary Education Commission. W. M. Ryburn compares the position of the Headmaster in a school to the Captain of a ship. P. C. Wren sums up the importance of the job of the Headmaster, "What the main spring is to the watch the fly wheel to the machine or the engine to the steamship, the Headmaster is to the school." It is stated, "He is an organiser, leader, governor, business director, coordinator, superintendent, teacher, guide, philosopher and friend."

Delicate Role of the Head. In the past the duties of the Head were confined mostly to routine work at school and beyond that he had practically no responsibilities. The new ideal of education entails heavy responsibilities. Now he is required not only to deal with correspondence, office work, scholar's register and cash books but also to discharge his duties to the society. Besides academic achievement of the students, he is required to look after their cultural, emotional, moral and physical development. He has to co-ordinate the efforts of teachers, students and the community at large.

The functions of Headmaster are very complex. He has to supervise each and every activity in the school. He has to play a very delicate and critical role. He has always to work with four varied interest of small groups: pupils, people, teachers and the authorities. He has often to come across and strike a balance in the practical fields among quarrelling and fighting students, grudging teachers, complaining parents and exacting departments. He is expected at various times and by various interests to play different roles. He must, by nature of his position, be—

1. A teacher of teachers. 2. A superviser not only of teachers but of service personnel. 3. A disciplinarian, just but effective. 4. A psychologist at least to the extent of being able to detect maladjustments, especially of teachers, which definitely hinder effective instruction or achievement of desired educational goals. A Financer in organising a budget. 6. A Lawyer at least to the extent of knowing his own obligations, rights and legal abilities as well as of those of all school personnel. 7. A Sociologist to the extent of at least being able to understand the relation of school with a social force. 8. A technical expert—in educational measurement and evaluation. 9. An expert in group dynamics to the extent of working effectively with staff, pupils, public and the authorities.

What is the Head Like?

1. The Head is the hub of the education process.
2. The Head is the leader of the school.
3. The Head is the seal and the school is the wax.
4. The Head is like the main spring of the watch.
5. The Head is like the flywheel to the machine.
6. The Head is like the engine of the steamship.
7. The Head is a liaison.
8. The Head is the strategic centre.
9. The Head is the solar orb.

10. The Head is a link.
11. The Head is a key-stone.
12. The Head is a social physician.

Duties and Responsibilities

The duties and responsibilities of the head are manifold and in fact he is concerned with each and every activity of the school. In the words of an educationist, "He should be a man who has finger on the pulse of the school, aware of the slightest rise in tempo."

Following are the six major duties and responsibilities of the head of an institution:

I. Duties and responsibilities relating to administrative matters.
II. Duties and responsibilities relating to supervision of teaching-learning programme.
III. Duties and responsibilities relating to educational leadership and human relations.
IV. Duties and responsibilities relating to students.
V. Duties and responsibilities relating to the community.
VI. Duties and responsibilities relating to the managing committee of the school and Department of education.

Duties and Responsibilities Relating to Administrative Matters

School Office

1. The head should see that a spacious, airy and well-furnished room is provided for the school office.
2. The head should ensure that the records are properly and systematically maintained and kept up-to-date.
3. The head should go through 'dak' carefully.
4. The head should be prompt in correspondence.
5. He should not, as far as possible, entrust office work to teachers.

6. He should provide every facility to teachers to use school office as service agency.

Time-table

1. He should see that school time-table is kept properly and the bell is rung at the appointed time.
2. He should take care to see that the school time-table is operative on the very opening day of the school.
3. He should equalize working load of teachers as far as possible.
4. He should make routine administrative assignments fairly to all teachers.
5. He should arrange his time and work in office in such a way that teachers may see him conveniently as often as necessary.
6. He should prepare the school time-table in consultation with teachers.
7. He should make school time-table suitable to local conditions.

School Budget

1. He should have the school budget for the whole school year carefully prepared well in advance.
2. The pupils as well as teachers should be allowed to participate in the preparation of the parts of the school budget which concern co-curricular activities.
3. He should see that provision is made in the school budget for all regular and anticipated needs so that the necessity of reallocations and re-appropriations may be minimised during the school year.

School Supplies

1. He should purchase educational supplies, viz., paper, pencils, pens, ink, chalk, dusters, blackboard, paint and laboratory chemicals, etc., only from reliable firms in accordance with rules.

2. He should invariably ask the firms to submit specimens of the commodities to be purchased.
3. He should always insist on purchasing matérials of good quality for use in the school,

School Plants

1. He should make arrangements for checking the cleanliness of class-rooms, laboratory, library, and play-ground regularly.
2. He should see that pupils' desks and seats and other articles of furniture in the school are kept in proper repair.
3. He should see that toilet and lavatory arrangements are suitable and adequate to the needs of the school.
4. He should see that the supply of drinking water is adequate for students and staff and it is maintained in proper sanitary condition.
5. He should see that school building is kept in good condition.
6. He should see that the school campus looks beautiful and attractive with shady trees, ornamental bushes, hedges and ornamental flower plants.

School Library

1. The principal should see that the school library is made a functional part of the school.
2. He should see that the person incharge of the library is well acquainted with the class room programmes.
3. He should see that adequate instructions are made available to the pupils on the use of the library.

Duties Relating to Supervision of 'Teaching-Learning' Programme

1. The principal should regularly pay supervisory visits to the class-rooms to acquaint himself with the learning situations provided to pupils.

2. He should stay in the class-room long enough to get an adequate picture of the teaching-learning situations of the class.
3. He should not interfere with the regular class work during his supervisory visits.
4. He should inspire confidence and friendliness in the teacher by his attitude during the class visit.
5. He should supervise not only class-room instructions but other activities of the school also.
6. His class visits should result in practical assistance to teacher.
7. He should regularly arrange for demonstration lessons for the benefit of the teachers.
8. He should recommend suitable instructional materials and professional books for the use of the teachers and should see that those are provided in time.
9. He should hold teachers' meetings to inspire and stimulate them in their educational thinking.
10. He should use democratic way of discussion in these meetings.
11. He should see that findings of research studies on "instruction and learning" are made available to teachers.
12. Class-room supervision should lead to research on problems existing in the school.

Duties and Responsibilities Relating to Educational Leadership and Human Relations

1. The Principal should be ever ready to consider new ideas on education coming from others and should be willing to try out those which seem to be useful.
2. He should consistently hold "progressive" views on educational matters.
3. He should try to apply such new methods as are suitable to Indian conditions.

4. He should encourage teachers to experiment with new procedures and techniques of education.
5. He should keep in touch with the latest developments in the field of education.
6. He should be democratic in his relations with teachers.
7. He should prove by his actions that he always means what he says.
8. He should not favour any of the teachers unduly.
9. He should show by his actions that he has confidence in his teachers.
10. He should give proper recognition to the good work done by the teachers.
11. He should not keep himself aloof from other members of the staff.
12. He should show in his dealings a real respect for the opinion of others.
13. He should not attempt to dominate his teachers by the force of his position.
14. He should have a due regard for the feelings of others.
15. He should never play one teacher against another in order to maintain his official superiority.
16. He should try to mutually reconcile differences, if they arise among teachers, between teachers and parents, and between teachers and the employer.
17. He should be ready to share with his co-workers the responsibility for any deficiency or weakness in the school programme.
18. He should share his work with and delegate responsibilities to staff members and committees.
19. He should provide all possible assistance to new teachers.
20. He should encourage and provide opportunities for in-service education of teachers.

RESPONSIBILITIES TOWARDS PUPILS

Health Services and Physical Education

1. The principal should see that the provision for regular and thorough medical check-up of the pupils is made.
2. He should plan for a follow-up programme of medical check-up.
3. He should see that equal opportunities are provided to all pupils under the physical education programme.
4. He should see that the energies of the teacher incharge of games, sports and physical education are directed towards the physical development of all pupils and not only to the production of winning teams or individuals.

Curriculum

1. The principal should develop a curriculum which provides experiences to meet the aesthetic, cultural, emotional, mental, moral as well as physical and social development of the pupils.
2. He should see that curriculum provides experiences which inculcate healthy moral and ethical standards.
3. He should see that curriculum provides ample opportunities for creative activities of the pupils.
4. He should as far as conditions allow develop a curriculum suited to the needs of pupils of ranging academic ability.
5. He should see that vocational subjects, appropriate to the community, are included in the curriculum.

Co-curricular Activities

1. He should provide for a varied programme of co-curricular activities in the school to develop the different-talents of all pupils.
2. He should get the entire programme of curricular activities prepare cooperatively by teachers and pupils.

3. He should also use the co-curricular activities programme to publicize the school and not to glorify his position.
4. He should see that all pupils are encouraged to participate in co-curricular activities.

Evaluation and Guidance

1. The principal should see that the evaluation programme of pupils is a continuous activity.
2. He should see that results of evaluation lead to a guidance programme.
3. He should encourage teachers to construct their own evaluation instruments.
4. He should see that pupils are assessed and guided before they choose different subjects for study.
5. He should see that school leavers get guidance on vocational choices.
6. He should see that school provides for individual and personal guidance to the pupils.

Discipline

1. The principal should believe in the concept of 'self' and 'social' discipline. He should encourage constructive solutions for solving disciplinary problems of pupils met by the teachers.
2. He should allow teachers to deal with the disciplinary cases of pupils and should deal himself only with cases of serious nature.
3. He should develop such traditions in the school as will socially shape conduct and behaviour of the pupils.

Responsibilities Towards Community

1. The principal should encourage the parents of the pupils to visit the school frequently.

2. He should see that parents are cordially received when they visit the school.
3. He should regularly inform the parents of the progress of their wards.
4. He should encourage the parents to or suit the teachers as well as himself on special problems of their wards.
5. He should organize parent study groups from time to time.
6. He should provide adequate facilities for the organization and proper functioning of the Parent-teacher Association in the school.
7. He should plan school programme with reference to the needs of the community.
8. He should encourage the use of community resources for vitalizing class-room instruction through excursions, field trips, study of local history etc.
9. He should encourage and organize social service programmes to render public services.
10. He should allow the community to use school facilities and services like school building, library, and dispensary ensuring at the same time that the work of the school does not suffer.
11. He should arrange social and cultural activities in the school and interpret the school programme to the community.
12. He should actively participate in the social and cultural functions of the community.
13. He should be above religion in organizing school programmes.
14. He should not allow the school to become a tool in the hands of any pressure group.
15. He should not allow his political beliefs to influence the administration of school.

Responsibilities Towards Managing Body of the School and the Department of Education

1. The principal should adopt suitable methods to raise funds and secure donations on behalf and with the consent of the Managing Body to finance the school programme.
2. He should present the case of the school fully to the Department of Education for getting timely grant-in-aid, recognition for teaching new subjects and opening new sections when needed.
3. He should acquaint the Managing Body with the school programmes.
4. He should give proper advice to the Managing Body in the selection and appointment of teachers.
5. He should inform the Managing Body about the work and conduct of the teachers.
6. He should regularly present to the Managing Body the various financial accounts of the school.
7. The principal should carry out the orders of the Department of Education in time.

Qualities of the Head

Significance of Each Letter of the Word 'Headmaster'

H stands for

(i) Hard work

(ii) Helpfulness

(iii) Honesty

(iv) Humility

(v) Humorous nature

E stands for

Enthusiasm

A stands for

(i) Accuracy
(ii) Adaptability
(iii) Alertness
(iv) Amicability
(v) Attentiveness
(vi) Attractive manners

D stands for

(i) Definiteness
(ii) Dependability
(iii) Desire for self-improvement
(iv) Devotion to the democratic ideal
(v) Devotion to the profession

M stands for

(i) Mastery of the subject matter
(ii) Maturity
(iii) Mental alertness
(iv) Morality

S stands for

(i) Scientific attitude
(ii) Self-discipline
(iii) Self-reliance
(iv) Sincerity
(v) Sociability
(vi) Steadfastness

T stands for

(i) Tact
(ii) Truthfulness

(iii) Teaching skill

(iv) Training

E stands for

(i) Ethics of the teaching profession

(ii) Experimental attitude

R stands for

(i) Readiness to serve others

(ii) Reasoning ability

(iii) Regularity

(iv) Relationships

(v) Resourcefulness

Staff Meetings

Efficient running of the school demands that members of the staff should occasionally meet for sharing responsibilities as well as experiences. These should be presided over by the head. These may be convened from time to time.

Briggs found that teachers expected the following things in a staff meeting:

(i) Help in their problems.

(ii) A wider outlook on education.

(iii) Meeting to be happy and wholesome.

(iv) Meeting based on appreciation of effort and accomplishment rather than shortcomings and faults.

Planning and Conducting Staff Meetings. The teachers should be informed in advance of the problems to be discussed in the meetings. It is very important for the head to listen to every teacher with attention and care. Minutes of staff meetings should be kept if possible.

A limit must be put to staff meetings and the best appears to be once a month. Of course, there need not be any rigidity in observing this principle. Occasional meetings for some particular purposes may have to be called. Sometimes it may become necessary for the head to convey staff meeting to clarify certain points of written order issued by him. An atmosphere of cheerfulness should prevail in all such meetings.

The head of the institution should take note of the teachers' problems and accordingly give his suggestions for the solution of the problems. His attempt should be to help the teachers as much as possible.

Time of meeting should be such as most of the members of the staff find it convenient to attend.

Purposes of Staff Meetings

1. To discuss the general progress of the school.
2. To discuss the admission policy.
3. To discuss the allocation of syllabus into various terms or quarters.
4. To discuss the organisation of examination.
5. To discuss periodical and annual results.
6. To discuss the distribution of teaching work.
7. To discuss the distribution of co-curricular work.
8. To finalise time-table.
9. To plan the organisation of functions.
10. To undertake new projects.
11. To discuss the institutional plan.
12. To evaluate the work of various clubs.
13. To prepare the annual report.
14. To discuss measures of observing punctuality by the students and checking late coming of the students.
15. To discuss measures for promoting punctuality and checking late coming of the staff.
16. To discuss tendencies of indiscipline among students.
17. To discuss internal cases of rift among staff members.

18. To arrange farewell and welcome functions.
19. To discuss social service programme.
20. To discuss celebration of festivals or functions.
21. To discuss about school inspection.

Essentials of Staff Meetings

1. Well-thought-out agenda.
2. Circulation of the agenda.
3. Notice of the meeting.
4. Convenient time.
5. Suitable seating arrangement.
6. Adequate preparation.
7. Congenial atmosphere.
8. Proper and meaningful discussion.
9. No disturbance.
10. Calm atmosphere.
11. Cooperative attitude.
12. Democratic attitude.
13. Time factor.
14. Recording of minutes.
15. Implementation of decisions.

Points to Remember

Relations with the Staff

1. Easy accessibility.
2. Recognition of individual differences.
3. Respect for the personality of staff members.
4. Sharing responsibility with the staff.

Relations with the Pupils

1. Due regard to their individuality.

2. Free access of the pupils.
3. Interest in their welfare.
4. Sharing some responsibility with them.
5. Sympathetic and affectionate attitude.

Relations with Parents

1. Parent-Teachers Association.
2. Utmost courtesy.

Relations with Community

1. Making school as a centre of community service.
2. Utilising community resources.

Relations with the Management

1. Due regard to the members.
2. Fair dealing.
3. Polite but firm refusal to their undue demands.

Relations with the Department

1. Prompt replies.
2. Timely submission of all records.

Educational which includes

1. Sound educational philosophy.
2. Wide general scholarship.

Professional. This implies:

1. Educational statesman.
2. Pragmatic leader.
3. Progressive outlook.
4. Professional pre-service and in-service training.
5. Professional ethics.
6. Professional pride.

Human Qualities. These comprise:

1. Appreciation of good work.
2. Proficiency in human relations.
3. Resourcefulness.
4. Sensitivity to the needs of the students, staff and the community.

Personality. This includes:

1. Creativity.
2. Cooperativeness.
3. Communication fluency.
4. Democratic attitude.
5. Duty-consciousness.
6. Enthusiasm.
7. Humorous nature.
8. Industriousness.
9. Integrity.
10. Mental alertness.
11. Open-mindedness.
12. Physical soundness.
13. Scientific temper.
14. Self-confidence.
15. Self-discipline.
16. Sociability.
17. Steadfastness.
18. Tactfulness.
19. Tolerance.
20. Truthfulness.
21. Unbiased attitude.
22. Understanding of the human nature.

Exercise

1. "The head is the hub of the educative process." State the role of the head in the management of the institution.
2. "Management of an institution is the art of human relationships." Explain the role of the head in developing human relations among various groups.
3. Explain the various functions of the head of an institution. How can he discharge his functions effectively?
4. Point out the significance of staff meetings. What are the principles of conducting staff meetings?

19

INTER-RELATIONSHIP

The inter-relatedness of the school and the community must be adequately understood in our country. The school should not be treated as an institution outside the community around it. There should be a friendly-oriented partnership between the school and the community. No education programme will be acceptable to the community if the school does not give due consideration to the culture and values of the community. Similarly a school will be able to discharge its functions effectively only when the community appreciates the work of the school and provides full cooperation to it.

The Secondary Education Commission 1952-53 has very aptly observed, "If the various agencies—the home, the school, the neighbourhood, the community, the religious organisations and the state—have no common outlook and agreed ideas but pull in different directions, the school will not be able to make an abiding and coherent impression on the character of students." It may be remembered that the students spend only one-fourth or one-fifth of the day in school. The rest of their time is spent in the community which can easily undo the goodwork of the school. This implies the establishment of the active association between parents and teachers.

School and Community

The relationship between the school and the community has been stressed by Prof. Dewey as "what the best and the wisest parent wants for his own child, that must the community want for all its children. Any other ideal for schools is narrow and unlovely; acted upon, it destroys our democracy." Again he has stated "the school is primarily a social institution. Education being a social process, the school is simply that form of community life in which all those agencies are concentrated that will be most effective in bringing the child to share in the inherited resources of the race to use powers for social ends."

In the words of S. Bala Krishna Joshi, "Close co-operation between the parent who is the first teacher and the teacher, who is the second parent, is the very foundation on which rests the fruitfulness of the training imparted in our institutions." Mr. George Tomlinson has stressed the need of cooperation between home and school in these words, "Let us fashion our schools with the well-being of children always in mind. In particular, remember that any clash between parents and teachers must always be harmful to the child. Harmonious working together can alone bring us the results we want." Teachers are interested in the welfare of the children.

They want their pupils develop culturally, ethically, mentally, morally, physically and socially. So is the case with the parents. Hence the need for united efforts on the part of parents and the teachers.

A school serves the community by:

1. providing training to the students in the art of living together.
2. developing democratic, moral, secular and social values in the students.
3. providing training in skills needed by the community.
4. making school as a centre of community service.

A community means a group of people with common interests and needs residing in a locality or village. Usually children of the community receive their education in the school located therein.

Parent-teacher Cooperation. Parent-teacher cooperation is helpful to the teachers in the following ways:

1. The teachers acquire maximum understanding about the child by getting relevant information from the parents.
2. The teachers ensure regular attendance of the child when they are in constant touch with his parents.
3. The teachers impress upon the parents, to provide proper equipment to their child.
4. The teachers stress upon the parents to have respect for the school laws.
5. The teachers motivate the parents to donate funds and gifts to the school.
6. The teachers discuss with parents various ways and means for the proper development and growth of the child.

Parent-teacher cooperation is also helpful to the parents. Following are some of the important advantages:

1. The parents acquaint themselves with the progress of their child when they are in constant touch with the teachers.
2. The parents come to know about problem situations before they become serious and take corrective and remedial measures.
3. The parents come to know about the work being done in school. They may also suggest some better ways of doing things.

It is extremely desirable to have close contacts of parents and teachers specially at the pre-school stage because the pre-school children are at the stage of habit formation. Parental cooperation and involvement goes a long way in providing effective pre-school education.

ROLE OF THE SCHOOL

The school should not only help the children but also assist in the education of their parents. For achieving better coordination between the pre-school and the home, it is necessary that there should be frequent contacts with the parents and the pre-school teachers.

The school teacher may organise parents association which could meet and discuss the needs and problems of the children.

Special lectures for parents on child care and development may be arranged.

The teacher may visit the homes of children to meet parents and may discuss problems relating to their food, health, habits and behaviours. Home visits will also enable the teacher to acquaint himself with the cultural and social background of the child.

Progress reports touching various aspects of life in school—academic, emotional, physical and social etc. should be sent to parents for their information and appropriate action.

Parents and School Days may be organised. Parents may be taken round the school. Parents may be shown the actual working of the school, classes and various activities. Children's work like calligraphy, charts, models, craft work etc., may be exhibited for the parents. Cultural and sports functions may be organised on the parents day.

Light refreshment for the parents may be served if the funds permit.

CONTRIBUTION OF COMMUNITY

The various institutions in the community such as Panchayats, Mahila Mandals, Youth Clubs etc., should be involved in different activities of the school.

Apart from cooperating in various programmes of the school, the community can offer assistance to the school in various areas like the following:

1. Electrification of the school building.

2. White washing and minor repairs of the school building.
3. Construction of compound walls.
4. Provision of sheds for cooking meals.
5. Donations of land for various purposes.
6. Painting of blackboards.
7. Supply of portraits of national leaders.
8. Supply of stationery and books to the poor students.
9. Supply of uniforms to the poor students.
10. Supply of utensils.
11. Supply of play materials.
12. Offering free services by individuals like doctors.

Community School

W. K. Mccharen writes, "A community school is one whose programme is designed for useful and effective learning on the part of the children and one which helps to improve the quality of living in the community, one which serves the total population of the community, and seeks to evolve its purposes out of the interest and needs of the people in community."

Ivol Stafford writes about the school programme and the community, 'The good school programme stems from community needs as an integral part of the life of the people. It is made by, for and of those, it would serve."

K.G. Saiyidian has pointed out, "A people's school must obviously be based on the people's needs and problems. Its curriculum should be an epitome of their life. Its methods of work must approximate to theirs. It should reflect all that is significant and characteristic in the life of the community, in its natural setting."

The school is not a place where merely the children of the community should receive education but the community itself also. With tons of money invested in school buildings and equipment, it is a poor economics, as well as bad educational philosophy to restrict its use a few hours each day, and for only a few months in the year. The school building and equipment must be thrown open for public use after the regular school hours are over.

If the school is taken out of its isolation, the tax payers will feel that they are really getting a fair return for their money and will take more interest in the school.

The teachers will get opportunities to become the leaders of the social group and improve their position and status.

Important Programmes of a Community School. Following are the important programmes which a community school must organise:

Curriculum Related to Real Life. The studies within the school must be related to the life outside. The subject matter of the various subjects of the curriculum should be carefully planned and brought into relation with the problems of society. The curriculum should reflect all that is significant and characteristic in the life of the community in its natural setting. "In the rural areas, the school" according to K.G. Saiyidain "should help the children to realize sympathetically the problems of rural life and train them to take part in it effectively when they have finished schooling, similarly in an industrial area the school should gradually make the child familiar with the industrial tools and processes and the conditions of life in the factories so that he may appreciate both the technical and the human elements of the situation."

Social Clubs. Social survey clubs should be organised in schools which should undertake to investigate some of the pressing needs and problems of the surrounding areas, e.g., the survey of the condition of roads, the percentage of literacy, the drainage of the street etc.

Social Service Leagues. As a corollary of the above, social service leagues may be organised, cleaning the lanes and streets, organising first-aid centres for the public, constructing some drains etc., are some of the activities to be undertaken by these leagues.

Adult Education Centre. In the evening or in the morning, literacy classes for the adults should be started in the school building.

The School as a Recreational Centre. Recreational programmes like games, dramas, bhajans etc., for children and adults of the community may be undertaken. Radio listening, film shows and exhibitions may be organised.

Celebration of National Days and Festivals. Important national days and festivals should be organised in the school premises at which the residents of the locality are cordially invited to attend and participate.

School Library and Reading Room. The adults may be encouraged to make use of the school library and reading room after regular school hours.

Parent-teacher Associations. Formation of the parent-teacher associations may be encouraged.

Utilisation of the Experiences of the Public. "What we would like to see is a two-way traffic" thus observed the Secondary Education Commission. In this context they have suggested that interested members of the community engaged in various useful vocations and professions should be invited to the school from time to time to talk about their particular work to show its place and significance in the life of the community.

Excursions. According to L.W. Kindred and O. W. Stephenson, the value of excursions for the pupils is, "to enlarge their concept of the school, cause them to look upon the community was laboratory where truth may be discovered and where they will see that not all learning is found between covers and books." Excursions bring reality, actuality and vividness in the subject-matter.

Vocational Efficiency. Opportunities should be provided in a school to increase the vocational efficiency of the students.

The head must show a paramount concern for the community otherwise school programme will fail to meet the objectives of modern philosophy of education.

The school of today is a vital part of the community—the focal points of its activities. Without the support of the public, the school cannot function and the contribution which public makes towards the school is in direct proportion to its understanding.

Exercise

1. Explain the need for the close cooperation between the school and the community.
2. Describe various ways through which a school can serve the community.
3. State the areas of collaboration between the school and the community.
4. How can a community help the school?
5. Elucidate the concept of a community school.

20

Managing Resources

Management of learning resources is a very broad concept. It includes all the elements that are needed for effective teaching-learning process. It means managing school programmes in such a way as to make the optimum use of resources; human as well as material. An efficient school management brings about harmony between plans and practices, goals and tasks so that there may not be any confusion in the working of the school. Proper co-ordination is necessary to make the best of learning resources. Planning is the basis of effective co-ordination.

Four Aspects of Management. Management in a school has four aspects.

Management of Material Equipment—This includes material things i.e., furniture and equipment, etc.

Management of School Plant—This includes school buildings, laboratories, playground etc.

Management of Human Equipment—This implies mobilisation of all people who are involved and interested in the educational activities of the school, i.e., pupils and their parents, school staff, experts, board of management etc.

Management of Ideas and Principles—This means organisation of ideas and principles into school system, curriculum, time schedule, norms of achievement, co-curricular activities.

School management is the embodiment of a spirit and of an ideal. School management should enable different limbs of the school organism "to function harmoniously in happy coordination blending themselves into a composite personality like the different rivulets which join together."

The Point of View of Society. Broadly speaking the school should be managed for the following objectives:

1. Consolidation of the spiritual strength of the society.
2. Maintaining the historic continuity of the society.
3. Securing the past achievements of the society.
4. Guaranting the future of the society.

Point of View of the Pupil. A school should be managed:

1. to train his faculties.
2. to widen his outlook.
3. to cultivate his mind.
4. to form and strength his character.
5. to develop and cultivate his aesthetic faculty.
6. to build up his body and give him health and strength.
7. to teach his duty to himself, the community and the state.

Fundamentally the purpose of school management is to enable the right pupils to receive the right education in the right way at the right time from the right teachers by bringing them together at a cost within the means of the state at a place specifically designed for the purpose of education. This objective can be achieved only when four categories of relationships within the school community, i.e., relations between organiser and teachers, relations between teachers and teachers, relations between pupils and pupils and relations between pupils and teachers—are pleasant and constructive, based on mutual goodwill and cooperation.

The Scope

It includes:

1. Planning
2. Budgeting
3. Organising
    (i) Human resources
    (ii) Material resources
4. Providing instruction
5. Providing co-curricular activities
6. Coordinating programmes
7. Directing
8. Coordinating
9. Providing for experimentation
10. Maintaining and developing proper school-community relationships
11. Evaluating

A Well-managed School

Density of India in the Class-room. The Education Commission 1964-66 rightly observed:

"The density of India is now being shaped in her class-rooms. This, we believe, is no more rhetoric. In a world based on science and technology, it is education that determines the level of prosperity, welfare and security of the people. on the quality and number of persons coming out of schools and colleges will depend our success in the greater adventure of national reconstruction whose objectives are to raise substantially the standard of living of our people and to create a new social order based on the human values of the dignity of the individual, freedom, equality and justice."

For the realisation of the objectives as stipulated by the Education Commission, a school should provide for the following:

1. Training in the art of living together.

2. Development of child's personality.
3. Provision of a stimulating environment.
4. Transformation into activity school.
5. Provision for experimentation.
6. Opportunities for developing self-discipline.
7. Provision for a well-qualified and suitable staff.
8. Making library as the hub of school activities.
9. Making school as a centre of community service.
10. Providing work experience and socially useful productive work.
11. Provision of progressive methods of evaluation of students performance.
12. Providing training for citizens.
13. Inculcating values of democracy, secularism and socialism.

A Well Organised School

Training in the Art of Living Together. School is not merely a place of formal learning. Its main concern is not to communicate a certain prescribed quantum of knowledge. It is primarily concerned with training its pupils in the gracious "art of living".

Development of Child's Entire Personality. The school should provide a richly varied pattern of activities to cater to the development of children's entire personality. It has to formulate a scheme of hobbies, occupations and projects that will appeal to draw out the powers of children of varying temperaments.

Provision of Stimulating Environment. The school's concern should also be to provide for its pupils a rich, pleasant and stimulating environment which will evoke their manifold interests and make life a matter of joyful experience.

Transformation into Activity School. The school must be transformed into an "activity school" because an activity has an irresistible appeal for every normal child and is his natural path to the goal of knowledge and culture.

The entire programme of the school is visualised as the unity and inspired by a psychologically congenial and stimulating approach. By planning a coherent programme of different activities rich in stimuli, the school will not be frittering away either the time or the energy of the pupils but will be heightening their intellectual powers also side by side while training them in other fine qualities.

Opportunities for Self-discipline. Discipline in the school should not be a matter of arbitrary rules and regulations enforced through the authority of the teachers. The students should be given full freedom to organise functions, to conduct many of the school activities through their own committees and even to deal with certain types of disciplinary cases. In this way, discipline will be maintained through the influence of the social group and gradually lead to the development of self-discipline.

The teacher should endeavour to win the love and confidence of his children and establish his prestige on sincerity, integrity, hard work and a sympathetic handling of their problems.

Library as the Hub of School Activities. The library may be the hub of the centre of the intellectual and literary life of the school.

The School as a Centre of Community. Another thing which will distinguish this school from most of the traditional schools is that it be organised as a centre of community service.

Work Experience and Socially Useful Work. The school should devote special attention to craft and other productive work and thus redress the balance between theoretical and practical studies.

Assessment of the Day-to-Day Work. The emphasis should shift from examination to evaluation. Teachers and children should concentrate on the real purpose of the school and take examination in their stride. Much greater credit can be given to the actual work done by the students from day today. Careful and complete records should be maintained. Moreover, in assessing their progress and position, factors other than academic achievement should be given due weight; their social sense, initiative, discipline, cooperation, leadership, etc.

This is the picture of the reorganised school. All schools may not be able to work up to it immediately. But it is not an impossible or unduly idealized picture and it does point out the correct direction of advance.

Effective Institutional Management

1. Principle of cooperation.
2. Principle of coordination.
3. Principle of democratic philosophy.
4. Principle of equality.
5. Principle of freedom.
6. Principle of flexibility.
7. Principle of human relations.
8. Principle of justice.
9. Principle of leadership.
10. Principle of optimism.
11. Principle of optimum utility.
12. Principle of professional growth of the staff.
13. Principle of recognition of individual worth.
14. Principle of sharing responsibility.
15. Principle of values.
16. Principle of budgeting.
17. Principle of economy.

Comprising Factors

(a) Principles of democratic administration.

(b) Scientific collection of the data.

(c) Efficient use of the school machinery.

(d) Judicious use of money.

(e) Target fixing.

(f) Periodic checking.

(g) Flexibility.

Principles of Democratic Administration. An efficient management must be based on the following principles of democratic administration:

(i) Principle of sharing responsibility.

(ii) Principle of equality.

(iii) Principle of freedom.

(iv) Principle of cooperation.

(v) Principle of justice.

(vi) Principle of recognizing individual worth.

(vii) Principle of leadership.

Democratic Educational Management. In a democracy all institutions, social, economic, political, educational, and others should be organised from the democratic point of view. The school is no longer regarded a place where students receive formal instruction but it is regarded to be "devoted" to and "engaged" in the service of the basic democratic principles, and goals.

This implies that the management and administration of a school should be done in such a way as it helps in the realization of the aims for which the school exists. Our managers and administrators must realise the significance of the fundamental character of democratic faith and must have faith in the philosophy underlying it. Then they will be able to evolve an educational system to meet the challenge of times. An eminent educationist observes, "It would be admitted by every administrator that the purpose of an administrative system is to help bring about a methodical and well-graded achievement of the educational and social ideals of the people. As such, the administrator's work has to conform in its concepts, structure and techniques to the kinds of ideals it is intended to serve.

Principle of Sharing Responsibility. A democratic manager and administrator acts upon the principle of sharing responsibility.

He does not himself usurp all powers but shares control and responsibility not only with his colleagues but also with the students. He does not make the mistake of thinking that he is born to rule. He delegates some of his powers to his colleagues. He avoids to be on the top of everything in the school. He introduces students' government in the school under the guidance of expert teachers.

Principle of Equality. R. R. Kumria writes, "A democratic administrator should look upon the personnel as socially equal to himself; he should not take decisions by himself, but with his colleagues; he should make them feel responsible and share in administration; he should have a code of set rules of administration which he and his colleagues should follow rigidly, making no discrimination in their application, and lastly, he should want no special privilege. He should avoid all 'bossing tendencies'. He should treat all those who work under him as his 'co-workers' as in democracy there are no subordinates.

Principle of Freedom. People are at their best when they have freedom to exercise their powers and talents. Unnecessary restraints imposed by the managers, and administrators curb all initiative and enthusiasm of their subordinates.

Principle of Co-operation. A democratic head will stress the importance of working together in a spirit of mutual help and co-operation. The school is said to be a co-operative society in which every member must work for all and all for each. A cooperative spirit must be reflected in every activity of the school-co-operation between the head and the staff, head and the students, head and the parents, head and managing committee, head and the inspector, etc. All engaged in the field of education have the same interests and purposes and there is no reason why there should not be co-operation at all levels of educational management and administration.

Principle of Justice. A democratic manager and administrator will not show undue favours to some. All will be treated on the same footing. All points of disputes should be promptly and judiciously settled. Lack of justice breeds disgust and frustration among the service personnel. Individual worth and not birth should be given due importance. No person should be above rules and regulations. The teachers and the students should feel that the head is an embodiment of fair play and justice. Most of our troubles in our educational institutions will vanish if once we recognise importance of fair play and justice.

Principle of Recognition of the Individual Worth. The democratic manager and administrator will respect the individuality of his co-workers. He will not injure their self-respect. He will realise the necessity of studying his co-workers individually.

The merit of the individual should be given its due recognition. Ryburn writes, "Nothing will more encourage a man or a woman, a boy or a girl, to greater effort, than an encouraging recognition of good work done, of sincere effort made, of good qualities shown. If those in charge of institutions, and those carrying on the administrative work of department wish to enable those working with them to do their best, they should always realize the value of ungrudging recognition of all that merits such recognition."

The Principle of Leadership. A democracy cannot function unless all the people are trained for discharging their responsibility and this involves training in discipline as well as leadership. An educational manager and administrator is a leader of various groups and he must possess qualities of leadership so that others may also follow him. In every sphere of human activity, leadership is beset with difficulties and the manager and the administrator must have a grasp of group and individual psychology, if he is to be successful.

The Advantages. The democratic management and administration develops friendly relationships among all the members working in every enterprise, educational or otherwise. In a school, if the Principal follows the democratic principles, he is sure to be successful in harnessing the talents and energies of the students and the teachers both to the maximum extent. In a democratic-atmosphere everybody works in a spirit of joy and makes a distinct contribution to the progress of the school. The moral enthusiasm of the teachers and the students is raised. The teachers become professionally mature when they share the planning of the school. The public in general also takes a keen interest in the school, if the head seeks its co-operation.

In the autocratic management and administration, the personality of the teacher is violated and he occupies a subordinate position. The personality of the child is also violated. The autocratic management and administration breeds the cult of blind obedience.

MANAGER AND ADMINISTRATOR

"The boss drives his men, the leader coaches them.

The boss depends on authority, the leader on goodwill.

The boss inspires fear, the leader inspires enthusiasm.

The boss assigns the task, the leader sets the pace.

The boss says, 'Get here on time', the leader gets there ahead of time.

The boss fixes the time for the breakdown; the leader fixes the breakdown.

The boss makes work a drudgery, the leader makes it a game".

Democratic Institutional Management Climate	*Autocratic Institutional Management Climate*
1. Cooperative planning is done by the whole staff.	1. Planning is done by the head of the institution.
2. The committees chosen by the group do the work.	2. The head chooses committees and dominates them.
3. The head discusses problems with teachers and offers suggestions.	3. The head tells teachers what to do.
4. The head respects teacher's personality and plans cooperatively with him.	4. The head sometimes embarrasses teachers before children.
5. The head gives co-workers credit for success.	5. The head takes credit for all success.
6. The head encourages faculty to make use of human resources in the community.	6. The head gives no recognition to parents and leaders.

Contd.

Democratic Institutional Management Climate	*Autocratic Institutional Management Climate*
7. Faculty meetings are cooperatively planned by the entire staff.	7. Faculty meetings are planned only by the head.
8. Teachers are encouraged to use cumulative records.	8. Cumulative records are only for the use of the head.
9. Teachers plan with the supervisors in special fields for work to be done.	9. Special supervisors outline course for teachers to follow in teaching special subjects.
10. Audio-visual materials are made available to the teachers.	10. Audio-visual programme is operated on a rigid time schedule, prepared by the head.
11. The head allows teacher to make flexible programmes which best suit the interests and needs of the children.	11. The teacher requires a set type of common programme.
12. The budget is prepared cooperatively, with teacher participation.	12. The budget is prepared by the managerial administrative staff.
13. Students are teacher-guided.	13. Students are teacher dominated.
14. The students are guided by the teacher in the choice of many activities.	14. The teacher plans activities without conferring with the pupils.
15. The pupils share with teacher in establishing standards of achievement.	15. The teacher sets up standards of achievement without conferring with the pupils.
16. The students share with the teacher the responsibility of appraising their work.	16. The students are not conferred with in appraising their growth.
17. Students are encouraged by the teacher to make suggestions concerning their work.	17. The teacher ignores suggestions of the pupils.
18. Students are encouraged to correct their mistakes.	18. The teacher directs pupil activities.
19. The teacher adopts an exploratory attitude.	19. The teacher gives directions in a firm manner.
20. The teacher tries to understand the child.	20. The teacher works according to set procedures.
21. The teacher is sympathetic.	21. The teacher springs awe and fear.
22. The teacher tries to find reasons for misbehaviour.	22. The teacher arbitrarily punishes pupils for misbehaviour.

Contd.

Democratic Institutional Management Climate	*Autocratic Institutional Management Climate*
23. The teacher takes into consideration the individual differences of the students.	23. The teacher treats all children alike.
24. Every child is provided with an opportunity to contribute and to lead a group.	24. Only the aggressive and brighter children contribute and lead.
25. Students are grouped properly.	25. Students are grouped on administrative reasons.
26. The students express themselves freely.	26. There is no such freedom of expression.
27. Curriculum is flexible to meet with the needs of each child.	27. Curriculum is definite and same goals are set for all the children.
28. Class teacher co-operates with other teachers to study problem students.	28. Class teacher does not participate in group study of problem pupils.
29. Teachers encourage parents to visit school for a closer relationship between home and school.	29. Teachers discourage parents from visiting school because it disrupts the schedule.
30. School atmosphere is reflected by student's remark, "I like school."	30. School atmosphere is reflected by student's remark, "I don't like school."
31. Students committee assume responsibility for selecting equipment and supplies needed.	31. Teacher or the head assumes responsibility for selecting and purchasing equipment and supplies.

A good manager and administrator would do well if he uses 'We' and not 'I' in emphasising the achievement of the department or of institution. This gives a sense of pride to his colleagues and they think that due regard is given to their merits.

Exercise

1. "A world whose schools are unreformed is an unreformed world." H.G. Wells. Explain this statement in the context of the management of the school.

2. State the scope of school management. What are the principles of school management?
3. How would you distinguish democratic management of an institution from that of an autocratic management?
4. "We and not I is the key concept in school management". Elucidate the significance of this statement in a democratic management.

Additional Reading

Bhaskara Rao, Digumarti (1994). *Scientific Aptitude*, New Delhi: Ashish Publishing House. ISBN 81-7024-658-X.

Bhaskara Rao, Digumarti (1995). *Animal Kingdom*. New Delhi: Discovery Publishing House. ISBN 81-7141-274-2.

Bhaskara Rao, Digumarti (1995). *Batracology*. New Delhi: Discovery Publishing House. ISBN 81-7141-279-3.

Bhaskara Rao, Digumarti (1997), *Scientific Attitude*. New Delhi: Discovery Publishing House. ISBN 81-7141-308-0.

Bhaskara Rao, Digumarti (1996). *Scientific Attitude vis-à-vis Scientific Aptitude*. New Delhi: Discovery Publishing House. ISBN 81-7141-308-0.

Bhaskara Rao, Digumarti, Editor (1996). *Encyclopaedia of Education for All*, 5 Volumes. New Delhi: APH Publishing Corporation. ISBN 81-7024-759-4 (set).

Vol. I *Education for All: The World Conference*. ISBN 81-7024-760-8.

Vol. II *Education for All: The EPA-9 Summit*. ISBN 81-7024-761-6.

Vol. III *Education for All: Quality Education for All*. ISBN 81-7024-762-6.

Vol. IV *Education for All: Planning and Monitoring*. ISBN 81-7024-763-4.

Vol. V *Education for All: The Indian Scenario*. ISBN 81-7024-764-0.

Bhaskara Rao, Digumarti, Editor (1996). *Global Perceptions on Peace Education*, 3 Volumes. New Delhi: Discovery Publishing House. ISBN 81-7141-319-6.

Bhaskara Rao, Digumarti, Editor (1996). *National Policy on Education.* 2 Volumes. New Delhi: Anmol Publications Pvt. Ltd. ISBN 81-7488-323-1.

Bhaskara Rao, Digumarti, Editor (1997). *Care the Child,* 2 Volumes. New Delhi: Discovery Publishing House. ISBN 81-7141-394-3.

Bhaskara Rao, Digumarti, Editor (1997). *Education for the 21st Century.* New Delhi: Discovery Publishing House. ISBN 81-7141-389-7.

Bhaskara Rao, Digumarti, Editor (1997). *Reflections on Scientific Attitude.* New Delhi: Discovery Publishing House, ISBN 81-7141-319-6.

Bhaskara Rao, Digumarti, Editor (1997). *Success Story of a Primary Education Project.* New Delhi: APH Publishing Corporation. ISBN 81-7024-850-7.

Bhaskara Rao, Digumarti, Editor (1997). *World Food Summit.* New Delhi: Discovery Publishing House. ISBN 81-7141-386-2.

Bhaskara Rao, Digumarti, Editor (1998). *Adolescence Education.* New Delhi: Discovery Publishing House. ISBN 81-7141-432-X.

Bhaskara Rao, Digumarti, Editor (1998). *Community and School Nutrition Education.* New Delhi: Discovery Publishing House. ISBN 81-7141-435-4.

Bhaskara Rao, Digumarti, Editor (1998). *District Primary Education Programme.* New Delhi: Discovery Publishing House. ISBN 81-7141-396-X.

Bhaskara Rao, Digumarti, Editor (1998). *Earth Summit,* 2 Volumes. New Delhi: Discovery Publishing House. ISBN 81-7141-435-4.

Bhaskara Rao, Digumarti, Editor (1998). *National Policy on Education: Towards an Enlightened and Humane Society,* New Delhi: Discovery Publishing House. ISBN 81-7141-426-5.

Bhaskara Rao, Digumarti, Editor (1998). *Reforming School Education.* New Delhi: Discovery Publishing House. ISBN 81-7141-403-6.

Bhaskara Rao, Digumarti, Editor (1998). *Teacher Education in India.* New Delhi: Discovery Publishing House. ISBN 81-7141-406-0.

Bhaskara Rao, Digumarti, Editor (1998). *World Summit for Social Development*. New Delhi: Discovery Publishing House. ISBN 81-7141-420-6.

Bhaskara Rao, Digumarti, Editor (2000). *Education for All: Achieving the Goal*, 3 Volumes, New Delhi: APH Publishing Corporation. ISBN 81-7648-152-1.

Vol. I *The Global Consensus*. ISBN 81-7648-155-6.

Vol. II *Mid-Decade Review Reports of Regional Seminars*. ISBN 81-7648-154-8.

Vol. III *Issues and Trends*. ISBN 81-7648-155-6.

Bhaskara Rao, Digumarti, Editor (2000), *International Encyclopaedia of AIDS*, 11 Volumes in 13 Parts. New Delhi: Discovery Publishing House. ISBN 81-7141-6 (Set).

Vol. 1 *Introduction to HIV/AIDS*. ISBN 81-7141-523-7.

Vol. 2 *HIV/AIDS—Issues and Challenges*, 2 Parts. ISBN 81-7141-524-5.

Vol. 3 *HIV/AIDS—Socio Economic Realities*. ISBN 81-7141-524-3.

Vol. 4 *HIV/AIDS—Law Ethics and Human Rights*, 2 Parts. ISBN 81-7141-526-1.

Vol. 5 *AIDS and NGOs*. ISBN 81-7141-527-X.

Vol. 6 *AIDS and Home Care*. ISBN 81-7141-528-8.

Vol. 7 *STD Case Management*. ISBN 81-7141-529-6.

Vol. 8 *HIV/AIDS Prevention and Care—Teaching Modules for Nurses and Midwives*. ISBN 81-7141-530-X.

Vol. 9 *HIV Prevention Education for Education for Educational Institutions*. ISBN 81-7141-531-8.

Vol. 10 *Instructional Modules for AIDS Education*. ISBN 81-7141-532-6.

Vol. 11 *School Health Education to Prevent AIDS and STD—A Package for Curriculum Planners*. ISBN 81-7141-5338-4.

Bhaskara Rao, Digumarti, Editor (2000). *International Encyclopaedia of Science and Technology Education*, 11 Volumes. New Delhi: Discovery Publishing House. ISBN 81-7141-548-2 (Set).

Vol. 1 *Science and Technology Education*. ISBN 81-7141-568-7.

Vol. 2 *Science Education in Developing Countries*. ISBN 81-7141-570-9.

Vol. 3 *Organisational Structure of Science*. ISBN 81-7141-570-9.

Vol. 4 *Science Education in Asia and the Pacific*. ISBN 81-7141-571-7.

Vol. 5 *Science and Technology Education for All*. ISBN 81-7141-572-5.

Vol. 6 *Values, Ethics, Talent and Girls in Science and Technology Education*. ISBN 81-7141-573-3.

Vol. 7 *Popularization of Science and Technology Education*. ISBN 81-7141-574-1.

Vol. 8 *Science, Power and Society*. ISBN 81-7141-575-X.

Vol. 9 *Information Technology*. ISBN 81-7141-576-8.

Vol. 10 *Teacher Training in Science and Technology Education*. ISBN 81-7141-577-6.

Vol. 11 *Teacher Training in Science and Technology: A Curriculum Framework*. ISBN 81-7141-578-4.

Bhaskara Rao, Digumarti, Editor (2001). *Distance Education in Different Countries*. New Delhi: APH Publishing Corporation. ISBN 81-7648-229-3.

Bhaskara Rao, Digumarti, Editor (2001). *Decentralised Management of Education (Management of Education in Panchayati Raj and Municipal Bodies)*. New Delhi: Discovery Publishing House. ISBN 81-7141-617-9.

Bhaskara Rao, Digumarti, Editor (2001). *Electrochemistry for Environmental Protection*. New Delhi: Discovery Publishing House. ISBN 81-7141-619-5.

Bhaskara Rao, Digumarti, Editor (2001). *Global Educational Studies*. New Delhi: Discovery Publishing House. ISBN 81-7141-616-0.

Bhaskara Rao, Digumarti, Editor (2001). *Global Synthesis of Educational Assessment*. New Delhi: Discovery Publishing House. ISBN 81-7141-613-6.

Bhaskara Rao, Digumarti, Editor (2000). *International Encyclopaedia of Human Rights*. 7 Volumes in 13 Parts. New Delhi: Discovery Publishing House. (Royal Size). ISBN 81-7141-567-9 (Set).

Vol. 1 *International Instruments of Human Rights*, 2 Parts. ISBN 81-7141-595-4.

Vol. 2 *Regional Instruments of Human Rights*. ISBN 81-7141-604-7.

Vol. 3 *Human Rights and the United Nations*, 2 Parts. ISBN 81-7141-605-5.

Vol. 4 *Fact Files of Human Rights*, 3 Parts. ISBN 81-7141-605-3.

Vol. 5 *Study Stories of Human Rights*, 3 Parts. ISBN 81-7141-607-3.

Vol. 6 *International Meetings on Human Rights*, 2 Parts. ISBN 81-7141-608-X.

Vol. 7 *Professional Training in Human Rights*. ISBN 81-7141-609-8.

Bhaskara Rao, Digumarti, Editor (2001). *Jomtcin Decade of Education*. New Delhi: Discovery Publishing House. ISBN 81-7141-618-7.

Bhaskara Rao, Digumarti, Editor (2001). *Nuclear Materials: Issues and Concerns*, 2 Volumes. New Delhi: Discovery Publishing House. ISBN 81-7141-611-X.

Bhaskara Rao, Digumarti, Editor (2001). *World Conference on Education for All*. New Delhi: APH Publishing Corporation. ISBN 81-7141-274-9.

Bhaskara Rao, Digumarti, Editor (2001). *World Conference on Higher Education*, New Delhi: Discovery Publishing House. ISBN 81-7141-610-1.

Bhaskara Rao, Digumarti, Editor (2001). *World Conference on Science*. New Delhi: Discovery Publishing House. ISBN 81-7141-612-8.

Bhaskara Rao, Digumarti, Editor (2003). *Inspiring Experience in Teacher Education*. New Delhi: Discovery Publishing House. ISBN 81-7141-656-X.

Bhaskara Rao, Digumarti, Editor (2003). *International Studies in Education*, 3 Volumes, New Delhi: Discovery Publishing House. ISBN 81-7141-647-0.

Bhaskara Rao, Digumarti, Editor (2003). *Military Conversion: Impact on Science and Technology*, New Delhi: Discovery Publishing House. ISBN 81-7141-578-4.

Bhaskara Rao, Digumarti, Editor (2003). *United Nations Millennium Summit*. New Delhi: Discovery Publishing House. ISBN 81-7141-632-2.

Bhaskara Rao, Digumarti, Editor (2003). *World Assembly on Aging*. New Delhi: Discovery Publishing House. ISBN 81-7141-637-3.

Bhaskara Rao, Digumarti, Editor (2004). *World Conference on Human Rights*. New Delhi: Discovery Publishing House. ISBN 81-7141-661-6.

Bhaskara Rao, Digumarti, Editor (2003). *World Education Forum*. New Delhi: Discovery Publishing House. ISBN 81-7141-639-X.

Bhaskara Rao, Digumarti, Editor (2004). *Education Employment and Human Resource Development*. New Delhi: Discovery Publishing House. ISBN 81-7141-681-0.

Bhaskara Rao, Digumarti, Editor (2004). *Successfully Schooling*. New Delhi: Discovery Publishing House. ISBN 81-7141-677-2.

Bhaskara Rao, Digumarti, Editor (2004). *European Education and Teachers*. New Delhi: Discovery Publishing House. ISBN 81-7141-702-7.

Bhaskara Rao, Digumarti, Editor (2004). *Teachers in a Changing World*. New Delhi: Discovery Publishing House. ISBN 81-7141-694-2.

Bhaskara Rao, Digumarti, Editor (2004). *Learning to Live Together*, 4 Volumes. New Delhi: Discovery Publishing House.

Vol. 1 *International Conference on Learning to Live Together.*

Vol. 2 *Globalisation and Living Together.*

Vol. 3 *Curriculum for Learning to Live Together.*

Vol. 4 *Science Education for the Contemporary Society.*

Bhaskara Rao, Digumarti (2004). *International Guidelines on Open and Distance Education*, New Delhi: Discovery Publishing House.

Bhaskara Rao, Digumarti, Editor (2004). *Adult Learning in the 21st Century*. New Delhi: Discovery Publishing House.

Bhaskara Rao, Digumarti, Editor (2004). *Educational Practices: Research and Recommendations*. New Delhi: Discovery Publishing House.

Bhaskara Rao, Digumarti, Editor (2004). *Chernobyl: Never Again*. New Delhi: APH Publishing Corporation.

Bhaskara Rao, Digumarti, Editor (2004). *Virology and Immunology*. New Delhi: APH Publishing Corporation.

Bhaskara Rao, Digumarti, C.A.P. Swami and B.S.V. Dutt (1997). *Self-Evaluation in Student Teaching*. New Delhi: Discovery Publishing House. ISBN 81-7141-374-9.

Bhaskara Rao, Digumarti and B.S.V. Dutt, Editors (2003). *Education: Programmes and Policies*. New Delhi: APH Publishing Corporation. ISBN 81-7648-470-9.

Bhaskara Rao, Digumarti and D. Naresh Kumar (2004). *School Teacher Effectiveness*. New Delhi: Discovery Publishing House.

Bhaskara Rao, Digumarti and D. Sridhar (2002). *Job Satisfaction of School Teachers*. New Delhi: Discovery Publishing House. ISBN 81-7141-652-7.

Bhaskara Rao, Digumarti and Digumarti Pushpa Latha (1994). *Achievement in Biology*. New Delhi: Discovery Publishing House. ISBN 81-7141-264-5.

Bhaskara Rao, Digumarti, C. Sridevi and K. Vijaya (1995). *Achievement in Social Studies*. New Delhi: Discovery Publishing House. ISBN 81-7141-281-5.

Bhaskara Rao, Digumarti and Digumarti Pushpa Latha (1995). *Achievement in English*. New Delhi: Discovery Publishing House. ISBN 81-7141-283-1.

Bhaskara Rao, Digumarti and Digumarti Pushpa Latha (1994). *Achievement in Science*. New Delhi: Discovery Publishing House. ISBN 81-7141-280-70.

Bhaskara Rao, Digumarti and Digumarti Pushpa Latha (1995). *Achievement in Mathematics*. New Delhi: Discovery Publishing House. ISBN 81-7141-278-5.

Bhaskara Rao, Digumarti and Digumarti Pushpa Latha, Editors (1998). *International Encyclopaedia of Women*. 5 Volumes. New Delhi: Discovery Publishing House. ISBN 81-7141-410-9.

Vol. 1 *Status of World's Women*. ISBN 81-7141-494-X.

Vol. 2 *Women, Education and Empowerment*. ISBN 81-7141-498-1.

Vol. 3 *Women Challenges and Advancement*. ISBN 81-7141-497-4.

Vol. 4 *Women and Family Health*. ISBN 81-7141-497-4.

Vol. 5 *Women and International Action*. ISBN 81-7141-498-2.

Bhaskara Rao, Digumarti, Digumarti Pushpa Latha and Digumarti Harshitha, Editors (2001). *Biological Warfare*. New Delhi: Discovery Publishing House. ISBN 81-7141-597-0.

Bhaskara Rao, Digumarti, Digumarti Pushpa Latha and Digumarti Harshitha, Editors (2001). *Women as Educators*. New Delhi: Discovery Publishing House. ISBN 81-7141-602-0.

Bhaskara Rao, Digumarti and Digumarti Harshitha, Editors (2001). *Education in India*. New Delhi: APH Publishing Corporation. ISBN 81-7141-207-2.

Bhaskara Rao, Digumarti, Digumarti Pushpa Latha and Digumarti Harshitha, Editors (2001). *Assessing Learning Achievement*. New Delhi: Discovery Publishing House. ISBN 81-7141-601-2.

Bhaskara Rao, Digumarti, Digumarti Pushpa Latha and Digumarti Harshitha, Editors (2001). *Energy Security*. New Delhi: Discovery Publishing House. ISBN 81-7141-598-9.

Bhaskara Rao, Digumarti, Digumarti Harshitha and K.R.S.S. Rao, Editors (1999). *Advanced Biotechnology*. New Delhi: Discovery Publishing House. ISBN 81-7141-516-4.

Bhaskara Rao, Digumarti and K.R.S. Sambhasiva Rao, Editors (1996). *Current Trends in Indian Education*. New Delhi: Discovery Publishing House. ISBN 81-7141-311-0.

Bhaskara Rao, Digumarti and K. Vijaya (1995). *A Text Book of Evaluation*. Ambala Cantt: The Associated Publishers.

Bhaskara Rao, Digumarti and N.V.M. Mohana Rao (2002). *Problems of Mentally Handicapped Children*. New Delhi: Discovery Publishing House. ISBN 81-7141-645-4.

Bhaskara Rao, Digumarti and S. Chandra Mohan (2002). *Sports Management*. New Delhi: APH Publishing Corporation. ISBN 81-7648-467-9.

Bhaskara Rao, Digumarti and Sk. Johni Basha (2004). *Teachers' Population Education Awareness*. New Delhi: APH Publishing Corporation.

Bhaskara Rao, Digumarti, V.V. Rao, V.V. Lakshmi and V.V. Krishna, Editors (1999). *Status and Advancement of Women*. New Delhi: APH Publishing Corporation. ISBN 81-7648-169-6.

Babu, P.C., Author and Digumarti Bhaskara Rao, Editor (2004). *Flowers of Wisdom*. New Delhi: Discovery Publishing House. ISBN 81-7141-695-0.

Bhagya Lakshmi, Lingineni, Author and Digumarti Bhaskara Rao, Editor (2000). *Reading and Comprehension*. New Delhi: Discovery Publishing House. ISBN 81-7141-543-1.

Bhuvaneswara Lakshmi, Gadde, Author and Digumarti Bhaskara Rao, Editor (2000). *Attitude Towards Science*. New Delhi: Discovery Publishing House. ISBN 81-7141-541-6.

Devraj, T.A.S., Author and Digumarti Bhaskara Rao, Editor (1997). *Trace Analysis of Uranium and Thorium*. New Delhi: Discovery Publishing House. ISBN 81-7141-375-7.

Durga Rani, K., Author and Digumarti Bhaskara Rao, Editor (2000). *Educational Aspirations and Scientific Attitudes*. New Delhi: Discovery Publishing House. ISBN 81-7141-555-55.

Dutt, B.S.V. and Digumarti Bhaskara Rao (2001). *Empowering Primary Teachers*. New Delhi: Discovery Publishing House. ISBN 81-7141-615.2.

Ediger, Marlow and Digumarti Bhaskara Rao (1996). *Science Curriculum*. New Delhi: Discovery Publishing House. ISBN 81-7141-321-8.

Ediger, Marlow and Digumarti Bhaskara Rao (2000). *Teaching Mathematics Successfully*. New Delhi: Discovery Publishing House. ISBN 81-7141-552-0.

Ediger, Marlow and Digumarti Bhaskara Rao (2001). *Teaching Science Successfully*. New Delhi: Discovery Publishing House. ISBN 81-7141-600-4.

Ediger, Marlow and Digumarti Bhaskara Rao (2001). *Teaching Social Studies Successfully*. New Delhi: Discovery Publishing House. ISBN 81-7141-596-2.

Ediger, Marlow and Digumarti Bhaskara Rao (2002). *Philosophy and Curriculum*. New Delhi: Discovery Publishing House. ISBN 81-7141-631-4.

Ediger, Marlow and Digumarti Bhaskara Rao (2002). *Improving School Administration*. New Delhi: Discovery Publishing House. ISBN 81-7141-633-0.

Ediger, Marlow and Digumarti Bhaskara Rao (2002). *Elementary Curriculum*. New Delhi: Discovery Publishing House. ISBN 81-7141-658-6.

Ediger, Marlow and Digumarti Bhaskara Rao (2003). *Language Arts Curriculum*. New Delhi: Discovery Publishing House. ISBN 81-7141-657-8.

Ediger, Marlow and Digumarti Bhaskara Rao (2004). *Teaching Language Arts Successfully*. New Delhi: Discovery Publishing House. ISBN 81-7141-678-0.

Ediger, Marlow and Digumarti Bhaskara Rao (2004). *Teaching Mathematics in Elementary Schools*. New Delhi: Discovery Publishing House. ISBN 81-7141-687-X.

Ediger, Marlow and Digumarti Bhaskara Rao (2004). *Teaching Science in Elementary Schools*. New Delhi: Discovery Publishing House. ISBN 81-7141-709-4.

Ediger, Marlow and Digumarti Bhaskara Rao (2004). *School Curriculum and Administration*. New Delhi: Discovery Publishing House. ISBN 81-7141-709-4.

Ediger, Marlow and Digumarti Bhaskara Rao (2004). *Modern Elementary School*. New Delhi: Discovery Publishing House.

Ediger, Marlow and Digumarti Bhaskara Rao (2004): *Relevancy in Elementary Curriculum*. New Delhi: Discovery Publishing House. ISBN 81-7141-751-5.

Ediger, Marlow and Digumarti Bhaskara Rao, (2004). *Teaching Social Studies in Elementary Schools*. New Delhi: Discovery Publishing House.

Ediger Marlow, B.S.V. Dutt and Digumarti Bhaskara Rao (2004). *Teaching English Successfully*. New Delhi: Discovery Publishing House. ISBN 81-7141-707-8.

Harshitha, Digumarti and Digumarti Bhaskara Rao, Editors (2004). *Educational Innovations*. New Delhi: Discovery Publishing House.

Indira Devi, Author and J. Prasanth Kumar and Digumarti Bhaskara Rao, Editors (2004). *Values in Language Text Books*. New Delhi: Discovery Publishing House.

Jayasree, Kandi, Author and Digumarti Bhaskara Rao, Editor (1999). *Correlates of Socialisation*. New Delhi: Discovery Publishing House. ISBN 81-7141-517-2.

John Babu, Chikati, Author and T.J.R. Prasad, G.M. Madhukar and Digumarti Bhaskara Rao, Editors (1996). *Problem Solving in Mathematics*. New Delhi: APH Publishing Corporation. ISBN 81-7648-273-0.

Lalitha, T., Author and K.S. Prabhakaram, D.S.N. Sastry and Digumarti Bhaskara Rao, Editors (2004). *Educational Philosophic Beliefs*. New Delhi: Discovery Publishing House. ISBN 81-7141-765-5.

Madhu Bala, Jampala, Author and Digumarti Bhaskara Rao, Editor (2004). *Adjustment Problems of Hearing Impaired*. New Delhi: Discovery Publishing House.

Marja, Talvi and Digumarti Bhaskara Rao, Editors (1996). *Educational Leadership and Social Changes*. New Delhi: Discovery Publishing House. ISBN 81-7141-320-X.

Nirmala Jyothi, M., Author and Digumarti Bhaskara Rao, Editor (2003). *Non-detention Systems in School Education*. New Delhi: Discovery Publishing House. ISBN 81-7141-654-3.

Prabhakaram, K.S., Author and Digumarti Bhaskara Rao, Editor (1998). *Concept Attainment Model in Mathematics Teaching*. New Delhi: Discovery Publishing House. ISBN 81-7141-424-9.

Prasanth Kumar, J., Author and Digumarti Bhaskara Rao, Editor (1998). *Effectiveness of Distance Education System*. New Delhi: Discovery Publishing House. ISBN 81-7141-437-0.

Prasanth Kumar, J., Author and G. Sundara Rao and Digumarti Bhaskara Rao, Editors (2000). *Open University Student Support Services*. New Delhi: Discovery Publishing House. ISBN 81-7141-550-4.

Ramatulasamma, K., Author and Digumarti Bhaskara Rao, Editor (2002). *Job Satisfaction of Teacher Educators*, New Delhi: Discovery Publishing House. ISBN 81-7141-655-1.

Rama Krishnaiah, D., Author and Digumarti Bhaskara Rao, Editor (1998). *Job Satisfaction of College Teachers*, New Delhi: Discovery Publishing House. ISBN 81-7141-438-9.

Rama Kumar Ratnam, M., Author and Digumarti Bhaskara Rao, Editor (1998). *Dukka: Suffering in Early Buddhism*. New Delhi: Discovery Publishing House. ISBN 81-7141-653-5.

Rathaiah, Lavu and Digumarti Bhaskara Rao, Editors (1996). *International Innovations in Education*. New Delhi: Discovery Publishing House. ISBN 81-7141-359-5.

Ramesh, Ganta and Digumarti Bhaskara Rao, Editors (1998). *Environmental Education: Problems and Prospects*. New Delhi: Discovery Publishing House. ISBN 81-7141-423-0.

Rathaiah, Lavu and Digumarti Bhaskara Rao (1997). *Achievement Correlates*. New Delhi: Discovery Publishing House. ISBN 81-7141-385-4.

Reddy, Sudhakar Y., Author, and Digumarti Bhaskara Rao, Editor (2003). *Creativity in Adolescents*. New Delhi: Discovery Publishing House. ISBN 81-7141-659-4.

Reddy, M.S., Author and Digumarti Bhaskara Rao, Editor (2004). *Creativity in College Students*. New Delhi: Discovery Publishing House. ISBN 81-7141-697-7.

Radramamba, B., Author and Digumarti Bhaskara Rao, Editor (2003). *Problems of Teaching*. New Delhi: APH Publishing Corporation. ISBN 81-7648-462-8.

Sanjeeva Rao, P.C., Author and Digumarti Bhaskara Rao, Editor (1996). *A Text Book of Geology*. New Delhi: Discovery Publishing House. ISBN 81-7141-313-7.

Satya Narayana V., Author and Digumarti Bhaskara Rao, Editor (2001). *Physical Education, Social Attitudes and Leadership Qualities*. New Delhi: Discovery Publishing House. ISBN 81-7141-593-8.

Srinivasulu Reddy, M., and K.R.S. Sambasiva Rao, Authors and Digumarti Bhaskara Rao, Editor (1999). *A Text Book of Aquaculture*. New Delhi: Discovery Publishing House. ISBN 81-7141-482-6.

Srinivasa Rao, Mandalapu, Author and Digumarti Bhaskara Rao, Editor (2004). *Achievement Motivation and Achievement in Mathematics*. New Delhi: Discovery Publishing House. ISBN 81-7141-674-8.

Vanaja, M. Author and Digumarti Bhaskara Rao, Editor (1999). *Inquiry Training Model*. New Delhi: Discovery Publishing House. ISBN 81-7141-515-6.

Vanaja. M. and N. Sneha Latha, Authors and Digumarti Bhaskara Rao, Editor (2004). *Student Shyness*. New Delhi: APH Publishing Corporation.

Valeri V. Koustiouk, Author and Digumarti Bhaskara Rao, Editor (2002). *A Text Book of Cryogenics*. New Delhi: Discovery Publishing House. ISBN 81-7141-642-X.

Valeri V. Koustiouk, Author and Digumarti Bhaskara Rao, Editor (2004). *Refrigeration and Environment*. New Delhi: APH Publishing Corporation.

Veena Kumari, Balusu and Digumarti Bhaskara Rao (1996). *Operation Black Board*. New Delhi: Ashish Publishing Corporation. ISBN 81-7024-711-X.

Veena Kumari, Balusu, Author and Digumarti Bhaskara Rao, Editor (2000). *Psycho-Social Correlates of Achievement*, New Delhi: Discovery Publishing House. ISBN 81-7141-547-4.

Vanaja, M., Author and Digumarti Bhaskara Rao, Editor (1999). *Inquiry Training Model*. New Delhi: Discovery Publishing House. ISBN 81-7141-515-6.

Venkata Rao, P. and Digumarti Bhaskara Rao (1989). *A Text Book of Zoology—Junior Intermediate*. Guntur: Vignan Publishers.

Venkata Rao, P. and Digumarti Bhaskara Rao (1989). *A Text Book of Zoology—Senior Intermediate*. Guntur: Vignan Publishers.

Venugopala Rao, K., Author and Digumarti Bhaskara Rao, Editor (2000). *Teacher Morale in Secondary Schools*. New Delhi: Discovery Publishing House. ISBN 81-7141-551-2.

Vidya, C., Author and Digumarti Bhaskara Rao. Editor (1996). *A Text Book of Nutrition*. New Delhi: Discovery Publishing House. ISBN 81-7141-309-9.

Vidya Bharathi, D., Author and Digumarti Bhaskara Rao, Editor (2000). *Educational Philosophies of Swami Vivekananda and John Dewey*. New Delhi: APH Publishing Corporation. ISBN 81-7648-309-9.

Books in Telugu Language

Bhaskara Rao, Digumarti (1986). *Dhrushya Sravana Bodhanapakaranalu* (Audio Visual Teaching Aids). Guntur: Nagarjuna Publishers.

Bhaskara Rao, Digumarti (1993). *Jeevasashtra Bodhana* (Teaching of Biology). Guntur: Nagarjuna Publishers.

Bhaskara Rao, Digumarti (1995). *Vignanasasthra Bodhana* (Teaching of Science) Guntur: Nagarjuna Publishers.

Bhaskara Rao, Digumarti (1997). *Vidya Manovignana Seshtram* (Educational Psychology). Guntur: Creative Press.

Bhaskara Rao, Digumarti (1998). *DSC Study Material*. Guntur: Nagarjuna Publishers.

Bhaskara Rao, Digumarti (1998). *Upadhyayudu Vidya*. (Teacher and Education). Guntur: Nagarjuna Publishers.

Bhaskara Rao, Digumarti (1998). *Vidya Drukpadalu* (Prespectives of Education). Guntur: Nagarjuna Publishers.

Bhaskara Rao, Digumarti (1999). *EdCET Teaching Aptitude*. Guntur: Nagarjuna Publishers.

Bhaskara Rao, Digumarti (2001). *Bharata Samajamulo Upadyayudu Vidya* (Teacher and Education in Emerging Indian Society). Guntur: Nagarjuna Publishers.

Bhaskara Rao, Digumarti (2001). *Bhoutika Sastra Bodhana Paddathulu* (Methods of Teaching Physical Science). Guntur: Nagarjuna Publishers.

Bhaskara Rao, Digumarti (2001). *Jeeva Sastra Bodhana Padhathulu* (Methods of Teaching Biology). Guntur: Nagarjuna Publishers.

Bhaskara Rao, Digumarti (2001). *Vidya Manovignana Sastram* (Educational Psychology). Guntur: Nagarjuna Publishers.

Bhaskara Rao, Digumarti (2003). *Patsala Yajamanyam/Paripalana* (School Management and Administration). Guntur: Nagarjuna Publishers.

Bhaskara Rao, Digumarti (2004). *Vidya Sanketika Sastram mariyu Computer Vidya* (Educational Technology and Computer Education). Guntur: Nagarjuna Publishers.